# Rock 'Til You Drop

## MICK JAGGER FORMS GROUP

MICK Jagger, R&B vocalist, is taking a rhythm and blues group into the Marquee tomorrow night (Thurs) while Blues Inc. is doing its Jazz Club gig.

Called 'The Rolling Stones' ("I hope they don't think we're a rock 'n' roll outfit", says Mick) the lineup is: Jagger, (voc), Keith Richards, Elmo Lewis (gtrs), Dick Taylor (bass), 'Stu' (pno), Mike Avery (drs).

A second group under Long John Baldry will also be there.

# Rock 'Til You Drop

## The Decline from Rebellion to Nostalgia

◆

John Strausbaugh

**VERSO**

London & New York

first published by verso 2001
© john strausbaugh
all rights reserved

uk: 6 meard street, london w1v 3hr
usa: 180 varick street, new york, ny 10014-4606

verso is an imprint of new left books

Design by hotwater

ISBN 1-85984-629-7

British Library Cataloguing in Publication Data
A catalogue record for this book is available from the British Library

Library of Congress Cataloging-in-Publication Data
A catalog record for this book is available from the Library of Congress

# CONTENTS

## ( 1 )

# Boom Boom Boom Boomer

## Colostomy Rock, and What It Says about My Generation

The crew was just kids—rock 'n' rollers with one foot in
the grave.
                                    —*Apocalypse Now*

How can you write about rock & roll? It's *silly*, it's supposed to be fun. How can you do that?
          —Charlie Watts to Chet Flippo, in *Rolling Stone*,
                                                    1978

[S]omeone's got to come along and say fuck you!
          —Alex Harvey, in *New Music Express*, 1973

IT'S THE AUTUMN OF 1999. Mike Doughty and I are looking at a photo of
his toiletries in the current issue of *Teen People*. Doughty was the founder/
singer/songwriter of the 1990s band Soul Coughing, a hiphoppy rock band that
made some successful records and toured extensively between 1993 and their
breakup in the spring of 2000. That made Doughty a bona fide rock star. I
knew him before he was famous, back when he was a youngster working as a
doorman at the Knitting Factory, the avant-garde music space in downtown
Manhattan, and writing about music for the paper I edit, *New York Press*.
He's young enough to be my son, a '90s kind of guy to my grizzled '60s old-
timer status.

In 1999, Doughty was enough of a rock star that a teenybopper magazine
like *Teen People* would want to do a silly little feature story regarding the toiletries he would take on the road with him. Doughty and I were looking at this
article together, and I was trying to explain to him that while I thought it was

1

great for him to be a teenybopper sex object when he was still in his twenties, I really didn't want him up on stage in his fifties, in the 2020s, fronting a session band pretending to be Soul Coughing, wheezing his 1999 hit single, "Circles," for the umpteen-thousandth time, for a nostalgic crowd of middle-aged lawyers and stockbrokers who've broken out their old baseball caps and worn them backward just for the occasion. "Soul Coughing—they *rocked!*" a bald dentist says, between woo-woos and air-fists, to his son and daughter, whom he's dragged along to this reunion-tour concert to show them what *good* music was really like. The girl rolls her eyes. "Dad, don't you mean they *rock?*" "What? Oh, oh yeah. *Woo!*" he cheers, gazing up at Doughty. . . .

What got me started was a monstrous Dorian Grey publicity photo of Kim Simmonds that was up on the wall of my office as a daily reminder of one major theme of this book. Simmonds, you may or may not recall, was the guitarist for Savoy Brown, one of those mediocre British blues-rock bands of the late '60s and early '70s, like Spooky Tooth and Free. A friend of mine remembers seeing Savoy Brown listed in a 1970s edition of the *Guinness Book of World Records* for having had the most personnel changes of any single rock band in a year. Simmonds passed through New York City in the fall of 1999 on a "reunion tour" with something calling itself Savoy Brown, and I had his horrific PR photo—he looked about seventy-five, with one of those terrifyingly runny melting-cheese faces old British guys get from a lifetime of hoisting pints. His hair, if it was his hair, looked like a dimestore "Rock Star!" Halloween wig, or as if a squid with hairy legs had clamped itself to the top of his skull and was sucking out what was left of his brains.

A central tenet of this book—so simple and obvious, the only thing remarkable about it is how easily you can start arguments with it—is this:

*Rock is youth music.* It is best played by young people, for young people, in a setting that is specifically exclusionary of their parents and anyone their parents' age. It is the music of youthful energies, youthful rebellion, youthful anxieties and anger—"a young people's (and by young I mean teenage) art form," as British novelist–essayist Will Self has written. "[U]nlike every other great genre of American pop," American rock historian James Miller concurs, "rock is all about being young, or (if you are poor Mick Jagger) pretending to be young."

Rock simply should not be played by fifty-five-year-old men with triple chins wearing bad wighats, pretending still to be excited about playing songs they wrote thirty or thirty-five years ago and have played some thousands of times since. Its prime audience should not be middle-aged, balding, jelly-bellied dads who've brought along their wives and kids. It should not be trapped behind glass in a museum display and gawked at like remnants of a lost civilization. That is not rock 'n' roll. Rock 'n' roll is not family entertainment.

The Rolling Stones are only the most obvious, and perhaps depressing, example of a once-great rock band that kept playing years and years after they'd gotten too old, had gone from the greatest rock 'n' roll band in the world to the greatest self-parody of a rock 'n' roll band. The Rolling Stones didn't make rock anymore after the mid-'70s; they made stadium events. I discuss them in depth in Chapter 2. The larger point to be made here at the outset is that by the 1990s, the Stones' brand of colostomy rock had become not an isolated freak show but a regular—and popular—feature of the summer concert season. Every year, ancient rock bands rise up from their graves and rule the nights again. Lynyrd Skynyrd, Jethro Tull, Yes, the Allman Brothers: pale ghosts of their youthful selves, they have become their own nostalgia merchandise. There can be only one motivation: as the Rutles declared, All You Need Is Cash.

I find this terribly dispiriting. When Journey's Steve Perry is having a hard time touring because of his arthritis, it's time for Journey to retire. When Eddie Van Halen needs to be careful how he moves onstage because of his hip replacement surgery, Eddie should sit down and become strictly a studio musician. When bands calling themselves Little Feat or Jefferson Starship are made up almost entirely of ringers and replacements and include none of the talents that originally made those names so recognizable, they should stop calling themselves Little Feat or Jefferson anything. When Pete Townshend decides in his mid-fifties that he wants to record a six-CD rock opera (*Lifehouse*) made up entirely of songs he wrote thirty years ago, the best of which he and his band already played to death during the 1970s ("Baba O'Riley," "Behind Blue Eyes," "Won't Get Fooled Again"), and that he is now going to rerecord in wimpy old-man's versions, with insipid string orchestrations laid on top for a false air of gravity... *someone* should say, "No, Pete, that's a bad idea," and lead him by the elbow back to the old folks' home—where Steve, Eddie, Mick, and the rest of the geezers might have a good laugh and remind him of the lyrics to a certain song he wrote decades earlier, famously addressing precisely this topic of aging. But no. Instead, Pete "reunites" one more time with what's left of The Who, sans Keith Moon—and really, what's The Who without Keith Moon?—and they go creaking off on another graybeards' summer concert tour of the States. Here comes the new one, not *quite* the same as the old one.

Neil Young, Graham Nash, the grizzled and addled Stephen Stills, and the rotund and liver-transplanted David Crosby gathered for a CSNY reunion tour in 2000. Even *Rolling Stone,* which had functioned for years as a CSNY fanzine, was reduced to praising their ragged vocal performances and ghastly physical appearance in terms so hollow, so un-musical, that only the most naive reader could fail to scan the truth between the lines. (*Rolling Stone* put Crosby on its cover yet again that year, not for any musical achievement but for his Frankensteinian love-child arrangement with Melissa Etheridge, an affirmative-action rock mediocrity better known for her lesbianism and her fawning friendships with more powerful rock industry figures than for any musical talent.)

Didn't any of these people see *Spinal Tap?* David Lee Roth's enemies started making fun of him when he'd been around so long that his big hair began visibly thinning. At least DLR never took himself too seriously and was always good for a self-mocking quip like, "Here today, gone later today." It should be the motto for all rock 'n' roll bands. The shelf life of rock credibility is too short for it to become a lifetime career. And yet every summer, like a parade of the Living Dead, here come the geriatric rock bands, people who made their last decent rock songs back when they were in their teens or twenties, now in their mid-fifties, pretending that they can still rock.

In principle, no one can argue against the abundant evidence that, with very few notable exceptions, middle-aged people make sad spectacles of themselves when they think they're "rocking out." It's when you start listing specific rockers and bands that the fights break out, because everyone has a special favorite or two whom they think are the exceptions. By "everyone" I mean, of course, my fellow baby boomers, technically defined as people born between 1946 and 1964. My definition: people who grew up in "the rock years." If you're in that group I can almost guarantee I can push one of your personal-hero buttons with a very short list of washed-up has-beens who should have stopped performing long before they did. I am now going to say rude things about some performers the reader may hold dear. This is a test:

Were you, for instance, a Fleetwood Mac fan? I never quite got their massive appeal myself. To me, Fleetwood Mac—the mid-to-late-'70s edition of Fleetwood Mac, "Rhiannon" and all that, not the earlier, bluesier version—was just ABBA with a decent drummer. Be that as it may, if you were a fan of Fleetwood Mac in the 1970s, why on earth would you want to see them reunited as middle-aged has-beens in the late 1990s, performing a nostalgia stage act of twenty-five-year-old hit songs you could hear livelier renditions of on the Muzak at your local supermarket or dentist's office? How could you look at the once-svelte Stevie Nicks and not cringe to see her overweight and stuffed like a sausage into some girdle or corset torture device so constricting she literally could not move in it, her pancake makeup thick and hard as china, her hair a straw fright wig, her once fetchingly crackled voice a scary croak? Yeah, you can go your own way, mama. Please. In the 1990s, a New York City drag club started an annual event "honoring" Nicks called "Night of 1000 Stevies"—a sure sign that she had achieved the status of a Cher/Liza kitsch icon.

Speaking of Cher, let us briefly note her 1999 life-after-love comeback. Let us grant her the song upon which that year's Cher revival—her third, fourth, fifth?—was based, since it was a catchy pop single, and if she wanted to go on making singles that listenable until she turned 120 you wouldn't want to stop her. But the once-famous Cher stage act, a highly calculated Las Vegas–style revue of dancers and acrobats and untold legions of backup singers, had by that point come to resemble a wax museum diorama. All the circus-act busyness that swirled around her could not distract your eye from the clear fact that she was so carefully and artificially composed, so stiff in her makeup and outfits, that she looked like a wax effigy of herself. She looked like a life-size Cher candle. For the finale they could have stuck a wick in her head and lit it. It would have been a grand pop-star way for her to go out.

But Cher was never really a rock performer anyway. She was always a pop star—a crucial distinction I'll return to shortly. Pop stars are by their very nature artificial constructs. We forgive them for that, and to some extent we even expect it of them. This is a book about rock, not pop, and for that reason I'll try not to mention Cher again. Or Madonna. Or Elton John. Or the terrible spectacle of Diana Ross, her hair a massive fractal globe of pure witchy static, "reunited" in 2000 with a couple of Supremes ringers—the "Subpremes," the *New York Post* acutely jibed—because her original compatriots refused to go on the road with her again. The sight and sound of her dragging her bony carcass through exhausted renditions of her old, *old* hits were not nearly as entertaining as watching the tour decompose like a disinterred corpse—Ross publicly queening and bitching at her crew between songs, the entire crew complaining about her in turn to the press, tour dates canceled left and right. The only thing supreme about it was Ross's evident narcissism. In the way of senior-citizen slugfests, its only competitor was that summer's Little Richard–Jerry Lee Lewis–Chuck Berry tour—call it the Reanimator Tour, proof that it was not only '60s acts who didn't have the good sense to lie down and die when they should. The three ancient egos openly feuded throughout; Berry reputedly insisted that he would be onstage one hour and not a second longer, and when the alarm on his wristwatch went off he'd go off as well, regardless of whether he was in the middle of a song.

How about the middle-aged Eric Clapton? Were you still thinking Clapton was God by, say, 1980? How about after the easy-listening Miller Beer commercials? How about after his son died and he wrote that hideously mawkish song for him and then would *not* stop playing it everywhere he went, year after year? At the 2000 Rock and Roll Hall of Fame induction ceremony (which I describe in depressing detail in Chapter 5), I watched Eric Clapton, paunchy and chinless, bearded and burghermeisterly, sit down onstage and cradle an acoustic guitar in his lap. He gave the impression more of an amateur ventriloquist than of a guitar god preparing to "rock out," and I sat there praying *Don't do it. Come on, man, don't do it.* But he did. He played that song. I won't even try to describe how the reunited Lovin' Spoonful sounded that night, croaking and shuffling through "Do You Believe in Magic?"

Peter Gabriel is a '70s rocker I once idolized. To me, Phil Collins was never anything but the drummer in Peter Gabriel's band, and Genesis without Gabriel was as much an imponderable as the Who without Keith Moon, or the Pogues without Shane. Then I saw the fiftysomething Peter Gabriel singing the theme song to *Babe—A Pig in the City* (alternate title: *Babe—A Pig Beyond Thunderdome*) at the Academy Awards ceremonies that year. Gray and concentrically rounded as a Botero figure, he sang "That'll Do, Pig," and I had to wonder for a second if he was addressing himself at the dinner table.

Who might we consider an exception to the rule? Iggy Pop? I will concede that of all the boomer rock heroes, Iggy was the best example, for many years, of a guy who could still rock well into middle age. I would argue that this is because Iggy always stripped rock down to its very simplest, stupidest, most primitive and primary elements. Iggy Rock was so *very* simple Iggy could get away with making it for years and years, like a Stone Age culture bashing away with the same style of flint ax eons upon eons. If the evolution of rock followed the scientific principle of punctuated equilibrium—long periods of stasis interrupted by quick bursts of massive change—Iggy was definitely one of rock's periods of stasis, remaining basically unchanged for most of his career. (I believe this also explains the way Motörhead could keep playing likably well into Lemmy's silver years. Music as simple and dumb as Motörhead's can't get old because it never changes. Motörhead was the RNA of rock, a bit of primary organic material so simple and unchanging it was effectively eternal.) Iggy was already forty-one years old in 1988 when he put together an absolutely killer band and toured behind the *Instinct* LP. It was a great rock tour, captured on one of the best live LPs in rock history, *King Biscuit Flower Hour Presents Iggy Pop.* He truly looked and sounded better than he had during several low points of his youth, including that Ziggy Pop period in the '70s when he was reduced to playing Pinocchio to Bowie's Geppetto. In the mid-1990s, *Trainspotting* introduced Iggy's music to a new, third generation of fans. Iggy toured some more, now in his mid-forties, and he seemed like a man ten, fifteen, twenty years younger.

But even Iggy couldn't keep it up forever, and by the turn of the century he was clearly running out of steam, making dreadful—and for Iggy Pop, demoralizingly low-energy—recordings like the bad beatnikisms of *Avenue B.* An even clearer sign of the heat death of Iggy Rock came that same year when Rhino released a six-CD limited collector's edition box set that included all the original tracks from the Stooges' seminal 1970 album, *Fun House,* along with five-CDs' worth of "the *Fun House* sessions"—take after take of Iggy and the guys hammering out what became the finished tracks. Five CDs of outtakes from a single Stooges' album was ludicrous, pompous excess. It was the very antithesis of everything Iggy and the Stooges meant to rock 'n' roll: economy, simplicity, no pretense, and, as Iggy himself declared, "no bullshit." This was a travesty. It was not the rock history it pretended to be; it was rock nostalgia— the very opposite and enemy of history. This was not the Stooges; it was just marketing and packaging, just an ant trap designed to attract boomers foolish enough to fall for it.

Patti Smith is another name angry boomers throw at me when I'm making the case for rock as youth music. Especially in New York, where Patti Smith is revered as an authentic local talent and "punk rock poet-priestess." My version: Patti Smith was one of the least talented posers in rock. Patti Smith was Jim Carroll with breasts, Lydia Lunch with anorexia, the Madonna of punk rock: everything bad and pretentious about the union of punk and poetry in one self-conscious package. Patti Smith was already, by my standards, a little long in the tooth to be making credible rock music by the time you and I first heard her. I was in my mid-twenties at that point and feeling a little too old even to be listening to punk rock, and she was a few years older than me. A thirty-, thirty-one-year-old "punk rock poet-priestess"? It seemed a stretch to me then, and the longer she stuck around, the farther the stretch. Granted, she'd had to spend all those years posing in front of the mirror, posing on the steps in front of Max's Kansas City, posing in front of a mic at the St. Mark's Poetry Project, memorizing Rimbaud, insinuating her mug into every photograph taken of William Burroughs at a certain point, before finally landing that record con- tract—for which, neo-beatnik punk priestess though she may have been, the careerist businesswoman in her remained eternally grateful (see Chapter 5).

When she disappeared from public view, you might think that at least she was showing the good grace to get out before she descended into complete self- parody. And then, years later, she made the inevitable rock-star "comeback" when approaching and then eclipsing fifty, an age at which rock stars should be, by law, man's or natural, dead or retired. She looked haggard and wan after years of widowhood and housewifery, and she put out a series of records of descending listenability. *Gung Ho*, released in 2000, was a terrible record. It's a cliché, but an accurate assessment, to say that it sounded like a *Saturday Night Live* parody of the kind of record a fifty-year-old Patti Smith might make. Her voice, lacking the faux-passionate, hiccuppy quality of her younger years, sounded flat and listless as damp laundry. It also sounded oddly unmatched to the musical accompaniment, like a kind of vocal appliqué glued onto the surface of prerecorded tracks, which by that point had given up sounding even remotely like rock, let alone punk rock, and were instead the kind of anonymous, almost-Muzak, adult-oriented global pop sound other aged former rockers, like Gabriel and Sting, had by then adopted as a pillowy cushion for their own increasingly de-energized vocals.

The experienced decoder of rock journalism could decipher how very bad a record *Gung Ho* was from the desperately overpraising reviews it earned from boomer rock critics in *Rolling Stone* and the *New York Times* and countless smaller venues. Stephen Holden, a middle-aged pop-culture journalist who should have been forced to stop critiquing rock music years earlier, reiterated the "punk rock poet-priestess" hagiography in a lengthy article in the Sunday *New York Times* (adding the absurdly pretentious notion that Dylan–Lou Reed–Smith represented a holy trio of rock poets that was a next-generation parallel to the beatnik trinity of Kerouac–Ginsberg–Burroughs, thus linking by analogy two false and pompous premises). "Towering, powerful music," cried the *New York Post*. "Easily one of the 10 best records of the year." The year wasn't half done at that point. "Her status as a world icon remains untarnished," *Newsday* assured its readers. In 1976, Smith told *New Musical Express*, "You know, I'd rather be remembered as a great rock and roll star than a great poet. To reach the highest point of something our generation created." She may be remembered as neither.

Look, I could go on doing this for another fifty pages, but I don't want you to think I'm just a bitch. The freak-show, fiftysomething versions of once-respectable bands like Little Feat or never-respectable hacks like Kansas creaking onto the stages of state fairs and open-air summer concert venues around the globe; the cross-generational exercises in tedium and faux-heavy skronk that were Neil Young's collaboration with Pearl Jam and Jimmy Page's with the Black Crowes; the Blondie comeback (fat, frazzled, barely wheezing out her twenty-five-year-old hit singles); Chrissy Hynde stumping for PETA; the aging scarecrows of Yes playing venues like the Foxwoods Resort Casino in Connecticut ("Somewhere," a *Newsday* reviewer quipped, "the hobbits are dancing"), a stage also graced by Paul Anka and Barry Manilow; the never-ending phenomenon of Bruce Springsteen; the return of the middle-aged Sex Pistols; the crotchety and droning Lou Reed; the severe case of hippie arrested development that was the Grateful Dead's never-ending road trip, a veritable Rolling Thunder of '60s nostalgia; David Bowie, Bono, Prince (almost as bizarrely eccentric and vain as Michael Jackson, and similarly sunk in inconsequentiality years before he noticed); the deathless and ever more inappropriately named Beach Boys; and, of course, Bob Dylan (Philip Guichard, who was then nineteen years old and immune to the youth fantasies of his parents' generation, wrote in Seattle's *The Stranger* in 1999 that "A Bob Dylan concert is a zombie show that requires self-deception from both the audience and the artist. While the audience pretends the wrinkled man with the scratchy nasal voice up on stage is the Bob Dylan they love, Dylan himself pretends that he's still the guy who wrote all those songs all those years ago. A certain amount of mood-altering refreshment aids both parties"). These are all examples my middle-aged friends have tossed at me to counter my argument that people their age have no business onstage. I call it the "You asshole, Kim Simmonds *rocks!*" list. If you think any of them are holdouts from the has-beens brigade, I can only say you're not hearing them as they are now, you're hearing them as you want to remember them. Colostomy rock is not rebellion, it's the antithesis of rebellion: it's nostalgia.

And nostalgia is the death of rock. We were supposed to die before we got old. Now look at us. Woo woo, Mick! Rock on, Bruce!

This is not just about getting old. No one has the right to tell Stevie Nicks or Deborah Harry she can't relax a little about her weight. No one can tell Gabriel he shouldn't grow gray and sleekly fat as Sebastian Cabot if he has a mind to. But you could certainly make the case that *rock stars* should not do those things. Obviously, rock grew old along with those who made it—and, more to the point, along with its biggest market, the baby boomers. Who doesn't get old, besides dead rock stars? My argument is not against aging, it's for aging *gracefully*. Plenty of people know how to do this, but rock stars, like movie stars, find it extremely difficult, and I suspect for the same reason: they have a pathological-professional need to continue to pretend they're young and sexy long after they've become neither. It's not about age so much as it is about the pretense of youth. Nobody says a word about old poets, jazz musicians, or tango dancers. If Mick Jagger wants to sit on a stool at the Blue Note and croak de blooz with Keith on an acoustic guitar, I wouldn't say a word. It's Mick butt-shaking and pretending to be really into "Satisfaction" for the millionth time that's unseemly. And it's what buying into this pretense does for us in the audience, we middle-aged boomers "recapturing the magic" of our teen years, that unsettles me.

Were we always so easily lied to by our rock stars? If so, what does this say about us as a generation? "We won't get fooled again"? Hell, were we fooling ourselves all along?

○

Of course, rock was a commercial enterprise from its start. Any romantic ideas that it was more than that, more important than that, were silly fantasies. But, as Ellen Willis, one of the first and best female rock critics in the '60s (see Chapter 3), put it to me, back then rock was something some young people shared, intently, to the exclusion of everyone non-rock. It was "like a generational language. You could play a song for somebody and they understood all sorts of things about you." And what we understood was that we were somehow "different." Rock was the soundtrack of change. We may not all have gone so far as John Sinclair, manager of the "revolutionary" rock band the MC5 and founder of the White Panther Party (also Chapter 3), did when he wrote "that our music and our culture constitute a *political* force, that the cultural revolution is inseparable from the political revolution, and that the revolutionary potential of our culture cannot possibly be fully realized as long as the capitalist social order continues to exist" (emphasis in original). But if rock turned out not to be a very useful aesthetic weapon of the revolution, if listening to rock music alone did not trigger sweeping political change—though perhaps it did stimulate in some young people the urge, effervescent and inchoate, to *cause* sweeping political change—at the very least there were some sweeping changes in attitudes that rock helped to promote at the time, and they were attitudes regarding some fundamental aspects of society and culture.

So of *course* the MC5 and Jefferson Airplane ended up selling out. Of *course* Mick Jagger was never a "Street Fighting Man." He went to an antiwar demonstration or two, same as everybody else, and it was the height of cynical, radical-chic appropriationism for him to pretend that he really thought the time was right for violent revolution. And yet maybe that song itself, having left Mick's hands and worked its way around the globe, variously interpreted and misinterpreted by young people, served *some* purpose as a rebellious anthem, some purpose beyond making Mick Jagger a richer man than he already was. At best one might argue that, through the '60s, rock's impact as an indirect agent of change was not always hampered by its blatant commerciality; that, in fact, the mainstream entertainment industry, by mass-marketing rock through records, radio, TV, and live appearances, actually helped spread countercultural ideas and rebellious attitudes to receptive young people everywhere.

Then again, I'd also agree with Sinclair that in the 1970s this somewhat unwitting cooperation with the counterculture on the part of the hipper establishment types became a wily co-optation of countercultural "style," reducing everything countercultural, including rock, to hollow gestures and advertising semiotics. That's why, when Rage Against the Machine's Zack De La Rocha played at being a third-generation Street Fighting Man thirty years later, with all the '60s-style rhetoric and gesturing preserved intact, as though he were some sort of ingeniously programmed animatron in a '60s Rock and Roll Hall of Fame exhibit, it could strike an old-timer like me as pure pantomime and clever spin, as serving no purpose but to help Zack, and the industry that supported him, sell more right-on records and righteous Che Guevara T-shirts.

The baby boom created a tidal wave of young people—in America, roughly 75 million baby boomers were born from 1946 through 1964. Compare this to "Generation X," named for a (tail-end-boomer) punk band, at 55 million. The so-called Generation Y, people born from 1981 through 1999, slightly eclipsed the boomers at 77 million. (Generation Y also goes by the more mellifluous "millennials" and the more strictly descriptive "boomer babies.") Generation Y is a "second baby boom" generation: by 2010, there will be more teenagers in America than at any point during the original baby boom.

America first discovered (and then began obsessing about) "teenagers" during World War II, when sociologists, educators, and other professional worrywarts became concerned that young people growing up during the violent years of the war and spending long hours without proper parental supervision might not be properly socialized. Talcot Parsons, the famous American sociologist, coined the term "youth culture" in 1941 to identify that adolescents and teens, for the first time ever, had a culture of their own distinct from that of their parents. It was thought that without proper acclimatization, these young primitives might go native and never properly develop into upright citizens. Thus the postwar era of black-and-white etiquette training films that kids would doze to or snicker at in darkened classrooms throughout the land—How to ask a girl for a date; Why snobs aren't popular; What to do if another student asks you to cheat. I remember these snoozers from my elementary school days.

Although boomers would later appropriate the notion of youthful rebellion, as well as assign to themselves all credit for rock 'n' roll, it was in fact teens in the 1950s—not baby boomers, mostly, but Parsons's war babies—who created the first "youth rebellion" and were the audience for the origins of rock 'n' roll, a "youth music" that was created, it's curious to remember, by men born in the 1930s (Elvis, Little Richard, Buddy Holly, Jerry Lee Lewis) or even 1920s (Chuck Berry). Indeed, the bulk of rock and countercultural heroes of the '60s were not boomers at all, but people born in the 1930s or during World War II: the Beatles, the Stones, Janis Joplin, Jimi Hendrix, Grace Slick, Jim Morrison, Abbie Hoffman, Huey Newton, and many others.

But it is true that youth rebellion developed momentum and cultural clout in the '60s and '70s, when the tsunami of baby boomers flooded through the high schools and colleges. Whereas some '50s teens might have felt alienated from their parents, many '60s and '70s teens were downright alien to them. It was in this period that sociologists began to identify "youth culture" as a potentially subversive subculture, existing within but at odds with the larger culture. (Eventually, a whole school of British sociology, Cultural Studies, would focus on the supposed subversion of youth music, fashions, and fads.) Indeed, between the long hair, the drugs, the rock, the free love, the pacifism, the no-work-ethic embrace of poverty, the flirtations with Eastern mysticism, and the radical politics, a subset of young people in the '60s came to be identified as inhabiting a completely separate culture from that of their parents and other, "straight," youth: the counterculture, the "freek nation." This was more than kids in black leather acting like hoodlums on the streets; this was a generation, or part of a generation, in what seemed to be open revolt.

This was my generation. We were born into the bountiful world of a long postwar boom, and we enjoyed the luxury, like no other generation before, to turn our backs on mundane matters like career and family and concentrate on changing the world. We were hippies; we were antiwar protesters; we were pro-drug and pro-sex; we rebelled against what we saw as the uptightness of our parents' generation and refused simply to plug ourselves into the sorts of dead-end jobs and lives they'd accepted; we were certain that "when the revolution comes" we would create a better, more equitable society for poor people, black people, gay people, and women. And our music, rock music, reflected and expressed all that. It was a music of youth, of the new, of now; a music of high energies and experimentation and change and revolt.

Thirty, thirty-five years later, many of the icons from the rock 'n' roll rebellion of the '60s were still up there onstage. *Rolling Stone*, the magazine that was born to document and champion the rock 'n' roll culture, threw itself a lavish, year-long thirtieth birthday party that was as dispiriting and distanced from the true spirit of rock 'n' roll as ... well, as a '90s Rolling Stones tour (Chapter 4). Even more antithetical to the original sense of rebellion and newness, the Rock and Roll Hall of Fame, godfathered by *Rolling Stone* mini-mogul Jann Wenner, remorselessly captured the entire rock generation behind museum display cases, making what was once new seem not just old, but ancient (Chapter 5). March 1999, when second-generation mock-rocker Billy Joel was inducted into the hall of fame, was truly the Day the Music Died.

It wasn't just the hairlines that had receded: the political commitment, the anger, the will to change that permeated the original music was also gone. This was a sorry transformation, for the generation that took on the mantle of world-changers to end up only as short-changers, flogging a rock 'n' roll long since eviscerated. We started out wanting to revolutionize the world and all we ended up doing was tinkering with the establishment.

Does every generation start out wanting to change the world and simply lose the energy and vision? Is it just a function of having responsibilities and rebellious children of your own? Or is there something particular about the failure of my generation to carry out the revolution it once promised itself? It can be argued that the movers and shakers of rock were always exemplars of hip capitalism, paying empty lip service to social change and "the revolution" but always far more focused on money and glamour and personal gratification. No amount of revolutionary signifying by Rage Against the Machine, no display of lumpen solidarity by Bruce Springsteen, no number of charity benefit performances by Sting and Jackson Browne can disguise how establishment rock became, decades ago. An industry that has made millionaires of its more savvy stars (Jagger, Bowie, Springsteen) and billionaires of its more ruthless businessmen (David Geffen) can hardly be expected to Fight the Power.

Can something very similar be said for my generation at large? I think it can. The revolutionaries of 1968 grew up, grew fat, grew complacent, withdrew from the world, and beguiled themselves with their own trivia. We went from Be Here Now to Remember When. This is not the revolution we thought we were going to make.

○

What are my credentials for making this argument? I'm a white middle-class American male, born in 1951, in Baltimore, Maryland. This is My Generation as much as it was ever Pete Townshend's (b. 1945). I'm not setting myself apart or above my generation by criticizing it. I'm as guilty as the rest. Working out some of the ideas for this book in *New York Press* over the previous couple of years, I was accused more than once of being a "self-hating" boomer. It's what gays call a gay person who dares to be critical of gay culture, what Jews call a critical Jew.

The first record I ever bought? When my twin brother, Richard, and I were five, our sister talked us into chipping in with her to buy this funny-sounding new 45 rpm single everyone was buzzing about: "Hound Dog," by some guy named Elvis Presley. First LP I ever bought? *Meet the Beatles.* In terms of rock 'n' roll history, they don't come any more boomer than I am. I had just turned twelve when the Beatles performed on *The Ed Sullivan Show.* By the end of that eighth-grade school year I and every guy I knew was in a band. The one my brother and I were in was called The Blenheims, because our drummer lived on Blenheim Road and I knew there was a Blenheim in England. The road was pronounced "Blen-hime" but I, already an insufferable pseud at twelve, tried to get people to pronounce the band's name the English way, "the Blenms." It didn't take. (Our next band we called The Prime Movers, same as one of Iggy's early bands in Detroit.)

My brother and I bought and shared a Kay guitar with punishingly bad action, played through a Vox amp with one ten-inch speaker and a killer reverb that sounded like you were coming from somewhere deep in the back of a walk-in meat locker. The Blenheims' first gig was at a backyard party thrown by our drummer's older sister. We knew only two songs, the inevitable "Louie, Louie" and a radically simplified version of "All My Loving," and we played them over and over all night, and the girls seemed never to tire of hearing them. This, I realized only much later, should have taught me pretty well everything I'd ever need to know about rock 'n' roll.

The big controversy among twelve-year-old rock musicians at the time was whether you were down with the bright, poppy Beatles or with the Dave Clark Five, whom we thought of as "dark" and "hard" because they had those stomping beats and that sax. Not much later the choice was between the Beatles and the Stones. I went with the Stones, once they started coming up with songs like "Under My Thumb" and "Satisfaction," songs that seemed to beckon to me from mysterious worlds of illicit, unknowable decadence. I didn't have the slightest idea what those songs were about. I just knew they were somehow bad, and bad's what I wanted to be.

My friends and I continued to play in little local bands all through high school. Didn't everybody in the mid-'60s? Early on my brother and I stopped hurting ourselves with that awful Kay and made a major investment, $350, in a real guitar: a Fender Stratocaster. We had to borrow most of the money from our father, and we spent a year delivering newspapers to pay him back. We put that guitar through a lot over the years. Eventually a drug addict "borrowed" it and we never saw him or it again. In those days equipment was hard to come by and often involved a real personal investment. A friend of ours scored a huge—well, it seemed mighty at the time—Silvertone amplifier when his dad had a heart attack mowing the lawn and died, because our friend's uncle, in a fit of desperation, ran our friend down to Sears and bought him the amp to

cheer him up. If a drummer had a basement or garage where we could practice, he was in the band, even if the rest of us kept better time than he did.

I have a photograph of the Prime Movers playing a teen-center dance; on
the back, written in my late mother's hand, it says "Sept. 1966." So my brother
and I are fourteen going on fifteen in this picture. (We were born on Halloween. It was said I was the trick, he was the treat.) There are five of us on the
stage—two guitars, bass, drummer, and me, by then the lead singer, with tam-
bourine. We're wearing our band uniform of polka-dot shirts, white pants, and
Beatle boots (except the drummer, whose mother disapproved of the whole
enterprise and refused to buy him a matching outfit). The drums and amps—
even that mighty Silvertone—look tiny.

Our bands played covers almost exclusively. In some lineups we tried to play
the popular songs the girls at the teen-center dance wanted to hear—"Young
Girl," "Hang On Sloopy," Paul Revere & The Raiders tunes, gloopy Top 40 ballads. In other bands we stuck to our aesthetic principles and played what we
really wanted to play. At first, that meant a lot of British Invasion material—
Stones, Yardbirds, Kinks, Who—plus the now more obscure singles that years
later would be remembered as "garage" rock and *Nuggets* rock. In the later '60s,
we picked up American rock again: hippie rock, blues rock, lots of long psychedelic workouts like "In-a-gadda-da-vida" and "Light My Fire," and rave-up
versions of "Psychotic Reaction" and "Hey Joe."

In the summer of 1969, after we all graduated from high school, the band
went "on the road": we drove a couple hundred miles from Baltimore up to
Atlantic City, New Jersey, the fading seaside resort, and played a gig in a roller-
skating rink. It was the first time we had ever "toured" outside Baltimore. It
was also one of our last gigs; by autumn, we'd all split off for various colleges.

That August, as a last fling, a few of us piled into the drummer's car and
drove up to Woodstock. I ate acid there for the first time, the first afternoon,
as Richie Havens played. I was seventeen. I was cold, wet, muddy, hungry,
thirsty, and sleep-deprived at Woodstock, and I spent much of the weekend
miserable, except when I was stoned, or skinny-dipping in that muddy pond,
or when the music was exceptional. The Who were great, even though they
were into their damned *Tommy* period by then; I watched, but I did not understand what I was witnessing, as Pete Townshend whacked Abbie Hoffman with

his guitar, knocking him off the stage. I made my way down through the sleeping bags and trash and got close to the stage as Jefferson Airplane played their dawn set. I heard Jimi Hendrix through the trees the last morning as we were trudging toward the car.

One hot Saturday afternoon in the summer of 1972, at the age of twenty, I was in the car, windows down, and I had the radio on one of Baltimore's great black radio stations. The disc jockey had a voice deeper and more rumbling than Barry White's. He was spinning soul and R & B singles; then this song came sliding out into the hot summer air, slow and sexy and slippery, quieter than everything else he'd been playing, with this guy talk-singing lyrics that seemed to be all about hookers and drug addicts, and when "the colored girls" sang the doop-doops I remember thinking "Walk on the Wild Side" was one of the coolest songs I'd ever heard. When it faded out there was an unusually long pause, just dead air and static, and then the DJ's whale-deep voice came back on and he purred, *That was so good . . . I'm gonna play it again.* And he did, the first and last time in my life I've heard a commercial-radio DJ play a single twice in a row. In Baltimore, a city very divided by race as well as by class, listening to that song linked, however tenuously and ephemerally, white and black radio listeners in *some* sort of three-minute bond, just as making the song united, however briefly, the white guy and the black girls who sang it. I think the DJ knew that, and it was part of the reason it felt so good. It was a small demonstration that in popular culture context is everything, and that everyone who receives a song contributes as much to its meaning at that moment as the artist who created it. That's one of the major reasons why, silly as it often is, popular culture is also important. Lou, Bowie, Roxy, Crimson, Genesis—that was mostly the rock I was listening to at that point. Arty, glammy, then still relatively obscure. In New York, punk rock was starting, but we didn't hear much of that down in sleepy Baltimore. Meanwhile, mainstream rock was heading into a dreadful patch with the coming of the Eagles, Dan Fogelberg, "A Horse with No Name," all that soft and folky rock, competing with the hollow bombast of Journey, Foreigner, Heart. Eventually, big, commercial rock would be so awful that disco seemed an improvement, an outcome that hastened the explosive spread of punk out of New York and London to the rock-deprived boonies and hinterlands.

I continued to play rock sporadically through my twenties. One cover band I played in had a long-term regular gig on Friday nights, churning out dance-able rock like "Brown Sugar" and "Rebel, Rebel" for a singles club in a motel banquet room on a semi-industrial strip of highway outside of Baltimore. That was depressing, but it supported the arty-rock band we were trying to get together. The last band I played in, at the end of the '70s, developed out of solo performances I was doing that I called avant-cabaret. Don't ask. A keyboardist joined me, then a drummer and a couple of backup singers, and I found I was in a band again. Three of us were white, two black. The drummer played in his mom's storefront Baptist church on Sundays. We enjoyed making music together and sounded pretty good, but after a few months I found I didn't have the heart to go through all the hassle of being in a band again. I was thirty, and that was just too old.

○

In *Rock and the Pop Narcotic*, a book that generated a lot of comment in the rock press when it appeared in the early '90s, '80s punk-label figure Joe Carducci stressed a distinction that's too often blurred: Rock is rock and pop is pop. Rock is made when some variation of a bass-drums-guitar group comes together because they just gotta rock. Pop is made when some congregation of disparate elements—often a producer, an engineer, a cute vocalist, and session men or machines (cf. Britney Spears, Michael Jackson, Backstreet Boys, Boyz II Men, 'N Sync, Bobby Sherman, the Monkees, the Spice Girls)—comes together with the express purpose of charting a commercially successful song. Carducci writes:

> A music that rocks can only be an active by-product of the playing of a band. Rock is not alchemy (adding black to white and getting gold), it is transubstantiation. It's not the notes, it's the jam between them. It is aggressive to the point of derailing from its rhythm and is unsafe at any speed. It is not identifiable by chart position, nor even by sound (say, fuzzed out guitars), volume or speed. Its special musical value is that it is a folk form which exhibits a small band instrumental language as in jazz, rather than mere accompaniment to a vocalist as in

pop. Rock is the place where rhythm and melody battle it out most intensively and in doing so they create something more. Traditional pop and folk uses of melody generally attempt to evoke a fairly refined emotional/reflective mood or trance. In rock, melody is present and its whiff of mood still distinctive; however, here it is pushed along by an explicitly physical, even carnal rhythm arrangement.

The Carducci principle is rife with imperfections and exceptions, as any attempt to codify popular culture must be. Carducci himself spent much of his lengthy book qualifying it. It's a rule of thumb, not an iron law, but useful all the same. It doesn't mean that rock is better than pop, only distinct from it. By this definition Motown was not rock, though you often hear rock historians refer to it that way. Jackson Browne was not rock. Funk is not rock, though in both historical roots and insistent rhythmic supremacy it is more closely related to rock than are either Motown or Jackson Browne. Over the years, rockers have incorporated influences from jazz and rap, the blues and classical music, the polka and the raga, but rock remains distinct from all those other forms, as they remain distinct from one another.

Savoy Brown was rock (if mediocre rock), but the Beatles, as most of us knew them, were not; the early Beatles, when they played in Hamburg, were straight rock 'n' roll, but by the time we all knew them they were a pop group that very occasionally rocked. An American punk wanting to anger his English counterpart might stretch this notion and claim that the Sex Pistols were not only *not* the zenith of punk-rock bands, but they weren't really a punk-rock band at all. They were a pop band mining and refining punk idioms and gestures that had already been created in New York and Detroit. (Some British writers have gone so far as to question the authenticity of *all* British rock. English music writer Michael Gray, in his Bob Dylan book, *Song and Dance Man*, speaks of the "gigantic difference between American and British pop. The best of the American stars had music that grew out of their own local roots. They picked up genuine skills and techniques unselfconsciously. Their English equivalents always had to imitate." Will Self puckishly opines that British rock is merely a form of music-hall imitation—sincere flattery from a cold-weather, very-white-skinned culture that simply didn't have either the black funk background or the southern white roots to make real rock 'n' roll. "British rock and roll is an oxymoron," he snipes. "*Pretending* rather well to be rock and rollers is a lot closer to the mark. . . .")

Noting the distinction between the more organic form that is rock and the more artificial construct that is pop is not to assert that pop can't sometimes rock or, conversely, that rock can't be popular. And I'd never claim that rockers don't want to be rich and popular. But when a rock band becomes primarily interested in making hit songs, it *isn't* making rock anymore. It has become a pop band. Among these pop-acts-who-look-like-rock-bands, Carducci lists, with wicked humor but aesthetic accuracy, such luminaries as KISS, Journey, Van Halen, Devo, the Go Go's, and Bruce Springsteen.

It's easier for pop singers to age gracefully than for rockers, because of rock's unique youth orientation. Rock is a distillate of youthful energies: innocence, ignorance, rebellion, discovery, hormones. It takes a very special forty-year-old, let alone fifty-year-old, to portray those qualities onstage or in recordings without appearing like a pathetic idiot. But a pop singer can go on crooning forever. Compare, for instance, the middle-aged David Bowie and the slightly younger Sting as they both continued to ply their diminishing wares at the turn of the century. Bowie, who made some credible rock in his day, still looked good by 2000, but his act had aged very poorly; when he wasn't plowing through his thirty-year-old greatest hits again (something he periodically vowed never to do again, only to periodically renege), he was trying to make Easy Listening adult contemporary Muzak, and he sounded awful. It was not in his chops or his training. I suspect he knew it, and that's why he was throwing up all the Bowie.com and Bowie Inc. flak, to distract from the low quality of the actual music. He was acting like Todd Rundgren had in the 1990s, unable to keep up musically but desperate to appear still with-it and high-tech.

Sting, on the other hand, seemed quite at home making Easy Listening Muzak for a fan base that was contentedly accompanying him into middle age; it was just the relaxed-fit version of what he'd always done anyway. Sting was the pop-vocalist version Kenny G. A photo of him in the *New York Post* in 1999 showed him doing a kick with a line of Rockettes. As a middle-aged performer, he was not making records I could like, but his records were not the excruciatingly painful listen Bowie's had become. They were not *failures* the way Bowie's were—they were just Sting being his usual mediocre, cheesy self. (See Chapter 3.)

In these pages I am writing about rock. Other forms of popular music are barely mentioned, and then only when I think they impinge somehow on rock. In fact, this is really only a book about '60s and '70s rock—boomer rock. What it meant then, and what its enduring presence on live stages and in museum cases says about boomers now. I don't spend much time discussing '90s or twenty-first-century forms of rock, like rap metal or riot grrrl—let alone hiphop, trip-hop or electronica—partly because I'm not well versed enough in them, but also because they're not germane to a discussion about my generation.

However, I want to distinguish my omitting contemporary rock from the typical boomer attitude that rock after the 1970s is simply not *worthy* of discussion. One often hears some boomer flatly declaring that "rock is dead." I've found rock writers in magazines from as far back as the '60s pronouncing rock dead. It became very fashionable to say this in the mid-'70s—when, admittedly, the predominance of soulless arena acts like Peter Frampton and formulaic faux-rock like Fleetwood Mac offered plenty of justification. Certainly by the time large numbers of boomers had crossed the forty-year-old mark it became a matter of historical faith that rock 'n' roll—the real, original, first-generation, living, breathing, Elvis-Beatles-Stones youth-rebellion rock we grew up with—had been dead for some time, and that everything second- and third-generation, from the Sex Pistols through U2 and Nirvana and on up to Limp Bizkit and whoever's still rocking today, is mere imitation.

No boomer ever summed up this faith more handily than James Miller, one of the most mainstream and establishmentarian of rock critics. The title of his 1999 book, *Flowers in the Dustbin: The Rise of Rock and Roll, 1947–1977*, telegraphs his message effectively: rock's "era of explosive growth has been over for nearly a quarter century"; "rock has many of the features of a finished cultural form—a more or less fixed repertoire of sounds and styles and patterns of behavior"; by the end of the 1970s, "the essence of rock and roll—as a musical style, as a cluster of values, as an ingredient in a variety of youthful subcultures around the world—had been firmly established," while, as a wing of the entertainment industry, rock and all attendant spectacle had become "ever more stale, ever more predictable, ever more boring. . . . Like such other mature pop music forms as the Broadway musical and the main currents of the jazz tradition, from swing to bop, rock now belongs to the past as much as to the future."

As a boomer I find much that's emotionally appealing about this thesis— which makes it all the more important, I think, to resist it, or at least question it closely. Boomers think we invented popular music, and popular culture in general, and that everything kids today produce is an imitation of things we did first and better in the 1960s and '70s. I repeat, this idea is not wholly unattractive to me; I have whiled away countless pleasurable hours deriding post-historical young colleagues for having missed out on sex, drugs, *and* rock 'n' roll all at once. I found myself staring darkly at televised highlights of Wood-stock '99 as Dave Matthews managed to desecrate both the memory of Jimi Hendrix and the honor of Bob Dylan with an absolutely imbecilic rendition of "All Along the Watchtower." I winced at Alanis Morisette's hippie twirl. Confronted by such an unimaginative, unabashedly reiterative, dull spectacle, a boomer like Miller or myself could find easy justification for treating rock as a dead language.

By 1999 Miller had long been a principal architect of mainstream rock history, along with Greil Marcus, Robert Christgau, and Peter Guralnick. He wrote his first rock review in the third issue of *Rolling Stone* in 1967 and kept going through the 1980s, writing for the *New Republic* and *Newsweek*, editing *The Rolling Stone Illustrated History of Rock & Roll*, consulting on a Time-Life home video *History of Rock and Roll*. In short, he *was* the establishment. He quit writing about rock in 1991, because he "no longer felt able to feign enthusiasm."

*Flowers* bears the hallmarks of this attitude. The dedication—"For Greil"— sounds a clear warning: this is History-of-Rock, written like the narration for a two-hour VH1 special, in strict chronological form. Miller begins with the conventional starting point of Wynonie Harris's "Good Rockin' Tonight" of 1947—not quite rock 'n' roll yet, but clearly an immediate, jump-blues antecedent. He ends, also conventionally, with 1977, the year Elvis died and the Pistols busted out internationally. His personal tastes clearly lean toward mainstream pop; his aesthetics as well as his historical perspective are very commercial. Broadly speaking, for him rock is a subset of pop music, which is a subset of the entertainment industry. This leads him to overdetermine the importance of various performers or trends based on their commercial success; figures like Dick Clark, Fats Domino, and Ricky Nelson get too much play in this kind of rock history, at the expense of people I consider much more significant and influential, like Zappa and the Ramones, to mention only two acts a commercial perspective like Miller's must perforce underacknowledge. He seems suspicious of any definitions of rock, such as mine, that hint at a purpose greater than selling hit records and making money. While there's plenty of worldly wisdom to this—there can be no doubting that rock 'n' roll was from day one seized on by entrepreneurs like Alan Freed, Dick Clark, and Colonel Tom Parker and sold with unprecedented vigor to the newly discovered teen market—it also seriously pushes one's view of the music toward a philistinism that undervalues rock's ultimate social meaning.

Miller is not deaf to the social repercussions of the music. He has clear memories of the excited rush of rock 'n' roll when it was new, the sense of discovery and wonder with which young people heard rock 'n' roll in the 1950s and '60s. He notes how Elvis's 1954 cover of "Good Rockin' Tonight" takes Harris's good-natured, rolling version and amplifies it with nervous, ungainly white-boy energy—thus creating something unheard before then. It was more a borrowing than an outright theft, and the borrowing has continued back and forth in both directions across the racial divide ever since—maybe even helping to close that gap a little.

Miller is also very good at recalling the extraordinary flush of exuberance that was Beatlemania. This is something I fear the Doughty generation cannot understand; you really had to be there. Miller, who would've been sixteen or seventeen at the time, never really got over it himself. To Miller, the Beatles were the apex of rock 'n' roll in every way—as pop music, as art, as a social movement, *and* as a highly successful business.

In Miller's chronology, David Bowie is the beginning of the end: the first overtly ironic reflection of rock's hype and its tropes back on itself. Springsteen is for him, in a sense, the American Bowie, without the irony or glamour but just as obviously plying second-generation rock mimicry, in which the hype eclipsed the modest talent. (I agree with him on that score.) Miller's take on punk rock is the boomer-approved, and I believe wrongheaded, view that punk rock begins and ends with the Pistols, in 1977, and that the Pistols, moreover, represent the apotheosis of what Bowie had begun: rock as a completed form, now eating itself up with self-referential irony. Post-1977 rock is barely mentioned in *Flowers*, shrugged off in a few lines of an epilogue.

Jim DeRogatis, a younger rock critic, summed up Miller's thesis: "It wasn't me who changed, it was the music. . . . Yet another Baby Boomer refuses to grant that the sun doesn't shine out of his ass."

Miller's logical error, DeRogatis argued, is common among boomers: we assume that because we stopped listening to the music at some point in the 1970s or '80s, it stopped having any merit or meaning.

On one level, Miller is making a purely formal statement—by the end of the '70s, rock's structural development was complete. Musicians and fans of new wave, speedcore, grunge, nu metal, rap-rock, or Soul Coughing's melange of funk-jazz-poetry rock might well quibble. Conversely, one could question why, besides narrative convenience, Miller chose 1977 as the end point of rock's growth. One could make a compelling case that rock's formal development was completed by 1967—or even 1957.

Miller is clearly not wrong to state that on the broad scale rock could never regain the sheer novelty it enjoyed in the 1950s and '60s. But it does not follow that rock isn't *experienced* as new by young people every day. A kid's first electric guitar is still his first electric guitar, and the first time he bashes out a chord on it is as much a thrill to him now as it was to me or Miller forty years ago. The sense of discovering something new, sexy, loud, and preferably unappreciated by one's parents is as exciting to fourteen-year-olds today as it was in the 1960s. Does that kid care if the "idioms" and "structures" and "tropes" of that musical language were first worked out fifty years ago? Does it lessen the pleasure?

At the same time Miller's book was published, a smaller, more obscure scholarly tome on the heavy metal subculture of the Midwest was released— Harris M. Berger's *Metal, Rock, and Jazz: Perceptions and the Phenomenology of Musical Experience*. Published by a university press, this book followed a curious subgenre of ethnomusicology studies that focused specifically on heavy metal, like Deena Weinstein's 1991 *Heavy Metal: A Cultural Sociology* and

Robert Walser's 1993 *Running with the Devil.* Academics had produced similar studies for folk music, R & B and other genres—why shouldn't the head-bangers get their turn?

Berger's deadpan academic approach is delightful and loaded with insight. The heavy-metal underground in the 1990s was inherently mysterious, like some tribal culture, rich with all sorts of social, political, and aesthetic complexities. Working like an anthropologist, Berger took his notepad into beat-down local rock clubs—often just a bar with a little stage in the back under the TV—and described the goings-on in precise detail: the parking lot ("I parked next to a Camaro and went inside the club"); the beer signs and arcade games; the way the audience subdivided into little all-girl cliques and "the Silent Men," his borrowed nickname for guys who stood off to the side, arms folded across T-shirts, nodding their heads slightly to the music, nursing their beers. A lengthy, carefully observed description of how a mosh pit forms, builds, and dies off is priceless. Berger interviews band members about what the music and the scene meant to them. Midwestern metal was largely a blue-collar scene: Dann, his principal informant, was in his mid-twenties, still lived in his parents' basement, and worked six days a week, ten hours a day, in a factory where he polished plastic parts. He and Berger discuss the scene's politics (mostly conservative to libertarian, with some ultra right patriotism) and religion (more Aleister Crowley–style do-what-thou-wilt individualism than the outright satanism that one might expect from the bands' overuse of satanic imagery). They touch on the scene's flirtations with racist ideologies and Nazi symbolism, the sense of community the metalheads maintain through zines and cassette-swapping, the sense in which metal could be seen as an inchoate expression of frustration and rage for the working-class young people involved in it. It is an absorbing exploration of a rock subculture that flies so far below the radar of establishment critics that Miller only mentions heavy metal once—and then only to make a joking reference to books like Berger's. Miller's top-down, trickle-down theory of rock is all about a few salient geniuses and their chart-busting hits. Berger's metalheads represent the masses way down below, whom those geniuses impress and influence. Just like Miller—just like Lennon and McCartney and Jagger and Richards in a bygone era—these lumpen rock kids were imitating the records they loved. Does it matter if formally the music stopped developing twenty years ago, as Miller argues? Not to those kids. That's only a rock critic's concern. The metalheads were just living the stuff when they were not at work. And I suspect it wouldn't concern them much to learn that Miller, or any other boomer, disapproved.

Indeed, every time someone declares rock dead, another bunch of kids seems to come along and discover it for themselves, all over again. In 2000, after its demise had been announced by fans of hiphop and electronic dance music throughout the later 1990s, a new wave of rockers started it up again. Yes, the "new" rock was as consciously retro as punk rock had been. That did not prevent it from kicking ass. For a dead art form, it sure sounded lively. The Donnas, the Go, Sleater-Kinney, Zen Guerrilla, the Unband, the White Stripes, the Mississippi All-Stars, the Dropkick Murphys, New York's Starr, and hundreds of other bands I can't pretend to know about were making great rock 'n' roll music. Yes, they were struggling to reach fans and sell records in a milieu dominated by corporate pop and hiphop; rock was "underground," nearly an illicit pleasure again. I'm not sure that's a bad thing. The upshot was that at the dawn of the twenty-first century one could safely say:

Rock isn't dead, Mr. Boomer. It's just dead *to you*.

○

Doughty insists that it's unfair and unrealistic of me to demand that the Kim Simmondses and Kansases stop dragging their horrifically aged bodies onto the world's stages. "Rock 'n' roll is all these guys know how to do," he argues.

They say that about football and baseball players too, but they don't let them keep pretending they can play when they can't play anymore. They make them retire and become coaches or do TV commercials or open hamburger joints. The same can be said of ballerinas. A supremely physical art form, ballet—like rock, I argue—can only be performed by young people at the height of their beauty, elasticity, strength, and suppleness. At a certain stage of maturity, the ballet dancer simply can no longer perform adequately and is forced into retirement. If this is cruel and "ageist," it's a cruelty and ageism built into the art form. Even the best dancers must finally submit to age. One thinks of Nureyev, who was so often called "the Mick Jagger of dance."

"What fans don't ever take into account," punk-rock critic Gina Arnold wrote in *Kiss This*, is that bands who won't retire "tend to look stupider than those who do. Who wants to see a Sonic Youth in their forties? Why aren't the Beach Boys now called the Beach Men? And what about that balding Danzig?" But people do come out for these acts, by the thousands. That it's nostalgia is painfully evident. When The Who or the Rolling Stones pretend to "rock out," their middle-aged audience can pretend to rock out *right along with them*. For a few hours, they can forget that they're middle-aged married professionals with pot bellies and chronic lower-back pain and kids in college. For a couple of hours they're kids again, rockin' with The Who, singing along with The Boss, grooving with the Mickster.

As we age, it's only natural that we feel nostalgia for our lost youth and seek out easy ways—like an old favorite song—to evoke old feelings of youth for a fleeting second. We boomers saw it in our parents' generation, carrying on its bobby-soxers' infatuation with Frank Sinatra decades after it became embarrassing. But we were the generation that wasn't going to become our parents. We were supposed to be the people our parents warned us about. Instead, we ended up becoming just like them.

Worse—we ended up envying them. In the late 1990s a neurosis appeared among middle-aged males. I call it Boomer War Envy. Steven Spielberg's 1998 blockbuster *Saving Private Ryan* was both a symptom and a vector of this disease. In the *New York Observer*, Terry Golway wrote a column called "Children of D-Day Refuse to Grow Up." Golway, who was then in his early forties, went to see the film, which stimulated him to reminisce about a trip he'd made to France in the 1980s, when "My buddy and I walked the D Day beaches of Normandy. . . . We went to Normandy not as tourists but as pilgrims intent on seeing with our own eyes the relics of another generation's sacrifice. Baby boomers and sons of combat veterans, we had never heard a shot fired in anger, but we surely had been reared in the shadow of conflict. We heard no stories about the glory of war . . . but we absorbed lessons about duty and honor and the common good, and of this nation's capacity for both greatness and goodness."

It was not the actual Normandy that spurred the middle-aged writer to such mawkishness, but Spielberg's recreation of it. *Saving Private Ryan* "has been interpreted, understandably, as a reminder to the succeeding generation that nothing it does will approach what [*New York Times* columnist] Maureen Dowd called the 'nobility' of the WW II generation," Golway noted. "The lives of most boomers are shallow, self-indulgent and indeed insignificant compared to their parents."

One saw this condition striking numerous other middle-aged journalists in the months surrounding *Private Ryan*'s massively successful release. Boomers share a neurotic guilt that we did not undergo what our parents did, that therefore we are less "noble" than they. Boomers envy our parents their war. World War II was our parents' finest hour, their generation's crucible, their defining moment. As kids we spent significant amounts of time playing army in our backyards, literally recreating World War II on a boy's scale, often outfitted with actual war surplus equipment. (I wore my father's Eisenhower jacket with his master sergeant's stripes on it.) When the time came, World War II envy was a factor in our resistance to the Vietnam War, a poor substitute for the glorious war our parents had enjoyed. We said it at the time—give us a clear evil like Hitler and we'll fight.

Steven Spielberg continued to play army as a boomer adult, recreating World War II several times—*1941, Empire of the Sun, Schindler's List, Saving Private Ryan*. Television newsman Tom Brokaw (although a few years too old to be technically included among boomers) wrote the booklength, best-selling summa of WW II envy, *The Greatest Generation*. But the supreme expression of Boomer War Envy was the way Bill Clinton, the first boomer president, played army in the White House, initiating remote-control air wars, fought with the best high-tech toys, as he reached into his war chest and hauled out great double-handsful of cruise missiles and smart bombs and stealth fighters to hurl at Eastern European civilians and (as it turned out) innocent Africans—make-pretend wars, just like we used to fight in our backyards as kids. Here was the perfectly murderous example of Golway's boomer refusing to grow up. In playing army on a global scale, Clinton was reliving his youth, just like the middle-aged guy playing air guitar to an old Zeppelin tune.

O

Undeniably, tradition runs strongly against rockers thinking that they can age gracefully, since it encourages them to think they have only two options: to keep playing rock the rest of their lives or to burn out and die young. The self-destructive lifestyle of rockers probably is predicated, at least in part, on this fatalism. The ones who die young—who commit suicide, in effect, most often by drugs—may feel that they just can't be here in fifteen, twenty years. They just can't still be rocking in their forties and fifties, and not knowing what else to do, they check out while they've still got it. Leave a beautiful corpse.

It doesn't have to be this way. Jimi Hendrix certainly could've grown old gracefully, mellowed into a jazz-blues statesman. Janis Joplin surely could have matured into a decent bluesy jazz performer as well. Friends of Kurt Cobain say that had he only lived another couple of years, spent that much more time being a father and getting away from junk, he could've survived for the long haul.

David Johansen strikes me as a '70s rocker who grew up gracefully—eccentrically, yes, but gracefully nonetheless. He just had to abandon rock to do it. Born in 1950, he became famous in the early '70s as the singer in the New York Dolls, a band that personified rock excess and outrageousness, from their high heels to drummer Billy Murcia's ODing on their first tour of the U.K. It was on that tour that the Dolls single-handedly introduced the New York rock scene's love of heroin into England; one of the long-term effects would be Sid Vicious's sad demise, while Dolls guitarist Johnny Thunders would go on to become one of rock's most infamous and longest-lived junkies, falling off stages all over the world until finally dying, reportedly of a methadone overdose, in 1991.

As a band, however, the Dolls displayed an admirable understanding of the need to get out while the going was good. They broke up early and young, leaving behind just two studio albums but having made a huge impression on other rock, and especially punk rock, musicians. Johansen continued to make rock, with varying degrees of critical and popular success, into the 1980s. Then he abandoned the genre and reemerged in the mid-'80s with an entirely new persona, the high-haired lounge lizard Buster Poindexter. Whether or not you liked this new act—a lot of his older fans found it offensively campy schlock—it made more sense for him to be doing this in his mid-'thirties than prancing around in gold lamé pedal-pushers and high heels. At least Buster was *intentionally* ridiculous and funny.

As the century ended, Johansen entered a third phase of his career. Under his own name (and hair) again, and backed by a great acoustic ensemble called the Harry Smiths (for the legendary New York City collector of folkways and traditional musics), he made an even more striking transformation: at fifty, he emerged as the middle-aged former rocker turned white bluesman and purveyor of old-fashioned, down-home American Music. Sitting on a stool on the stage of the Bottom Line in the heart of Greenwich Village, not too shy to slip on his reading glasses when he needed to scan a lyric or a chart, he offered lovely renditions of old standards by Lightnin Hopkins and Mississippi John Hurt, Muddy Waters and Rabbit Brown, as well as even older, anonymous traditional tunes with roots sunk deep into America, such as the heartbreaking "Delia" and the magnificent country dirge "Oh Death." In his own way he was taking rock, there at the beginning of the twenty-first-century, back to where it started. It wouldn't make him millions of dollars or attract screaming teenage fans, yet it felt and sounded like exactly the right music for him to be making at the time. For a man who'd acted so outrageously in his earlier career, it was a startling, wise, beautiful, and, yes, *respectable* turn.

I sat in the back of the Bottom Line with the sixty-six-year-old Giorgio Gomelsky, whom you'll meet in Chapter 2, and the thirtysomething punk rocker George Tabb (Chapter 6), wondering why more older rockers couldn't make career and aesthetic choices as smart and appropriate as this one. All Johansen was doing was acting his age. Why was that so amazing?

# 2

## Steel Wheelchairs

### The Historical Reenactment of the Once-Great Rolling Stones

"You once said that you didn't want to be singing 'Satisfaction' when you were forty-two."
"No, I certainly won't."

—Mick Jagger, interviewed by Jonathan Cott,
*Rolling Stone*, June 1978

They're like Levi Strauss to me now, the Rolling Stones.
They're still great musicians and they still deliver the
goods, but one has to be realistic and say they are a
brand name.

—Tony King

IN FEBRUARY 2000, when Giorgio Gomelsky decided to throw himself a sixty-
sixth birthday party, he held it at the Green Door, an "underground" rock club
in what used to be Manhattan's Garment District. In the middle of a block of
storefronts, the nondescript brick building housed a British fashion designer's
showroom and workspace until the late 1970s. The Green Door got its name
from the dull paint on the industrial steel doors at the entrance. Otherwise
there was no sign, nothing on the street (except, sometimes in the wee hours,
stoned and drunken rock fans spilling out of those doors) to tell the uniniti-
ated that the legendary club was there. Lacking the various state and city
licenses an official nightclub must have to operate in the open, the Green Door
kept a discreet profile, advertising events mostly through photocopied hand-
bills and word of mouth in the New York rock community. The ground-floor
space, as in many other good rock and jazz clubs around the world, was tiny,
narrow, dark, and funky, with a small, low stage in the back and too many hard

surfaces for the music to bounce off. There were also small rehearsal rooms in the basement and on the second floor; halfway down the block, you could often hear a lone guitarist or drummer practicing at odd hours of the day or night. Fortunately, most of the Green Door's neighbors were daytime-only businesses, which helped to minimize, if not entirely eliminate, complaints about the noise.

A funky little rock club may seem an odd place for a sixty-six-year-old Russian émigré to throw a party for himself. But not for Gomelsky: he was, after all, the founder and proprietor of the Green Door, and when he tired of the partying, he needed only to toddle up to his bed on the third floor, where he lived and worked.

Gomelsky is no household name to those of us who are only music consumers, but to music industry insiders he's long been a legend. He was effectively the Rolling Stones' first manager, and his showcasing them at his Crawdaddy Club put them on the road to superstardom. It was Giorgio who introduced the Stones to the Beatles. He managed and produced the Yardbirds, organized major jazz and blues festivals, put the Animals onstage with Sonny Boy Williamson, put Soft Machine in St. Tropez, and partied with *everybody*. In the early 1970s he was a major force behind European art-rock. After coming to New York in the late '70s, he was a godfather–mentor to several successive New York rock scenes.

Giorgio's sixty-sixth birthday party was packed with young New York rockers and a sprinkling of demi-famous old-timers, and several bands played. The Rolling Stones did not. Jann Wenner did not send a photographer from *Rolling Stone*. Kurt Loder did not wish him a happy birthday on MTV News. It's not that Loder wasn't an admirer (he was; he and I discussed it); Giorgio just wasn't newsworthy. He was not famous or glamorous, he was not wealthy, and he had long ago slipped off to the sidelines of the record industry. Though I was unaware of it until recently, he produced one of my favorite albums from my teen years—it says it right there on the back of my ancient copy of the *Having a Rave-Up with the Yardbirds* LP, "A Giorgio Gomelsky Production." He lived four blocks from my office at the newspaper, and it was only by coincidence that I met him.

Giorgio supported the Stones when they were just schoolboys emulating their black American heroes. He remembers the years that led up to their arrival, and the London club scene that made them possible. It's an instructive point of view from which to begin a consideration of what they later became.

○

Gomelsky was born on the road, in Soviet Georgia. His father, a surgeon and medical researcher, was fleeing Stalin's crackdown on the professional classes. His mother was a French-speaking milliner from Monte Carlo. He grew up in Italy and Switzerland, hitchhiked all over as a kid, spent significant years living in England, France, and the United States, and spoke all the relevant languages. "I don't have a homeland," he says. "I guess in a way jazz became my homeland. . . . I'm a jazz and blues fan from way back, since I was ten, eleven years old, which, since I was born in 1934, puts you back toward the end of World War II," he says. "The Germans had been marching up and down the town in Northern Italy where we had temporarily ended up on our way to Switzerland. My dad, a dedicated antifascist, was on their blacklist, and we had to duck and dive." His first memory of jazz is of finding a stack of American records in an attic and hearing songs like "Caravan" and "Take the A Train" and "a Louis Jordan record, something about chickens. We played those again and again and again."

By the end of the war the family had reached Switzerland, where Gomelsky got hooked on the late-night jazz and bebop programs on Armed Forces Network (AFN) radio. He started an adolescents' "jazz society" at "the Benedictine monks' school I went to for a while. Great teachers, the Benedictine monks, but you want to talk to them about jazz? Forget it. We were also practicing playing boogie-woogie stuff. They had this great organ in the church, and three of us . . . would sneak into the church at night when the monks were asleep. One was pumping [the organ], one was playing the left hand part and the other the melody." The precocious jazzbo left home a month before his thirteenth birthday and hitchhiked his way around Europe, finding the arty jazz scene and existentialists' cafés everywhere he went. At "fourteen or fifteen" he started writing reviews for an Italian jazz magazine and organizing jam sessions. He also became interested in filmmaking. When he returned to school in Zurich, "a bunch of us decided to try and put on an open-air jazz festival in the streets of the city, and off we went to ask the city elders for permission. They gave us the most amazing runaround, so one Sunday in May, we went down the Bahn-hofstrasse [the main drag], where all traffic was barred and the burghers and their families went window-shopping, gazing at gold watches, silks, jewelry and other such Swiss luxuries, and on the precise stroke of four, about two hundred of us knelt in the middle of the street, took our pants down, and showed our asses to the sky. You call it 'mooning' here, I believe. Well, next day it was in the papers—and guess what, we got our permits. However, the day of the festival it pissed with rain like it hadn't done in fifty years! Nevertheless, it was a great success, and I think the ZuriFest is still going."

His parents had divorced, and his mother had moved to London, where she worked for "the last of the great Parisian hat designers," making millinery for the royal family and nobles—those big hats they always wore when going to the horse races." He learned English reading the copies of *Melody Maker* she sent to him every week, and he moved himself to London in 1955. "I didn't really speak English, but I could read it and understand it. Of course, my mum was there and she soon sorted me out."

At a club called the Jazz Centre he met Harold Pendleton. "He later became the owner of the famous Marquee, and he founded the National Jazz and Blues Festival in Richmond, and later the Reading Festival, which is still going now." The London clubs were full of what the English called "trad jazz, which really meant some form of early New Orleans or Dixieland music." Chris Barber (who, with Van Morrison and Lonnie Donegan, put out a very retro CD called *The Skiffle Sessions* in 2000) was one of the top bandleaders.

"So there is the beginning of a scene, where you might even be able to make your living at either writing about jazz or promoting jazz or playing it," Gomelsky recalls. "And this is why I went there. I saw it as an awakening of some kind after what that country went through in World War II. I mean, when I got to London, pubs were closing at nine-thirty—forget it! This fog and smog, it was like Jack the Ripper country. You couldn't see three feet in front of you. They were heating their houses with coal, that's why they had the smog. . . . There was no nightlife to speak of, everything was gray and depressed. They had won the war and lost the peace, so to speak. I was used to being up all night in cafés and clubs on the continent, discussing the future of humanity and scheming away at stirring things up. This bohemian culture just didn't exist in London."

Gomelsky got a Greek friend to import an Italian espresso machine. "So now we have this FAEMA coffee machine, in a little place, the Olympic Coffee Bar, around the corner from King's Road, near Sloane Square. King's Road goes through Chelsea in London, and Chelsea was always the artists' district. But at that time it was all dead. There was the old Artists' Club, but it was almost in ruins. But we had a coffee bar, three tables, nine chairs, and no legislation governing this kind of establishment. So now after the pubs close we go to the coffee bar, and drink coffee all night.

"Soon, all the young heads with something to say showed up. People like Mary Quant, who was still unknown, and her boyfriend, Alexander Plunkett-Green. She went on to invent the miniskirt, and he started the modern restaurants on King's Road, beginning the whole revolution that led to Swinging London. There was a bunch of people like this. A friend of mine and I rented an old painter's studio—funnily enough in Edith Grove, where later Brian Jones, Mick Jagger, and Keith Richards got their infamous pad—a big, very cool place, and I organized jam sessions, and some young but impoverished aristos played Chemin de Fer—'Chemmy' they called it—you know, illegal gambling parties.

"Finally, and I'm jumping a bit here, the Greater London Council changed the licensing laws, so if you were serving food in a place you could go on drinking until three a.m. That was the beginning of the glorious and famous London clubs of the sixties. It started with Blaises, then the Cromwellian, the Scotch of St. James, the Bag O'Nails, and ended up with the Speakeasy, the best of them all." (There's a great reference book on all the clubs of the era, Tony Bacon's *London Live*, published in the U.S. by Miller Freeman Books in 1999. Giorgio is acknowledged in it as a source.)

In the early '60s, London's jazz club scene, mostly in Soho and the West End, began slowly to give up some nights to bands playing British versions of the blues, R & B, and "skiffle," the peculiarly British amalgamation of acoustic blues, hootenanny folk, and Chicago "rent party" music that became very big in England—the Beatles started as a skiffle band, the Quarrymen. Local blues bands could find work in the back rooms of London pubs. Guitarist Alexis Korner and Cyril Davies on harmonica formed Blues Incorporated, which over the years included pre-Stones drummer Charlie Watts. Mick Jagger, Keith Richards, and Brian Jones, calling himself Elmo Lewis after the blues legend Elmore James, honed their skills playing as "the interval band" between Korner's sets (while Korner and his band were up in the front of the pub downing a few pints). Jack Bruce and Ginger Baker played with Korner as well.

"Harold Pendleton agreed to give Korner and Davies a Thursday-night residency at the Marquee, and within weeks it became *the* hot spot in London," Gomelsky recalls. "Matter of fact, we were lucky, because there was a big sex scandal going on at the time in London involving Secretary of State for War John Profumo, and in our second week, Christine Keeler and Mandy Rice-Davies, the two girls involved in the scandal, showed up with their entourage of paparazzi. The next day the club was in the papers! Great publicity! I mean, there's like forty of us blues freaks in a place that holds five hundred, and in the middle of the evening these two very hot girls show up and pffft! [He makes a rocket sound.] Now the Marquee—and the pub around the corner where everybody went between sets to get tanked up, because the club had no booze license—becomes the meeting place of all the blues fans in the land.

"It's there I met Brian Jones for the first time," he recalls. It was 1962. Jones "was twenty and just down from Cheltenham, which is a spa city, very genteel, a bit snob, like all such places."

Given the bad-boy, tough-guy image they would soon be cultivating, it's hard to think what nice young lads the Stones were when Gomelsky met them. Jones was the most posh of the group—Gomelsky remembers the rest of them, London boys, making fun of his accent, as well as his lisp. He was small and handsome, well-educated, fey, sort of the deacon's son from the suburbs slumming in the big city. Mick and Keith had known each other since they were five years old; Keith would later remember being as attracted to Mick's great collection of Muddy Waters and Chuck Berry records as to Mick himself. They were both students—Keith at art school, Mick at the London School of Economics. "Mick had not much to say," Gomelsky says. "He was a singer, that's it. He was going to school. Economics. He had wonderful handwriting. I saw him once with this notebook, and I said let's find out what he had learned that day. Open it up, it says, 'Karl Marx, eighteen-whatever to eighteen-blah blah blah,' neatly written. So I open this, 'Hey, Mick, what year was Karl Marx born? Let's hear what you learned today!' He didn't know." When the band moved in together on Edith Grove, Gomelsky recalls, Keith's mother used to drop by periodically with gifts of cash and a stack of clean, pressed shirts. Charlie Watts would later say that "It was more of a family than a band." He'd never been in a band for more than three months, and he figured this one would be over in a year.

It was their next manager, Andrew Loog Oldham, who invented the Stones' bad-boy image. He "made sure we were as vile and nasty as possible," Mick would later say. "Andrew pitched it so that we were very much the antithesis of the Beatles. . . ." In reality, "they were just as cynical as us, but they'd been pitched as clean-scrubbed, they'd got the suits. We were sort of billed as this black version of them. And of course when you look at the pictures now you can see how really clean and sweet we were." Keith later revealed that behind the scenes the Stones and Beatles were almost "a double act," and he spoke of their "meticulous" coordination on timing record releases so as not to conflict in the marketplace. "In the beginning of all this, in the early '60s, nobody took the music seriously," he has said. "It was the image that counted, how to manipulate the press and dream up a few headlines."

The Stones did not start out thinking of themselves as a rock 'n' roll band. Especially Jones: a blues purist, he had founded the band, with piano player Ian Stewart, as a blues "tribute" outfit. (Oldham, in the image-building phase, would soon force the big, '50s-looking Stewart out of the official lineup, though he continued to play and tour with them his entire life.) They played covers—"tributes"—of songs by black American blues and R & B artists such as Jimmy Reed, Muddy Waters, Howlin' Wolf—though Mick and Keith's taste for more rock 'n' roll material like that of Bo Diddley, Chuck Berry, Buddy Holly, and Elvis would soon get them in trouble with the older purists, whose favor they needed to curry if they wanted gigs. There was a sense, Gomelsky remembers, in which they were college-boy snobs about it, the same way that college rock fans would later consider their tastes in Half-Japanese and Yo La Tengo more refined than the rock lumpen's love of Kiss and Iron Maiden. To be a blues fan in London in 1962 made you part of a knowledgeable elite, apart from and above the fans for what Mick called "waffly white pop. But I mean there's always going to be good-looking guys with great haircuts. . . . That's what pop music is about." In the frontispiece to this book, a small notice from a 1962 *Jazz News*, Jagger (incorrectly cited as having "formed" the "rhythm and blues group") is quoted saying, "I hope they don't think we're a rock 'n' roll outfit." Note that Wyman and Watts are not yet in the group; Mike Avery, as "Mick" Avery, would soon become known as the drummer in the Kinks.

Jones was the band's acknowledged leader. "Brian was actually a very good instrumentalist," Gomelsky says. "His mum was a musician and he had gotten piano and violin lessons early in his childhood. He had a very open mind to music. He listened to jazz. Except for Charlie, a bebop fan, none of the others did. Jagger had no idea about jazz. Neither did Keith. Years later, I remember a friend of mine telling me he got the job of accompanying Mick Jagger into every jazz record store in London to buy jazz records. He wanted to educate himself."

Harold Pendleton, the older jazz traditionalist, was reluctant to push this new, "raw" blues thing, so Gomelsky found "dying jazz venues" around Central London where he could plug in R & B nights. "Among other places, I find this one around the corner from Piccadilly Circus. Until a few months before it had been the Piccadilly Jazz Club. . . . I took it over and started putting on R&B shows on Friday nights. One of them was the small-scale but very comprehensive first London R & B Festival, which featured all the five or six exponents of the style, including, of course, Blues Incorporated and the Rollin' Stones [as they called themselves at first]. Harold hears about this and feels I'm trying to steal his thunder, which of course is not true. But to prove my point that R & B would find its audience no matter where, I decided to start another venue as far away from the Marquee and Central London as possible. Some young friends of mine, the Rustics, were running a venue at the back of the Station Hotel in Richmond, the very last stop on the District tube line, fifteen miles from the West End. So I go down there to have a peek.

"I'm checking it out and I see they have this nice room in the back of the pub with phony palm trees, a stage with wooden cutout music quavers on the back wall and a small white grand piano. The place held about one hundred, one hundred fifty people at most, but I thought the odd juxtaposition would be hilarious—Palm Court Blues Orchestra! 'Palm Courts' were big in England way back—dancing and beer, pretending to be on a beach on some tropical island."

Only Sunday nights were available, but he took them. The first group he booked was the Dave Hunt R & B Band, who'd also play at the Piccadilly. Ray Davies was in this band. When they proved unreliable, Giorgio went looking for a replacement.

"At the Marquee and in the music pubs, Brian Jones had been bending my ear constantly, which I didn't mind because I was on his side anyway," Gomelsky says. "He used to say to me—[he affects Jones' whispery lisp] 'Giorgio, Giorgio, you gotta come hear my band. *Thith ith the betht blueth band in the land. Weally. Weally.* Why are you not coming?'" When Hunt didn't show one Sunday night, Gomelsky called Ian Stewart, "who worked at Imperial Chemical Industries, one of the biggest U.K. corporations, and was the only one you could reach on the phone. I told him the gig was theirs."

The Stones had just "gotten themselves thrown out of the Marquee by Cyril Davies, a blues purist who thought their versions of Chuck Berry and Bo Diddley were rock 'n' roll-infected, and they badly needed a regular gig," Gomelsky explains. On their first Sunday night in Richmond, all of three people showed up. "I had completely goofed printing the fliers and the sign outside the pub. I couldn't draw—or spell," Gomelsky chuckles. The sign he wrote for outside the pub announced:

*Sunday night, 7:30 pm*
*Rhythm and Bulse*

"Rhythm & Bulse!" he laughs. "No wonder hardly anyone showed up, right? Not that it would have made a difference had I spelled it properly. The audience just wasn't there yet. But the three guys who did show up I'll never forget. They all joined the music business. One of them, Paul Williams, became a blues singer; another, Little H, a famous roadie who worked for Jimi Hendrix and later died in the crash with Stevie Ray Vaughn; and the third started his own venue somewhere and became an agent. They were cool guys.

"So Brian says, 'Giorgio, there'th sikth of us, and there'th three of them. Do you think it'th worthwhile? Thould we play?' I said, 'Brian, how many people do you think can fit in here? A hundred? Okay, well then play as if there were a hundred people in here.' And they did. And that was one of the reasons I rarely went to see the Stones in later times, because in some ways, that was like the best show they ever did. For three people."

Within weeks, lines were forming outside the pub for the regular Sunday night Stones gigs at Gomelsky's Crawdaddy Club, as he'd dubbed it, after a Bo Diddley song. He remembers packed houses of reticent young Brits, just standing and gawking at the band, afraid to dance. "There were a few tables in the joint, and I convinced my friend and assistant Hamish Grimes to get up on one of them and start waving his arms about while shouting 'Yeah! Yeah!' and whistling as loudly as he could. There wasn't anything else you could do, the place was so crammed. So, during the last number of the first set, an extended version of a Bo Diddley song, 'Pretty Thing' I think, Hamish gets up there and starts waving away. [He windmills his arms over his head.] Everybody looks up and in a split-second they catch on and two hundred pair of arms were undulating like crazy! Man, that was something." A young reporter named Barry May, from the small and conservative newspaper *Richmond and Twickenham Times*, wrote a full-page rave of the show:

> A musical magnet is drawing the jazz beatniks to Richmond. The attraction is the Crawdaddy Club at the Station Hotel, the first of its kind in an area of flourishing modern and traditional jazz haunts. R & B is replacing traddy-pop. The deep earthy sound is typical of the best R & B, and gives all who hear it an irresistible urge to stand up and move. . . . A patch of light from the entrance doors catches the sweating dancers and those who are slumped on the floor, the long hair, suede jackets, gaucho trousers and Chelsea boots . . .

To cajole the London press out to Richmond on a Sunday night, Gomelsky let it be known that he was filming the wild, "ritualistic" behavior of the Stones crowds, and that he had put the band in a small studio to record two tracks for it, a Bo Diddley and a Jimmy Reed song. Peter Jones of the *Record Mirror* sent a reporter. Patrick Doncaster, "a drinking pal and old 'jazzer,' who played very fair Dixieland trombone in a semipro band of journalists *and* was the entertainment editor of the awesome *Daily Mirror*," came and wrote a rave that had much to do with suddenly vaulting the Stones to national attention:

> . . . In the half darkness, the guitars and drums twang and bang. Pulsating R&B. Shoulder to shoulder on the floor are 500 youngsters in black leather and sweaters. You could boil an egg in the atmosphere. Heads shake violently, and feet stamp in tribal style with hands above heads, clapped in rhythm. Shaking figures above the rest, held aloft by their colleagues, thrashing and yelling, like a revivalist meeting in America's deep south . . .

Unfortunately, this was not the sort of attention the pub's owners wanted. On the same day that the Crawdaddy was invited to find a new home—April 22, 1963—Gomelsky "got news that my father had died in Switzerland. The next day I left for Switzerland. I thought I would be back in a few days, but my father had left behind many instructions regarding his legacy and I had to take care of that, and it took three weeks.

"Luckily I had a cool girlfriend at the time, Enid Tidey, who knew the business. She was secretary to Denis Preston, who was the first independent record producer in England with his own studio and label. So she and Hamish looked around, and with the help of Harold Pendleton found the perfect spot for the Crawdaddy to move to, not even half a mile away, on the grounds of the Richmond Athletic Association, where Harold had been putting on the Richmond Jazz Festival. There was this sports complex with a grandstand, and underneath the grandstand was a bar. So when I came back from Switzerland we had moved from the Station Hotel to this place. Here we could fit nearly a thousand people."

The Stones played there, and the Paramounts (who became Procol Harum), and the Muleskinners (who in part turned into the Small Faces), and the Moody Blues, and the Animals, who came down from Newcastle. Later that year Gomelsky convinced Pendleton to let him book the Stones into the Richmond Jazz Festival, bringing the highly controversial R & B to the purists; the effect was much like that of Dylan at Newport. Gomelsky would also produce his own festival, the first British Rhythm & Blues Festival, in Birmingham in 1964. Featuring the Yardbirds with Sonny Boy Williamson, the bill also included the Spencer Davis Rhythm & Blues Quartet—with Stevie Winwood, all of fifteen—a Liverpool band called the Roadrunners, and Long John Baldry, with an uncredited vocal turn by one of Baldry's roadies, a youngster named Rod Stewart.

Meanwhile, the Stones had met Andrew Loog Oldham, an ambitious young guy who'd done some publicity work for Brian Epstein and the Beatles. Gomelsky by this time had met the Beatles himself. He'd seen them, before they were famous, in Hamburg. "Oh, I liked them. They were a good, fluent band. . . . I didn't know they were from Liverpool at first, but they didn't sound German. I was in Hamburg on a Chris Barber tour, so we said hello to them, talked a while." They were still in their black-leather-jacket rock 'n' roll phase. "They were playing long hours, so they needed to know a lot of songs and covers. Later on . . . I was asking how they wrote all their original songs, and John Lennon said, 'When you have to play five hours a night you get to know a lot of songs. We just pinched from here and there. You arrange it so people don't know where you pinched it from. It's not a big science.'"

In his autobiography, *Stone Alone,* Bill Wyman records that it was Giorgio who brought the Beatles to meet the still-unknown Stones:

> Our link with the Beatles, which was always friendly, began on 14 April 1963. . . . Giorgio was talking to the Beatles about making a film. He told them about us and invited them to visit our show in Richmond, only three miles away, later that night.
>
> The room was packed and we were in good form, driven on by the Crawdaddy regulars that now formed our core audience. Soon after we began our first set, we were staggered to see the four Beatles standing and watching us. They were dressed identically in long leather overcoats. I became very nervous, and said to myself: "Shit, that's the Beatles!"

"After the Crawdaddy we went back to Edith Grove and stayed up 'til the wee hours talking about music," Gomelsky adds. "Then they invited us to go to the Royal Albert Hall [four days later, on April 18]. Every year the BBC had this concert the light entertainment music department was putting on. The Beatles were just hitting at the time. [They topped a bill of fifteen acts.] We

[Brian, Keith, Mick, and Giorgio] went there and met them again, and at the end of the evening, Brian Jones and me were helping Neal and Malcolm, the Beatles' roadies, great guys, to carry equipment out of the artists' entrance, and there's this bunch of girls. They start grabbing Brian Jones, 'Oh can I have an autograph? Can I have an autograph?' And Brian was like, 'But I'm not a Beatle!' The girls hadn't been inside, so they didn't know. He had the long hair, looked like a pop star. I told him to sign anyway, and he did. As we're walking down the steps of the Albert Hall to go to my apartment not far from there, Brian looks at me and says, [he does the Jones lisp, with fervid intensity] 'Giorgio, Giorgio, *that'th* what I want. That'th what I want!' And I said, 'Brian, you're going to have it. Don't worry about it. But when you get it you might not want it.' I was wrong—he never got enough of it. . . ."

It was Jones who brought in Oldham while Gomelsky was in Switzerland a few weeks later. "When I came back, the first thing I did was to show not the rushes but a rough cut of the first part of film I had shot before leaving. I wanted it to be a twenty-minute thing. This was up to like eight or nine minutes. And Brian Jones brings this guy to the screening. He introduces me to him and says, 'This is Andrew. We went to school together and he's visiting me.' So Brian—perfidious Brian as it turned out—manipulated the whole thing. Of *course* he never went to school with Andrew. Brian stabbed me. . . ." Shortly thereafter, Gomelsky was informed that Oldham was the band's new manager. "Of course, I think Andrew offered him personally some money. I think that at some point later on, the other Stones found out that Brian was getting a cut above them. They didn't like that very much." In *Stone Alone*, Wyman writes that Jones "planted the seeds of his own demise . . . when he held back cash from the earliest shows, saying they were for band expenses. Nobody disputed his leadership but he always maintained that we were working cooperatively, that it was a five-way partnership in every sense. Yet right from the start we all had this nagging feeling that he was conning each of us out of several pounds at every gig."

Both Wyman and Keith Richards would later say they felt bad about how they'd treated Gomelsky. Wyman wrote that "here was a fairly brutal example of how useful allies and kindred spirits were jettisoned when an act got a sniff of success. Giorgio was an enthusiast who had provided the Stones with an anchor when it was needed. Giorgio's contribution to our success has since been belittled. But while he may not have been right as our future manager, just chopping him out of the gang was insensitive, to put it mildly." Richards, in an interview in *Rolling Stone* in 1971, remembered that Oldham and his partner Eric Easton "fucked Giorgio because he had nothing on paper with us. They screwed him to get us a recording contract."

Asked what he did after Oldham stole the band from him, Gomelsky scoffs, "He didn't steal it, he bought it from Brian, cheap! Whatever. Well, I was choked and shocked, obviously. My friend Brian deceived me. Years later I had it confirmed from Bill Wyman that Brian had manipulated the situation. One of the reasons he had put forward to the others was that they shouldn't trust a 'foreigner' like me to manage their affairs. Talking about Brit xenophobia! The other reason? Eric Easton [an older showbiz type, Oldham's partner and mentor] gave him [Brian] the money to have a custom-made suit."

And what of that film he'd made of the Stones? It "got lost," Gomelsky says. "Nobody knows where it is. It would be worth a fortune today. Perhaps Mick Jagger has it and he's waiting for me to pass away."

If he's mentioned at all in Stones histories, Giorgio disappears at this point in the story, written off as the "mad Russian" whom the Stones had to outgrow to become a worldwide success. His vision was too small; he concentrated too much on live performances and developing a club circuit; he was no match for Oldham's promotional skills. (Giorgio's style did tend toward running small, silly listings in *Melody Maker* promoting "the thrilling, exhilarating, GALVANIC, intoxicating, incomparable ROLLIN' STONES.")

But Gomelsky did not entirely disappear from the industry after the Stones severed their relationship with him. A brief accounting seems in order.

Giorgio has, for example, another story he can tell about the Beatles. Peter Clayton had written for *Jazz Beat* and done liner notes for Decca in the 1960s. By the '70s he was a columnist with London's *Sunday Telegraph.* In 1971 he wrote a funny "confession," "How I Didn't Join the Beatles," that began:

Normally I keep quiet about how I didn't make a film with the Beatles in 1963. . . .

The near miss began when a man named Giorgio summoned me to his flat near the West London Air Terminal. . . . [On arrival] I went into a living room where four young men were sitting around eating omelettes off their laps. I suppose I should remember some of those tart witticisms which became such a feature of Beatles press conferences, but all I can recall are the omelettes, each in the centre of a big plate, like a stranded yellow fish, and the Beatles' pale faces and grey suits and prolific hair (by today's standards, of course, they were short-haired; you could see their ears).

Giorgio's idea was to make a day-in-the-life film about the band. "They are fabulous," Clayton remembered him enthusing. "So hip. Part of a new culture; they are going to be enormous and we are going to write a film for them." He and Clayton, with the Beatles' help, did in fact produce "a detailed synopsis of a story which I'm still convinced would have worked," Clayton wrote in the *Telegraph* column, and "in April 1963, we were ready to make the first Beatles film. All that was needed was the approval of Brian Epstein. . . ." But the Beatles' manager (whom Clayton recalled as exhibiting "a combination of shyness [and] profound suspicion of the ways of showbiz") "probably mistook Giorgio's explosive enthusiasm for just another attempt to stampede him into something," and their film never got made.

"Can you imagine sitting there with the four Beatles and inventing a funny, 'dadaistic' film, off the cuff?" Giorgio reminisces today. "Apart from anything else, we had a great time. But Epstein didn't know his ass from his elbow in those early days. He came from Liverpool, the sticks really, compared to London—although he had wanted to become an actor, and even studied in London for a while, I think. . . .

"A few weeks after our meetings, United Artists, which was run by hustling American producers who wanted a quick 'in' to the nascent London scene, and were ready, as usual, to fork out big money to buy themselves a lion's share, offered the Beatles a three-picture deal. There was no way we could compete with that—our budget was twenty thousand dollars and our aesthetic approach well outside studio conventions. But in any case we didn't get the opportunity to even compete. Epstein, naively—and unethically, in my opinion—just gave them our treatment without ever informing us."

And that treatment, of course, became *A Hard Day's Night.*

"A couple of years later Epstein wrote me a letter, which unfortunately I misplaced somewhere, in which he apologized. He said he didn't know, he was naive, blah blah."

After the Stones fiasco, Gomelsky's friend Hamish Grimes took him to hear a young band "rehearsing on top of a pub in East Sheen, near Richmond," he recalls. "As we were going up the stairs I heard [getting faster and louder] ta-ta-ta-ta TATATATA. Resting on a chord—later known as a 'power chord'—they were playing a sort of manic accelerando, and it caught my ear instantly. I thought, 'Oh, oh, very interesting!' Open the door and there they are—the Yardbirds. The first thing I told them when the song finally stopped was: 'You got the job.'"

Giorgio worked with them for a few years, producing their albums, managing, arranging their tours, which included opening for the Beatles. On their first U.S. tour he arranged for them to meet the legendary Sam Phillips and record "Train Kept A-Rolling" in his Sun recording studio in Memphis. They were touring on a bill with Chuck Berry and the Beach Boys. "Our first show was in Pittsburgh and our equipment hadn't arrived," Giorgio recalls. "I said, 'Now we have to go around begging people to let us play on their instruments.' Chuck Berry wouldn't lend them to us. He wanted us to buy it from him. We ended up borrowing them from the Beach Boys. Jeff managed to blow an amp. Little Fender amp."

From 1967 through 1969, with financing from Polydor and Deutsche Grammaphon, Gomelsky started a public relations and artists' management firm, Paragon, and his own record label, Marmalade, which put out, among other titles, John McLaughlin's first LP, *Extrapolation*. With the lavish backing of the Germans, it was a high-rolling time for Gomelsky. He had a studio built in the middle of the offices, in which visiting artists such as Otis Redding and the Doors could rehearse.

"We were also booking acts and doing PR for all the hip clubs in town. Monday nights at the Speakeasy was humor night, and we'd put on Goon Show, pre–Monty Python events where the actors were people like Brian Auger, Eric Burdon, Jimi Hendrix, Keith Moon—real pissers. It was the first late-night kind of scene, because the musicians were gigging and couldn't get there much before midnight. . . ." Daevid Allen, original guitarist with Soft Machine and founder of the band Gong, once told Giorgio about the time he was at the club "tripping on acid and falling about, hitting his head against the wall. He felt sick and went into the toilet, and there this guy taking a leak took pity on him, got him a glass of water, straightened him out. That guy was John Lennon."

When Gomelsky's German backers pulled the plug on him at the end of 1969, he moved to France, where he managed '70s prog-rock bands such as Magma and Gong and developed a French touring circuit for them and other art-rockers. A job with RCA then brought him to Manhattan, where he was more or less permanently living by 1977. He moved into the Chelsea building that became the Green Door in 1978. There were still fashion display mannequins on low platforms lining the walls when he moved in. With his apartment on the third floor, the rest of the space was given over to a music center and unofficial rock club. Untold numbers of New York bands rehearsed and recorded, performed and partied there over the years. In the '80s it was known as the Plugg Club, with a logo designed by *Punk* magazine's John Holmstrom; as a launchpad for avantist–downtown–No Wave musics, it was a precursor to and incubator for later spaces such as the Knitting Factory. The first Green Door parties were thrown there in the late '80s as an alternative to the club scene by a teenage rocker, Jesse Malin, who'd go on to found the band D Generation. Bill Laswell lived there for a time, and old friends of Giorgio's like Niko would sleep on the floor when visiting New York. For a while, the ground floor was occupied by an S & M club called Paddles; a whole generation of New York rockers has fond memories of filing past customers who were being whipped and nipple-clamped as the musicians headed upstairs to meet with Giorgio.

He keeps his hand in to this day. He has videotaped priceless interviews with a wide range of rock music figures—not so much the musicians as the more behind-the-scenes people like himself, managers and producers and club owners whose insiders' views of the music and the industry are crucial to an understanding of rock's history. And in 2000 he convinced me and George Tabb to co-produce with him an event we called "Rock in New York: The Sounds and the Stories," described in an addendum to this book.

○

Another émigré to New York, Peter J. Swales, talked to me about his memories of the Stones and Giorgio from the 1960s. Today Swales is best known as an historian of psychiatry and a critic of Freudian psychotherapy, one of the so-called Freud bashers who got the psychoanalytical community riled up in the 1990s. He is among the small group of contrarians who adhere to the alternative psychological theories developed by Thomas Szasz and R. D. Laing in the 1960s. It was odd and interesting to learn that in a previous life, as a very young man who'd left school in Wales to move to London, this same Peter Swales worked for Giorgio at Paragon and became Mick Jagger's personal assistant in the late '60s. Handsome and slight, his hair gone gray (at age fifty-one, when I first met him in 2000) but still swooping across his brow in a boyish cowlick, he must have been a fetching lad in those teen years.

Like me and James Miller and countless other boomers, Swales has precise memories of hearing the Beatles for the first time as an adolescent. It was a life-altering experience, whether you were in a small city on the East Coast of the United States, as I was, or in a small town on the coast of Wales.

"When I was a kid of fourteen I heard 'Love Me Do' for the first time, then 'Please, Please Me,' and I was just not the same person after that," he recalls. "My folks had a record store, so I would get to learn about these things before anybody, and more, if you like, encyclopedically, more intensively. [This was] as far as you could get from London heading west—Pembrokeshire, a little peninsula on the coast of Wales. So that was it. I heard the Beatles and it changed my life. And by some stroke of fate that to this day I don't understand, the local tobacconist-newsagent had the newspaper *Mersey Beat*, edited by Bill Harry, published in Liverpool. With all the stories on the Beatles, the Mersey-beats, the Four Pennies, and also by extension a bit of Manchester stuff like Freddy & the Dreamers—who by the way were a great little band—and the Hollies. I used to read it religiously. Brilliant.

"The Beatles, that was just mind-blowing. You might say that in microcosm they condensed everything that had gone before and anticipated everything that would come after. During the year or eighteen months after 'Please, Please Me'—bear in mind this is way before they broke in the States—things happened so fast, moved so fast. First come all these other bands from Liverpool, the Swinging Blue Jeans, all that. Then Manchester; then it opens up. Sheffield,

Birmingham—the Red Caps, Dave Berry & the Cruisers—then Newcastle, Eric Burdon and the Animals, what a brilliant band. Then London.

"Luckily, all this stuff had been able to gestate out of the eye of the media. The media, London-based, London-centric, had completely lost touch—in their own narcissism, in their incestuous little ghetto—with what was going on in the rest of the country, in the body politic. So they catch up late, and of course they want to get their pound of flesh. So what you had was a bunch of much more, say, pretentious, arty [London] bands like the Rolling Stones, Mannfred Mann, Graham Bond Organization, the Yardbirds. Good for them all, but what I mean by pretentious is they had pretensions in a sort of college, quasi-academic way—they thought it was really cool digging up obscure blues music and all that. Like Brian Jones, little Cheltenham kid playing bottleneck blues, never heard before in Britain. Fucking brilliant . . .

"On my seventeenth birthday I fled school and fled home. Through my mother, because of our record store, I was able to get a job at EMI [in London]. So I worked from the age of seventeen as a management trainee—read 'office boy'—learning the ropes for two and a half years in Manchester Square and then in Hayes, Middlesex, where the factory was. So somebody like Giorgio was familiar to me, as were the Yardbirds, the Beatles, from seeing them in EMI's offices. They'd come in." He can remember the Yardbirds swooping through the offices, the swashbuckling Gomelsky in the lead, followed by Clapton and the rest, with the band's roadie, a stooped older man who happened to be lead singer Keith Relf's father, bringing up the rear. "I was working for EMI from September '65 through March '68. By then I'd come to be living with a rock group, in a house between Fulham Road and Kings Road in Chelsea, that was financed by Giorgio's apparatus. That's how I got to know Giorgio. He'd always say [in Gomelsky's Russian accent] 'Pee-tair, one day you will come work for me.' I never really believed it, but it came to pass."

In 1967, "I got to know this group called the Ingoes that Giorgio had sent for a year's apprenticeship to Paris, to get themselves together. . . . I was sharing an apartment with the guy who became their drummer, this guy Kevin. I fell in with the Ingoes and got 'adopted' by them. They were all three or four years older. They called me Little Peter. I was this cute kid, like a little waif off the street. I paid my way by making them tea, cooking them crumpets, stuff like that. They all moved into the apartment I was sharing with my friend. This was impossible. We wrecked that place. We'd all become an extended family with Julie Driscoll [the singer, whom Giorgio managed] and others. So suddenly we lose our place—we've wrecked it—and Giorgio's secretary Madeleine puts us in this house. To my disbelief, but my total relief and gratification, the band said, 'Peter, you're coming too.'

"I remember, Giorgio would call me at ten at night. Maybe the band was out on a gig. He'd call me. 'Pee-tair, who is there?' 'Nobody, Giorgio, just me.' 'Okay, doesn't matter. When they come home, tell them there is a party at twelve-thirty. I got Paul McCartney and Eric Burdon and Frank Zappa and Captain Beefheart. We are coming for a pahr-tee!' He'd give me a list of alcohol to go buy. Fuckin' 'ell, the alcohol! I'd be rushing off to the off-license.

"By the way, when I went to work in his office, part of my job was to keep Giorgio's drink cabinet supplied. Pilfer the odd bottle of whiskey for myself. He didn't care. Giorgio's whole life was an extended party. . . .

"Giorgio, in the context of the mid-'60s London scene, had such a charisma," Swales recalls. "It was quite amazing. Giorgio had this real Mephistophelian charisma. On the other hand, when you came a bit closer he was a fucking big teddy bear. These guys in the band and so on, we referred to him—in a friendly, loving way, but with a bit of a sting in it—as Rasputin. You gotta understand, we were so unworldly we only had a limited number of stereotypes to which we could relate. Given that Giorgio was something-Russian-Jewish, we weren't sure quite what, and he looked to us like Rasputin." Swales remembers listening in September 1974, when John Lennon was the "guest DJ" on a rock radio program on WNEW in New York (to which Swales had moved in 1972, beginning his second, nonrock career): "Lennon was playing his faves from the early '60s. . . . In the middle of all that he lapses into a kind of trance state and recollects on Giorgio, this 'Rasputin character.' It was amazing to me."

Swales only worked at Paragon for six months. In 1968 he went to work at the Rolling Stones' office—which, by then, effectively meant working for Mick Jagger. The Stones had by that point "outgrown" Oldham, just as they had Gomelsky; in his autobiography, Wyman remembers that after Oldham the band was "virtually managed" by Jagger: "He brought into our Maddox Street office as 'personal secretary' Jo Bergman, an American girl who had been help-ing Brian Epstein in the running of the Beatles fan club, and had latterly been assistant to Marianne [Faithfull]. Not surprisingly, she took all her instructions from Mick, and, with Andrew gone, it was a Jagger-Faithfull-Bergman organi-zation, with Jo catering to Mick's every whim."

When Bergman called Swales and offered him a job with the Stones, Swales recalls, "I went round to Jagger's for a couple of hours. Drank tea, got stoned, worshipped at his altar, and went to work for him. I went to a Mothers of Invention concert with them, funnily enough, at that time, still while the job was provisional. The five Stones. Must have been one of the last times publicly when the five originals, with Brian, were ever together. I mean there were times subsequently for business meetings and photos. They were in the royal box at Royal Albert Hall.

"By the way, they were not particularly impressed with the Mothers."

Interestingly, Swales remembers that "Just about the first question Jagger asked me that first time I went round the house, of which I have a very vivid memory, was, 'And how is Giorgio?' It had been five years. So I answered the question. But then I realized it had been a pure formality. Jagger was being nice, polite, welcoming. It was obligatory."

Asked if he agrees with the notion that the Stones had to leave Giorgio to find success, Swales is philosophical. "Yeah, it may be true, maybe Giorgio wouldn't have been the right man for the long haul," he concedes. "Giorgio was, I would say in retrospect, much too much an altruist and an idealist. And a bit too untogether to be a successful businessman in the long haul. . . . On the other hand, if they hadn't run away, maybe everything would have been dif-ferent. No knowing."

○

Did the Stones have to leave Gomelsky behind to find success? No knowing indeed. What is clear, though, is that they did have to leave behind Giorgio's "rhythm & bulse." Let me offer a minor historical thesis:

The Stones didn't become the Stones until 1965, when they started writing their first rock songs for themselves. Before that they weren't the Stones, they were just another cover band. They had to stop being a "tribute" band and start being a rock band.

"We got the feeling we were running out of standards, so we just had to start writing our own," Jagger explains in *Stone Alone*. "We never wrote any blues numbers to start with. Original blues are very difficult to write. The tunes we wrote were more like ballads or pop songs." Wyman records that "The first Jagger-Richards titles were 'It Should be You' and 'Will You be My Lover Tonight,' and were recorded by an Oldham protégé, singer George Bean." For themselves they wrote a few good R & B imitations such as "Tell Me," which appeared on their first LP, *The Rolling Stones*.

It was Oldham, with the support of the Beatles, who convinced the Stones to stop being a rhythm-and-blues tribute band and start being themselves. "It was Andrew who pointed out to us that if we didn't start finding a source of new material this thing wouldn't last," Keith Richards remembered. "So for me the greatest contribution Andrew ever made was to lock me and Mick in the kitchen for a day and night and say 'I'm not letting you out until you've got a song.' Mick and I learned very quickly in retrospect. It seemed a long time at the time until we were able to say 'Do we have the balls to give this to the rest of the boys to play'—until we came up with 'The Last Time.'"

"The Last Time" appeared, with "Satisfaction" and "Play with Fire," on their 1965 LP *Out of Our Heads*, which was still dominated by R&B covers. *December's Children*, tossed together for the Stones' burgeoning U.S. market and released at the end of 1965, included a few other great originals: "As Tears Go By," "I'm Free," and "Get Off My Cloud." After that came "Under My Thumb," "Paint It Black," "Lady Jane," "Stupid Girl," "Think," "It's Not Easy," "I Am Waiting"—all on the truly great, first all-Jagger-Richards-composed LP, *Aftermath*, released in the United States in the spring of 1966. *That's* the Rolling Stones. Up until then, they were just another bunch of skinny white British kids paying homage to black American acts. On their second American tour, in 1964, they hit New York City and raced straight to the Apollo in Harlem, where, Keith Richards would later say, they were completely aware of the "honor to be allowed into this inner sanctum of soul." That same year, they introduced the teenybopper audience of the TV show *Shindig* to the mysteries of Howlin' Wolf. "I think it's about time that we shut up and had Howling'

Wolf onstage," a beaming, clearly tickled Brian Jones told the show's jabbering MC.

As Gomelsky recalls in detail, the Stones were part of a whole generation of young Brits who were studying and reverently copying the blues and R&B. There were the Yardbirds (with, in series, Eric Clapton, Jeff Beck, and Jimmy Page), John Mayall, the Animals, Them, the High Numbers (later The Who), Steampacket (later Rod Stewart and the Faces), Spencer Davis, Long John Baldry, and many others, many of whom were connected with Giorgio in one way or another. The results of their infatuation with black American performers were not always happy. Giorgio organized a famous recording session for the Yardbirds and old blues legend Sonny Boy Williamson that turned into a glaring demonstration of the huge gulf separating the British teens from their idol. The LP is stiff, disjointed, not very good. As teenage rock fans in Baltimore, my friends and I used to shake our heads over it, wondering why it sounded so stilted and formal compared to the Yardbirds' live recordings of the same material. In his 1997 Led Zeppelin history, *Hammer of the Gods*, Stephen Davis records that the session was "total chaos. Sonny Boy kept the musicians guessing with long pauses and arcane blues structures that he seemed to be improvising on the spot." The Yardbirds, nervous and "awestruck," couldn't keep up. Returning home, Sonny Boy collaborated much more easily with a white R & B group who called themselves the Hawks—later the Band. "According to the guitarist Robbie Robertson," Davis reports, "Sonny Boy derided the English players he had been working with, saying how miserably the Yardbirds and the others had played."

For their part, even if there was a lot to it that was mannered and stagy, when the Stones played the blues it was intriguing, it was sexy, and they electrified it with an intuitive Chuck Berry/Bo Diddley funkiness few other white kids' bands quite managed in those days. At their best—"Heart of Stone," "Not Fade Away," "Time Is on My Side," "It's All Over Now"—they were very good at it. At their worst, they were no stiffer than, say, the well-meaning but plodding John Mayall.

The Stones and other British bands such as the Yardbirds unarguably served a crucial role in introducing white kids in both the U.K. and the U.S. to all-important strains of black music they may have never heard otherwise. Rock historians would later disagree over how important this cross-fertilization was. In his Beatles-centric *Flowers in the Dustbin*, James Miller writes off all the Stones' early efforts as mere "burnt-cork minstrelsy." In Chapter 1 I cited British writers such as Will Self who would basically agree, relegating all British rock to a genre of music-hall mimicry that, even at its cleverest and most sincere level of imitation, can never quite be the real thing, because the blues, R & B, and rock 'n' roll are indigenous American art forms. On the other side of the argument, as far back as 1971 American blues and rock historian Peter Guralnick was declaring that "whatever else they have been, The Stones have always proved the best advertisement for American black music outside of the music itself. Where a group like The Beatles retreated quickly into studio seclusion and, more important, never really did anything to see that their influences were recognized, The Stones from the first have paid their respects."

Still, if that was all the Stones had done, just brought their blues "tribute" music to the kids, they most likely would have disappeared from view in a few years, after having put out a handful of memorable but not earthshaking albums, like the Animals, like John Mayall, like all those other British blues purists. Because ultimately this "tribute music" was a dead end, and carried on too long it would have appeared to be mere schtick.

That's the importance of the move Oldham forced the Stones to make. You can see the difference in the old videos of Jagger's performances (excerpted, for example, in the documentary film *25 x 5*)—the great leap forward from 1964 to 1965, from a studious, uptight young Jagger assaying a Muddy Waters classic with great care in 1964 to a new Jagger on *Shindig* in 1965 presenting his own material to the world, sashaying through "The Last Time" and "Satisfaction." He's tremendously more energized, more involved—and, behind the mask of bravura, more scared. Anyone who's ever played music in front of an audience knows why. It's one thing to play someone else's music, to be a mere conveyor, more or less competent, of someone else's song. It's something else entirely to get up in front of people and sing *your* song. There's a lot more at stake: you're putting not just your "interpretation" and your "competence" on the line—it's *you* the audience is judging, your songs, your vision. In great performers this inspires blind terror and strutting bravado in equal measures, and you can see that mix in Jagger in 1965, swinging his hair, swinging his mic stand, swinging his little hips, and swinging the whole auditorium along with him. You are literally watching him *become* "Mick Jagger." He's smiling through the lyrics, showing off; he knows he's become a sex symbol. He's also become a real performer and frontman, playing both the band and the audience. He has developed by 1965 this way of bending away from the mic between lines, ducking, then swooping back up to the mic to deliver the next line, then ducking away again in a theatrical hunchback crouch Johnny Rotten would later exaggerate. It's a call-and-response gesture—sing a line, duck out of the way, then pop back up to sing another—a way of allowing space for the musicians to play and the girls to scream. By allowing that space he becomes the grand master of ceremonies. It's a very African move in that way. (The African-inflected, call-and-response elements in R & B, rock, and rap musics have been well documented and commented upon.)

*That's* rock 'n' roll: a skinny white guy amping up rhythm & blues, channeling those ancient spirits and straining them through his Anglo uptightness, tapping into the music's dance-ritual roots and electrifying them. Rock 'n' roll really is, in the words of an early *Billboard* writer who intended the term as an insult, "mongrel music." Proud, loud, strutting, sexy mongrel music. It was not enough for white British kids merely to imitate black American music; they had to mix with it, mess with it, start making music of their own.

This brings us circling back to that unanswerable question: Did the Stones have to break with Giorgio to break with the rhythm & bulse? Giorgio's history with the Yardbirds suggests otherwise. It was at Giorgio's insistence—over the protestations of young Eric Clapton—that the Yardbirds, who also thought of themselves as an R & B band, recorded "For Your Love" in 1964, a pure pop tune written by Graham Gouldman (later of 10cc). It was their pop-chart breakthrough (followed by another Gouldman song, "Heart Full of Soul"). Clapton the blues purist considered recording "For You Love" as selling out. Supposedly it's one of the reasons he quit the band. Gomelsky adds that Clapton also didn't get along so well with bassist Paul Samwell-Smith, the band's "musical director," who "could be a little officious. He enjoyed the power a bit, I think." He goes on:

"Of course, doing 'For Your Love' *was* a break with pure blues. But I kept thinking, 'The Beatles opened up a vast opportunity for English artists, we can't afford to miss out here. Reaching a wider public is important—once we have access we can tell them about the blues and real music.' Everybody else that came from the blues was making pop records—the Stones, the Animals, Spencer Davis. We had gathered an audience, but we couldn't get past the radio. And in England, remember, there was only one radio station, with only like one pop program a week. Until [pirate] Radio Caroline came along and really changed everything. So we had to figure out a way of getting in there. We all had done blues songs as singles—the Stones had done 'Come On,' we had done 'Good Morning, Little Schoolgirl.' But we forgot that in England there wasn't really a blues audience that bought singles—they bought albums. By the way, that's why I recorded the *Five Live Yardbirds* album before they had a single hit record.

"And then there was the commercial music scene, as bad in the U.K. as in the U.S.—worse really, because of a lack of regional markets and independent labels, and radio producers controlling what and who went on the air. They were working hand in hand with the music publishers, and if they didn't have some kind of a financial interest in it, you wouldn't appear. So one day Ronnie Beck, who was a nice, young, pretty hip 'song plugger' for a major publisher, came with this song, 'For Your Love.' As soon as I heard it I said, ah, we could use harpsichord here, and on the demo there was a bongo drum and I said, oh, interesting. We'll do a pop song, but we'll inject some stuff in there that will indicate to people with ears that we're doing this a little bit tongue in cheek, but we're also doing it as an opportunity to reach a bigger audience and put in some experimental stuff. Which we did, and it worked. Same with sitar and tablas-like sounds on 'Heart Full of Soul,' Gregorian chants on 'Still I'm Sad,' and a jazzy walking bassline on 'Shape of Things.'"

Peter Swales adds that "even those blues purists like Clapton came around to a more broadbased pop tradition by around '67, in one fashion or another. . . . I don't doubt his sincerity when he quit the Yardbirds, because Giorgio *was* trying to popify them. But within a year he's doing stuff aimed at a mass market [too]."

So there's the Stones, in 1965, inventing themselves as a rock band and help-ing to invent rock in the bargain. From the moment they stopped being a trib-ute and cover band and started writing their own songs, they kept growing and improving, up to their peak, the plateau of *Beggars Banquet, Let It Bleed,* and *Sticky Fingers.* Can it be denied that this was their finest sustained moment, 1968 into 1971? The songs included "Street Fighting Man," "Sympathy for the Devil," "Gimme Shelter" (still the sexiest rock song ever recorded), "You Can't Always Get What You Want," "Let It Bleed," "Salt of the Earth," "Live with Me," "Monkey Man," "Brown Sugar," "Can't You Hear Me Knocking," and "Dead Flowers."

This era of the Stones, this version if you will, is the Stones most people remember and love. This was their peak, and very shortly after it they began to slide downhill, though it took a lot of people a long time to admit it. Let alone the Stones themselves.

Grant them 1972's *Exile on Main Street,* a fine, down-to-earth juke jam, very misunderstood and underappreciated at the time—but understandably so, because, for all its high spirits and boogie and woogie, it was, consciously, a step down from the rock-heroic heights the band had scaled on those previous three LPs. It was simpler and more straightforward, and it's still fun to hear today. . . . But it wasn't *Sticky Fingers* or *Let It Bleed.* (It was also largely constructed by Keith Richards and a bunch of American session men in Keith's mansion in France, while the rest of the band was far-flung around the globe and only jetting in occasionally to punch in the parts that Richards couldn't play or sing himself. It helps explain the rawness of it, its throwback-to-basics juke-joint appeal: that's where Keith's heart was, even if he did go on for another thirty years being Jagger's enabler in all the bombast and spectacle.)

That 1972 U.S. tour—the post-*Exiles* tour, the one captured notoriously on film by documentarian Robert Frank as *Cocksucker Blues*—was also arguably their last truly great tour as a rock 'n' roll band. Face it: as musicians the Stones had always been a precarious proposition. Even as basic rock musicians, their live playing always teetered on the brink of disaster—and not intentionally, in the punk sense of *courting* disaster, either. They were all just barely competent rock musicians. Many's the live gig preserved on audio or videotape in which Keith is out of tune and slightly out of time, Charlie's dropping the ball, and Bill Wyman is a barely audible sludge of bass noises. Many's the night that what held them together was a huge act of faith on the part of their audience and the undeniable natural force of Mick Jagger, an onstage performer of riveting genius in his heyday.

Of course, barely achieving musicianly competence is a hallmark of rock 'n' roll; some of the great fun and energy released by rock music is in the tensions of a band barely able to hold it all together, desperately flailing away. Still, shambollocking incompetence is just as likely to leak energy, lose propulsion, become flat and boring. As Gomelsky points out—and the documentation attests—the famous Hyde Park/Brian Jones tribute concert of 1969 is a great example of how awful the Stones could be onstage. Effectively, they hadn't played in front of an audience in two years, and they sounded like it. But that's when they started playing onstage again, and it's in that period, 1969–1972, that they hammered themselves into a great onstage touring unit, maybe even "the greatest rock and roll band in the world" for a while. Go back and listen to *Get Yer Ya-Ya's Out*, watch *Gimme Shelter* or, if you can, *Cocksucker Blues;* for all the ominous anti-Stones import of both those films, the live performance footage is to this day exciting and impressive—what a great rock show the Stones were putting on in those years, despite it all. The Stones tour in '72 was the ultimate sex, drugs, and rock 'n' roll tour (watch Keith in *Cocksucker Blues* nod out backstage, gaunt and skeletal, wilting before your eyes in slow motion like a dying lily in a time-lapse film). The Stones of 1972—*that* I can understand feeling nostalgic for. Who among us boomer rock fans *isn't* nostalgic for that?

But 1972 was the last you ever saw it. Charlie Watts would later say that at the time he'd thought it was going to be their last tour.

It certainly should have been. This is the grim truth boomer Stones fans refused for decades to admit: 1972 was the last great Stones tour, and also the beginning of the end. Every tour after that was like a reenactment of '72, an attempt to reproduce the Stones at their peak—only the reproductions had less and less fidelity as the years ground on; the image became ever fuzzier and degraded, like a photocopy of a photocopy of a photocopy, until you ended up with senile, senior-citizen horror shows like *Voodoo Lounge* and *Bridges to Babylon.*

The quality of their recordings sank even more quickly and depressingly. *Exile*, their last really good LP, was followed by the descent into *Goat's Head Soup* in 1973, the forgettable *It's Only Rock and Roll* in '74, and the awful *Black & Blue* in '76. In 1978 they rallied and made a conscious effort, like an over-the-hill prizefighter, to work off the fat and the lethargy, to stage a comeback. In

1978, those of us who by then had been Stones fans for fifteen years took *Some Girls* as a last memento, an aloha from a band entering its sunset years. This was Silver Age Stones, a magnet of instant nostalgia, a last hurrah. Had it been the last album they ever put out—had they the decency and good sense to tour one last time behind that LP and then break up for good and all—no one could've have blamed them. After all, hadn't they'd given us these last little gifts—"Beast of Burden," "Shattered"—as a kind of peace offering, a way of saying, "Sorry about *Black & Blue*, folks. We weren't ourselves"?

Unfortunately, they didn't stop in 1978. It was only the point at which they utterly and completely stopped being the Rolling Stones and went back to being just a cover band: a Rolling Stones cover band. They were the Rolling Stones, Inc., a corporation whose business was to mass-produce and mass-market Rolling Stones nostalgia products. They did that very well, but it *wasn't* rock 'n' roll, and it wasn't the Rolling Stones. The Steel Wheelchairs tour wasn't even a rock concert anymore: it was a stadium spectacle, something very much more like a football game than rock. Complete with fireworks display. And that's the crowd such events attract, that's how they respond, like they're at a sporting event. Go Stones.

○

Peter Swales went to work for the Stones at a historically felicitous moment—when they were beginning to peak. It was the era of "Jumpin' Jack Flash"/*Beggars Banquet:* we're back and we're bad Stones. He remembers that before this, he'd seen them "live in the Finsbury Park Astoria. It must've been either the end of '65 or early '66. Coincidentally, I saw them something like a month later in Tooting, because a friend of mine had a spare ticket. At the same time, a woman at EMI—who was, unbeknownst to me at the time, the lover and then second wife of George Martin—used to sneak tickets for *Top of the Pops*, for me and my little buddies. She thought I was a cute little kid. Understand, I was seventeen. So I'd go to *Top of the Pops* looking like a Mod, hair [combed] back, and the Stones were there one day, much to my surprise, miming—except for Jagger, he sang live, that was how they did it—miming '19th Nervous Breakdown.' I remember standing in the back with another so-called Mod. He was chewing gum. His name was Bob Thacker. We're standing way at the back, not dancing. [He mimes leaning against the wall, looking cool and bored.] And Keith Richards looks over with pure menace in his eyes, as if to say, 'You fucking cunts, get on that floor and dance!'"

I ask Swales about his position in the Stones organization.

"When I first met with him, Mick had in mind to start a record company, for which he liked the name Mother Earth," he replies. "And I did know quite a bit about records and distribution and promotion and all that. So ostensibly I was taken on to do record promotion. But inherent in that gray notion was a conflict. You can't promote one or two records a year. It's a full-time gig. A record company issues product every week or every two weeks, at least every month, and employs somebody full-time to go lobby the BBC, Radio Luxembourg—'For fuck's sake, play this record!' You cultivate relationships, you rub shoulders, you take these people—in those days—to the pub, hang out with them. What Mick wanted wasn't very clear to me. We talked in that first meeting about selling *Beggars Banquet*, privately produced, off the back of trucks—lorries, as we called them. Which was mad."

Jagger wanted to get the Stones out of their existing contract with Decca Records, and in effect create for the Stones what the Beatles had with Apple Records.

"That was the analogy. So I was taken on ostensibly to do promotion, but virtually did none. I mean, a bit here and there. I set up the big 'Beggars Banquet' for the press, all that shit—104 invitees is the number that sticks in my head—in a restaurant in Kensington. But I instantly fell into the role of factotum, personal assistant. Across the board. Anything and everything that was needed, I had to fix it. 'Peter! Gotta find three sax players.' So I'd be like, 'Mick, that last Fleetwood Mac album that we were talking about the other week, pretty good, no? How about those sax players?' 'Peter, that's a fucking great idea.' Or, 'Peter! We need a keyboardist.' I'd heard that Al Kooper was on a promo visit. He was with Columbia-CBS. So I just called up Columbia-CBS. 'Hi. My name is Peter Swales. I'm calling from the Rolling Stones' office.' Red carpet. 'I'm wondering if Al Kooper is still in England.' 'Yes he is.' 'Well tell me, hypothetically, in principle, would he be available for a Stones session?' So I call Mick, 'Mick, listen, the keyboard player on *Blonde on Blonde*, so happens he's in London.' 'Peter, that's fucking great.' So next thing he's playing on 'You Can't Always Get What You Want,' which I think he's traded on for the rest of his life. It's as though he'd gotten a Purple Heart or Victoria Cross in battle action.

"So music. Album covers. All at the last moment. I'd have to sometimes— which was humiliating for me—go get a taxi for Mick in the rush hour. You know, anything. Anything. Dead exciting, but very difficult."

Both Giorgio and Swales speak about what a small circle of people the London rock community was, up through the later 1960s. "You have to remember, the rock scene in London, from '63 through '68, '69, was a little village. All these things were cottage industries," Swales says. "Bizarre for me in retrospect is that I could go to the Marquee Club and see what I conceived of at the time as world-renown bands—the Spencer Davis Group, the Yardbirds, the Animals, Jimi Hendrix, Pink Floyd in the earliest stage—in this little club, maximum capacity I guess seven or eight hundred. Today it's unthinkable. These bands had had Top Ten hits all over the world, and yet they were playing these little gigs. . . . Little could we foresee the gigantic scope on which things were going to be mounted imminently, the whole transformation."

As a less pleasant example of the scene's intimacy, he notes that the Stones' offices where he worked were on the top floor on Maddox Street, and "next floor down was the Kinks. And Jagger used to send up the Kinks something rotten to me. Gawd, you know the German word *schadenfreude?* To take pleasure is someone else's misfortune? That's how he'd talk about Ray Davies and his brother. I remember him telling me that he'd seen them live at the Whiskey-a-Go Go in L.A., and they were the worst fucking band he'd ever seen in his life—and he really enjoyed that."

It was in this setting that the Stones pulled together (if just barely) their TV special, *The Rolling Stones Rock & Roll Circus*, featuring a gaggle of rock star friends including The Who, Eric Clapton, and John Lennon. The show was not seen for years because in the end, Jagger decided the Stones' performance on the show was not up to snuff. For one thing, they had not, at that point, played together in front of an audience for a couple of years. For another, Brian Jones was so out of it he could barely stand up, let alone play. He'd be dead in half a year.

"Oh my god, what a disaster that was"; Swales smiles wryly. "First, we had rehearsals in the Londonderry Hotel. We rented a floor that was ordinarily a banquet hall. It was Bill Wyman's favorite hotel in London, overlooking Hyde Park, on Park Lane. I think that was the reason we decided to have rehearsals there. So you're talking about The Who, Taj Mahal—we'd hoped to get Dr. John and Graham Parsons, but they couldn't make it through—long, complicated stories having to do with visas and Musicians Union. Taj Mahal we smuggled in, virtually. There was Clapton. . . . Originally I'd been sent round by Mick to Steve Winwood's, whom I knew a little bit, to convince him to play with Keith Richards, Clapton, and a drummer as yet unknown—who eventually would become Mitch Mitchell. Steve wouldn't do it. . . . So Jagger pulled a trump card by calling Lennon.

"So this is November, December '68. I had not seen them perform, by the way, since those times in 1965. Possibly I'd seen them in the studio. Okay, so toward the end of the day, early evening, in terms of the peer pressure and the camaraderie of musicians, it's like, when are we going to hear from the Stones? That's the way all those guys, Townshend and that lot, are thinking. I'm in suspense. 'Oh my god, Peter, get ready for a fucking abortion,' that's what I'm thinking. I could see Brian was completely out of it. So they go, take their places, and they start 'Sympathy for the Devil.' Brian is still trying to tune up. He's fumbling away. But it's recognizably 'Sympathy for the Devil'; they're holding it together. Then it starts to fall apart. And this totally impressed me about Mick Jagger; I found it awesome: He suddenly became a different person. Figuratively speaking, he whipped that band into shape. As they're doing it, as they're delivering, he's looking at them with menace, with sheer you might almost say *odium* in his face. And they just pulled it together. But not Brian. In that moment we knew this was a disaster. Ain't gonna happen. Did a couple of other songs. The Stones acquitted themselves.

"Okay, so when we get to the television studio, everything takes longer, inevitably. There's all kinds of setbacks. Everything took longer than scheduled. By the time the Stones finally are going to do their stuff, it's one or two in the morning. And we're going to have to go through the night. You can't just keep the studio for tomorrow. Well, I don't know how they made the segment of the film even as good as it is, to be honest. Given the state that they were in. I'll tell you this, Brian couldn't even play. He's miming. If you check out 'You

Can't Always Get What You Want,' incredibly, Keith laid down the acoustic guitar track, and they played with it. It's very difficult for a drummer to play along with an acoustic guitar track, but that's what they did.

"We—I mean the collective, the family—we should have said, 'That's it, Brian. You can't be in this band anymore.' It was manifest that he was going down the tubes. As it happens, that's how charitable Mick and Keith really were, and Charlie and to an extent Bill, I guess—no, Bill had no say in it, really. It dragged on for another six months before we said, 'Brian, that's enough.' At least three times, maybe four or five times, Mick put it to me with certain gestures, eye signals, telling me what he really meant. 'Peter, call Brian. Tell him he better be at the fucking photo session on Thursday. Or. . . .' Right? 'Or.' That was tantamount to a threat. 'Otherwise you're out of the band.' I call Brian . . . [here Swales imitates Jones's fey, slight voice—though without the lisp Giorgio affects when he's doing his Jones imitation] and he says, *'Oh, but Peter, on Thursday I'm going . . .'* Whatever. I say, 'Brian, I'm sorry. Mick says you've got to be there. And so does Keith.' It got heavy for me."

Swales is skeptical of the traditional Stones conspiracy theory—that Mick and Keith stole Brian's band, and Keith stole Brian's girlfriend, and together they drove him to the drink and drugs that killed him. "That's a very superficial perception. There are certain facts that could be adduced toward supporting a kind of conspiracy theory like that, but Brian dug his own grave, years before. I can't stress enough how far they bent over backwards to try to accommodate and oblige him. They really did. Yeah, it's true that in the beginning it was Brian's band. He was the leader, by his own declaration. And he was potentially very despotic. And yet he didn't have the creative talent—I'm not talking about the musicianship, but the creative talent to keep that band going, to produce a new repertoire. Which Mick and Keith did, to their credit. With few exceptions, all those rock groups and beat groups and R & B groups from the early '60s were spontaneous democracies, and a tyrannical dictator, even of a benevolent bent, couldn't get away with it for that long. That just wasn't the way it worked. Especially when it came to money. You know, Brian can't keep twice the amount that anybody else is getting. Especially when you're struggling to make ends meet. And about stealing his girlfriend, well, this kind of crap goes on all the time among young guys. . . .

"Brian was also, in modern psychiatric language, this narcissistic type. He had such a vanity about him, and such a conceit that he's the kind of guy who's going to fall soon enough into self-deceit. He's what you can really call an addictive character, much more than Keith even."

Swales pauses. Sighs. Then he adds: "Lovely guy, by the way, Brian. He was so well-mannered, and he spoke such lovely, pristine English. None of this Cockney shit, Mick and Keith, this fake Cockney accent. Middle class. And half Welsh. His father, an aircraft engineer, was Welsh."

Swales says that something about the Hyde Park Brian Jones tribute concert in July 1969 struck him as the first sign of the way things were going to go—toward the big spectacle and bombast that became the Stones in the 1970s. "I'd been working for them eight or nine months. We learn that Blind Faith is gonna play in Hyde Park, a free concert. Black Hill Enterprises had gotten the sort of franchise to do free concerts in the park. Mick comes to me one day. He looks at me in a very pointed way, a way that betokens, you might say, a command or instruction, and says, 'Peter, I need you to do something for me on Saturday. Go to the park, check it out.' You may ask why he didn't go himself. Maybe he had a prior commitment. More likely he didn't think it was too easy for Jagger to just go to the park. . . .

"So I go and report back, 'It was fucking great.' I seem to remember we ended up talking about how good Steve Winwood and Clapton were, and who's this bass player Rick Gretsch. What I loved was they did that Buddy Holly song 'Well, All Right,' and Jagger, Clapton, and Lennon had jammed on that in the de facto dressing room at the television studio where we made *Rolling Stones Rock & Roll Circus* seven months earlier or whatever it was. . . .

"So this coincides with Brian being out of the band. 'Brian, you gotta go. You're out. Fired.' I had quite a lot to do with Mick Taylor coming into the band, though in a very incidental way. Mick Taylor came in. First thing he did—the Stones had laid down a beautiful version, much clearer version of 'Honky Tonky Woman,' without that squealing lead guitar, those chords at the top. You could hear the saxes—the Fleetwod Mac saxes, that bunch. Beautiful. But it did lack something. And Jagger—quite rightly, as was proven in the fullness of time—knew that it was a single. Frankly, I couldn't quite hear that at that point. So Mick Taylor came in, overdubbed the guitar. And at that very time Mick, now secure in the knowledge that Mick Taylor can pull it off, agrees that the Stones will do Hyde Park. Which was a big thing for him. They couldn't have faced an audience properly in, oh, two years at least, two and a half years . . . through the drug bust period and all that.

"Anyway, something had changed. There was a watershed that had happened in the meantime, though I doubt Mick could've anticipated it. Up till '65, '66, bands like the Stones couldn't hear themselves playing. All you heard was screams. Deafening. You couldn't hear anything. But by Hyde Park, now people want to sit down and listen. . . . And then, a week before the concert, Brian goes and dies, right? So the whole thing became, through some weird synchronicity, a tribute to Brian Jones. Pity the poor fucking butterflies that Mick let go off the stage that day!" Swales laughs. "They all come crashing down. Oh, it was weird."

It was the U.S. tour later that year, the one that culminated in Altamont, that Swales says was the turning point. "The scale and the scope of it was mind-boggling to us," he says. "Don't forget, those five Rolling Stones had been to the States, traveled most of the world and come back to tell the story. So they were worldly wise in ways that I surely couldn't be. I was just a kid, five or six years younger than them. They'd had this bizarre five years of experience. But even they couldn't have known the scale that things were going to start happening on, festivals and all that. I mean, in those days the P.A. systems, there were no monitors. A few people were beginning to experiment with them. So it was very difficult to make that leap. It needed a reinvention of the technology to accomplish it. Also in terms of lights, transportation, the whole organizational apparatus you're going to have behind that."

I put it to him that the benign way to describe what happens to rock as it goes from the 1960s to the 1970s is that there's more equipment, more skill for putting on these bigger shows—

"And more money," he quickly adds.

Which is all to the good, and produces, in the early '70s, a Rolling Stones touring outfit that really could claim to be "the greatest rock 'n' roll band in the world." The less benign interpretation is that the drive toward bigger and better becomes an impulse toward too big and puffed out; that the music stops being rock 'n' roll when it starts being a stadium spectacle.

"Sure," he nods. "In a manner of speaking, Charlie Watts was the conscience—and therefore, necessarily, the *guilty* conscience—of the Stones. And he was always saying to me, 'You know, Peter, this is absurd. We're a little club band. What the *fuck* is all this?' I suspect it was probably Charlie, then, who motivated the move, it must have been '72, when the Stones returned to the Marquee Club. Much as they loathed John Gee and Harold Pendleton [who'd kicked them out years earlier for not being blues purists], much as they hated their fucking guts, they returned to the Marquee Club to do something for Granada TV. And when Ian Stewart died, poor Stew, the Stones had a private party in the 100 Club on Oxford Street. So you might want to read it this way for convenience: In a sense, the Stones have had a guilty conscience about just this, the absurdity of playing these vast stadia with these props, these fucking huge penises and whatever. It's nonsense. That's been for me the source of a certain deep disappointment vis-à-vis the Stones and Jagger. We, meaning the Stones office when I was there, we brought over Taj Mahal for *Rock & Roll Circus*. What a lovely little blues band that was. And I know that was Keith's model of how the Stones would get old with grace and dignity. But they became too famous, too celebrated to be able to."

When discussing his own aging, Mick Jagger liked to use that same model, to compare himself to old blues and jazz men, the way they can go on doing their thing credibly until the day they die. But the minute the Stones stopped being a blues homage band and became rock 'n' rollers, that comparison became invalid. Rock has blues in its roots, but the two are, in the end, completely different art forms. Blues is a grown-up's medium. Young people can get the blues and play the blues, but they only get better at it as they become adults. Rock is youth music, and you only get *worse* at it as your youth fades.

Besides, the blues is about chilling and illing, not jumping up and down and sashaying around. Muddy Waters would look just as ridiculous as Mick Jagger does now if he pranced around and wiggled his butt. Conversely, when the elder Mick sits on a stool and simply sings a nice, bluesy number, it's much easier on the eye and the ear than his sexy-senior-citizen antics. Partway into the abominable *Voodoo Lounge* tour of 1994, the Stones broke from their routine show, walked over to a separate area of the vast stage, and did an Elvis-'68-style acoustic segment. Stones Unplugged, just a bunch of good old boys settin' around on stools, playing some old tunes. One was "Angie," which was awful, but the other was a wonderful acoustic rendition of "Sweet Virginia." For the first time in the show, everyone else onstage looked as if they were actually grooving and having as much fun as Mick. It was a totally charming few minutes. If they'd played the whole concert that way, just a bunch of old white bluesmen plucking away on hollow-body guitars and honking on the harmonica, it would have been a lovely evening out with the elderly Rolling Stones. But, of course, you can't play an evening of acoustic blues to a stadium crowd of yahoos who've paid way too much money and drunk way too many beers not to hear "Satisfaction" and see some fireworks, so the Stones soon dragged their old bones back over to their amps and went back to pretending to rock out.

In a 1972 TV interview, talk-show host Dick Cavett asked Bill Wyman if he could picture himself still playing rock 'n' roll at age fifty or sixty. Wyman says no, he sees himself retiring. (He would finally do so after the disastrous *Steel Wheels* tour of 1989.) Asked the same question, Mick just says, "Yeah, easily . . . there's a lot of people that still do it at sixty. I think it's a bit weird, but they seem to still get their rocks off at it. Marline Detroit, she still does it, and she's more than sixty."

Six years later, in *Rolling Stone* number 268 (June 29, 1978), a very different Mick Jagger, age thirty-four, was interviewed by Jonathan Cott. Cott began the article with a then-controversial statement: "I've been missing the Rolling Stones for years," he writes, noting that the mid-'70s era, between 1972's *Exile* and the upcoming *Some Girls*, had been "musically dispiriting." No kidding: *Goat's Head Soup, It's Only Rock and Roll, Black & Blue*. . . . As Cott observes, ". . . during their post-'Exile' period, the Stones seem to have been around more in body than in spirit." They went from a period of incredible fertility during which they were creating some of the greatest rock songs of all time to "Angie" and "Starfucker." The spark was gone, never to be rekindled.

Cott goes back and forth throughout the interview between asking Jagger typical rock-journalist questions about his lyrics (giving Jagger opportunities to show he knows a thing or two about Jung and Artaud) and coyly needling him about the band's age and its lackluster performance record in the '70s. His very first question is, "You've been a Rolling Stone for about fifteen years now. How does it feel?" And Jagger's response, defensive yet already capitulating, as though he knows where this is heading: "What a funny question! It's a long time, perhaps too long. . . ."

Cott persists: "Along with The Who, the Rolling Stones are two of the last Sixties English rock groups that are still together."

Jagger: "I think both groups are very fragile."

Cott notes rumors that the Stones might break up.

"That's rubbish," Jagger snaps.

Asked what he's done with his life in the '70s, Jagger quips, "Wasting my time." It's a joke and a throwaway—and maybe one of those lines that's more revealing than the teller means it to be.

Later, Cott judiciously calls *Exile* "probably the last of your albums to have been widely admired," and he asks, "How successful were your last few albums?" Jagger goes into a long, again defensive, response, but he concedes, "I think there are some good songs on our last albums, but they probably lacked direction."

Near the end, Cott zings him with: "You said that you didn't want to be singing 'Satisfaction' when you were forty-two."

"No, I certainly won't," the thirty-four-year-old replies. But twenty years later he'd still be at it, in his mid-fifties.

Chet Flippo followed up in *Rolling Stone* that September (number 273, September 7) with a generally unhappy piece covering the *Some Girls* U.S. tour. The Stones and their management were unhappy with *Rolling Stone* for not having been fully supportive of the band recently. Flippo records how he was eventually disinvited from the touring press, but not before he'd gathered ample impressions of the "old pros, crippled by age and by dissipation . . ."

Reporting on one concert, Flippo observes: "In 'Beast of Burden' when Jagger pleaded, 'Ain't I *tough* enough?' it was a real question, not a rhetorical one. Thirty rows back, though, with everyone still standing, I was thinking: I'm thirty-four years old and I've seen rock & roll for seventeen years and I'd kinda like to sit down. Jagger is also thirty-four and he's been doing rock & roll for seventeen years and most of the time he acts like he'd like to sit down, too. Why does he keep this up? Just for the few moments of glory? I studied him through binoculars and his face showed no emotion whatsoever." That was at a good show; the bad ones, Flippo notes, were "really painful." Typically, he writes, the crowd would be buoyant at first, "ready for the old Stones magic to wash over them." But as the concert proceeds and "the magic wanes, a certain listlessness sets in."

A certain listlessness. Remember, he was writing this *in 1978*. The Stones—"old pros, crippled by age and by dissipation"—would continue dragging themselves through world tours for another twenty years. Keith and Ron Wood were bored and doing side projects by 1979. Keith and Mick feuded and spat through the early '80s. In 1980 the Stones released *Emotional Rescue*, the first in a long line of what I consider post-Stones LPs, or, to put it more directly, bad Stones-tribute LPs: *Tattoo You* in '81, *Undercover* in '83, *Dirty Work* in '86, *Steel Wheels* in '89, the utterly forgotten *Urban Jungle* in '90, *Voodoo Lounge* in '94, *Bridges to Babylon* in '97 (with subsequent touring around the world through 1999). In 1981 they did their first really huge outdoor stadium tour. From then on, over the next two decades, the show became ever more bombastic—the vast stages and catwalks, the fireworks, the pyrotechnics, the theatrical sets and props that look like castoffs from roadshow productions of *Cats*, Mick's weirdly sports-inspired costumes, the ever larger cast of backing musicians and singers and guest artists. It was with the *Steel Wheels* tour in 1989 that large numbers of people finally began to smirk; the jokes about it being the "Steel Wheelchairs" tour were as apt as some fans felt they were cruel. It didn't help that the music from the album itself sounded so frankly imitative of younger, then-popular acts. As a youngster, Mick Jagger had imitated Muddy Waters. Here he was now as an old fart, imitating . . . *Prince?* Could one sink any lower? The stage was so vast that when the band spread out to play they looked like ants on a picnic table; they probably couldn't see one another unless they were wearing their contact lenses.

There was something sadly metaphoric about the huge empty spaces separating them from one another. They weren't a band anymore; they were the board of directors of Rolling Stones, Inc., called together for their annual meeting. Not a rock band anymore, but a handful of middle-aged men acting like a rock band. The stages and sets and fireworks only kept getting bigger in the '90s, the show more and more soulless, less like rock—even outdoor stadium rock, a dicey proposition in the best of times—and more like a truck pull. On tour in the mid-'80s, a serious, tired-looking, gray-haired Charlie Watts was asked on film if he still liked touring with the Rolling Stones after twenty-five years. He scowls and rubs his neck, looking like any laborer leaning on his shovel. "It's work, innit?" he replies. "I mean I just don't think about it, actually. Best not to. I'd have been dead years ago if I thought about it. It's quite hard work, some of it."

Look at the 1988 video for "Just Another Night," which was another one of those now-forgotten late-late-model Stones singles—this one from Mick's misbegotten solo LP and tour. He looks like a dirty old man, scrawny and leathery as an iguana, in ridiculously heavy eye makeup, with a pretty young girl pretending to find him sexy and fawn on him. It's just awful.

Presenting them their award at the third annual Rock and Roll Hall of Fame induction ceremony that year, a gray-bearded Pete Townshend facetiously tells them, "Guys, whatever you do, don't try and grow old gracefully, it wouldn't suit you." (He should know.) Mick, in a tux, opines, "We're being rewarded for twenty-five years of bad behavior." He quotes Jean Cocteau's line about how Americans are funny people—first you shock them, then they put you in a museum.

In the concert video from the *Voodoo Lounge* tour of 1994, Whoopi Goldberg comes out onto the stage to introduce them. Why Whoopi Goldberg? What did she have to do with anything? It didn't matter by that point: it was just celebrity glad-handing, just one star(fucker) giving the nod to another. "I'm here to introduce the band that brought music to us that our parents told us we probably shouldn't be listening to," she announces, and then adds: "But a lot of our parents are here tonight!" Which doesn't make any sense, but you figured she'd probably gotten high backstage, and anyway, you knew what she meant . . . and it was *really* depressing.

○

We could make this easy and just accept the cynical notion that the Stones were faking it all along. Faking it as young Stones, imitating black artists; faking it as old Stones, imitating the younger Stones; faking it as satanic Stones and street-fighting Stones and all the other Stones along the way. There is ample firsthand reportage, from a variety of people who knew him, that the real Mick

Jagger, behind all the guises and costumes, was Jagger the economics student all along, Jagger the cold businessman who would build himself a reported $200 million personal empire—Jagger, that is, as the oily Turner in *Performance*, sneering at us that we all work for him. All the rest is showbiz. Or, if you will, dance-hall schtick.

There's the curious way Jagger—Oldham's supposedly dark, wicked tough guy—always turned docile and obedient when the money spoke. Of singing "Satisfaction" on *Shindig* and having the line "trying to make some girl" bleeped out, he shrugged and muttered what difference did it make: there's a washing-machine commercial and then you sing and then there's a soap-powder commercial. After being busted for pot at Keith's house, on TV Mick was grilled by some old farts, including a quintessential vicar type; the setting was some English garden. Jagger was on his very best behavior, very polite, using his most posh schoolboy accent. "I don't really want to form a new code of living or code of morals or anything like that," he murmurs to the elders. "I don't think anyone in this generation wants to." This, from the future Street Fighting Man.

In January 1967, the band appeared on Ed Sullivan's show to plug their latest hit, "Let's Spend the Night Together." Informed he was not allowed to sing that suggestive line on camera before millions of innocents, he modified it to "Let's spend some time together." He rolled his eyes comically each time the line came around, in mute, weak protest. "We could have just walked off the show I suppose," he would later concede. "It became rather a *cause célèbre* later on, but I mean, I thought at the time that nobody would really care or ever remember."

We know. It's only rock 'n' roll. Years later, when it came time to censor "Starfucker" and promote it as "Star Star" for public consumption and promotional purposes, the Stones hardly batted an eye, and neither did anyone else.

I mention to Swales that Grace Slick in her memoirs relates the first time she met Jagger at his house in London—the meeting was about organizing the Altamont concert, in 1969, when Swales was working for him. She says it was like going to meet your banker. Jagger was very polite, very businesslike. "Oh, he could be," Swales smiles. "He was a multiple personality. Not in an incontinent way, but in a very controlled way. That was one of his personas, even to the extent of putting on a suit sometimes." Slick writes that Jagger "opened the door in an expensive business suit. The place was immaculate; Mick had magnificent Oriental rugs covering hardwood floors with Louis XIV furniture and expensive artwork hanging on the walls. He was like a kid dressing up in his rich daddy's accessories. He offered us no dope, just tea. . . . It was all business. . . .

"It turned out Mick had gone to business college, and apparently, when he told you he'd be talking business, that's *all* he did. He was one of a small group of rock stars—Frank Zappa and Kiss's Gene Simmons were also members of the club—who never got irreparably jerked around financially, because he paid close attention to what the managers and record companies were doing when it was time to shuffle the deck.

"A smart businessman."

"There you go," Swales grins. Of the suit he says, "I bet it was a brown one with pinstripes. He was very adept at doing that. Other times he'd come in in virtual rags—another performance—looking ragged, too much acid over the past few days, that sort of thing. Other times he'd be somebody else again. There was this contradiction for me, this discrepancy if you like."

Swales remembers wondering, "'Well, wait a minute. Is this theater, or is this really political?' What I'm alluding to is, when I went to work for the Stones they recorded virtually all of *Beggars Banquet*. That includes 'Street Fighting Man.' What interested me precisely was its social, political—even at times, you might say, mystical and sexual—dimensions. Of course, this was the time of Vietnam. Jagger had very strong opinions about Vietnam. Especially when he learned that Stones' money was being misused by Decca to fund radar for the American military. Boy, was he indignant. I mean, Jagger marched on the American embassy in Grosvenors Square.

"And yet, this political dimension more and more began to seem to me to be posturing. Not necessarily disingenuous, but . . . look, within the first month I was working there I'm sort of commanded to get things together for *The Rolling Stones Rock & Roll Circus*." He thought to himself, "'Ah! So it's all a circus, is it?' You know what I mean? The theatrics of that."

There's Jean-Luc Godard's *Sympathy for the Devil* (a.k.a. *One Plus One*), filmed in 1968, not seen much anymore for the very good reason that it's a crashing bore of a film, half documentary, half diatribe. The Stones' rehearsals of "Sympathy for the Devil" are inherently interesting; we watch the song get built up from Keith's original shuffle to Charlie Watts's inspired evil mambo. One notices Brian in the background, barely involved, as Mick and Keith run the show. Otherwise, only the interspliced scenes of black "revolutionaries" have any interest today. A black man reads from Eldridge Cleaver's *Soul on Ice*, some very funny lines, such as: "Any group of middle-class white boys who need a haircut and male hormones can be a pop group. That's what pop means. Which is exactly what cool was . . . exactly what Dixieland was. Complete with funny hats and funny names."

How apt. Beyond that, the film is an exercise in pretentious tedium. Its only saving grace, as an historical document, is that Godard's silly enjambment of the Stones' endless rehearsals with the interminable scenes of geeky British guys and brainless actresses droning great bollocksy swaths of leftist theory and revolutionary literature is as close as the Stones ever really got to "the revolution"—far closer than on "Street Fighting Man."

About the song itself: Younger people will find this impossible to believe, or perhaps just mortifyingly naive, but in the context of its day it was possible to take "Street Fighting Man" seriously. When the Stones reached Oakland on their 1969 U.S. tour, a flyer was distributed that declared, "Greetings and welcome Rolling Stones, our comrades in the desperate battle against the maniacs who hold power. The revolutionary youth of the world hears your music and is inspired to even more deadly acts . . ." (cited in Booth). This was an era in which rockers, hipsters, blacks, and young people generally spoke of "the revolution" as a sure and imminent event. To hear Mick Jagger speak of it that way was at the time a very great thrill. I don't know that anyone really thought Jagger was actually going to be out on the barricades when "the revolution" came; but if it did happen, the song suggested, he'd be . . . behind it. Somewhere.

The key term is "suggested." It was possible, given the tenor of the times in 1969, not to notice that the most clever aspect of the song, besides its great timing, is the now-oft-remarked-upon ambiguity of the lyrics. Whereas the Beatles flatly told us all to shut up about the revolution, Jagger's sentiments were far murkier, his politics much more slippery. The lyrics to "Street

Fighting Man" are the political equivalent of his ambidextrous sexuality: politically, these lyrics definitely swing both ways. The time is right for fighting in the street, but I'll just be singing in a rock 'n' roll band. The time is right for revolution, but "where I live" (which I think we can read as a variant on the '60s term "where I'm at") the game is compromise. Because ultimately, don't you know, there's just no place for a street-fighting man. The last verse, removing it all into some fairytale or historical realm with its kings and servants, further distances the singer from any serious intent that may be deduced from the rest of the song.

In the end the revolution never happened, and Jagger was off the hook. The closest the Stones came to manning a barricade was Altamont. If you believe Sonny Barger, they were certainly faking it playing the satanic Stones at Altamont. At Altamont, when push literally came to shove—when the Stones' music actually seemed to be inciting a crowd to violence—the Stones turned recalcitrant and peckish. To borrow a phrasing from my punk-rock friend George Tabb, they pussied out.

That's definitely how Sonny remembered it. In the spring of 2000, Don Gilbert and I went to the Hell's Angels' New York City clubhouse to interview Barger, the Angels' lifelong spokesman. At sixty-two he was still built like a man sculpted in iron. He was giving interviews, a rarity in itself, to promote his long-rumored autobiography, *Hell's Angel: The Life and Times of Sonny Barger and the Hell's Angels Motorcycle Club*—written with Keith and Kent Zimmerman, the twins who, interestingly, also worked with John Lydon on his autobiography, *Rotten*.

In *Hell's Angel*, Barger recalls the ill-fated evening the Angels found themselves "playing the part of bodyguards for a bunch of sissy, marble-mouthed prima donnas." He remembers being "escorted to a backstage area and introduced to the Rolling Stones. They came out of the trailer in their prissy clothes and makeup and we shook hands, then they disappeared back inside. It was like they were little kids as they ran back into the house to hide or something. They didn't say anything." He continues:

All the opening bands had finished playing, and it was time for the Stones to come out. The sun was still out and there was plenty of daylight left. The crowd had waited all day to see the Stones perform, and they were sitting in their trailers acting like prima donnas. The crowd was getting angry; there was a lot of drinking and drugging going on. It was starting to get dark.

After sundown the Stones still wouldn't come out to play. Mick and the band's egos seemed to want the crowd agitated and frenzied. They wanted them to beg, I guess. Then their instruments were set up. It took close to another hour before the band finally agreed to come out. A cold wind was blowing through the valley.

As violence between the restless crowd and the Angels escalated, Barger says, "the Stones were talking a lot of 'brothers and sisters' type of hippie shit":

Richards walked over to me after finishing "Love in Vain" and told me the band wasn't going to play anymore until we stopped the violence. "Either these cats cool it, man, or we don't play," he announced to the crowd. I stood next to him and stuck my pistol into his side and told him to start playing his guitar or he was dead.

He played like a motherfucker.

Barger grinned when Gilbert and I asked him about it. "Keith Richards denies it happened," he said. "Of course. He's supposed to. But all you have to do is realize, he stood up there and said, 'If the violence don't stop, I'm not playing no more.' The violence got worse and he continued to play." He smiled and shrugged. "The thing is," he went on, "everybody loves them. They sing really really well. That don't make them nice guys. They were goddamned jerks as far as I was concerned. There's nothing more I can say about it. They're prima donnas. They take advantage of their public. They come over here to the United States, they wanted to act like they were tough. They seen what tough was like, they went home with their tail between their legs. And they're never gonna get over it."

○

"Them touring at their age is like Evita going on tour stuffed in that glass case of hers," Motörhead's Lemmy has said of the Stones—and Lemmy's no spring chicken himself. Announcing that he planned to quit making rock when he turned thirty-three, the Foo Fighters' Dave Grohl said, "I'm 28 now. Why 33? I don't know—what the fuck. Look at Mick Jagger. You see this man in tight yellow pants, bouncing around as if he's in a step-aerobics class. . . . [You think] 'This is not going to happen to me.'" In the October 1999 *GQ*, Will Self begged the Stones to stop touring, ranting about how embarrassing he found their "senescent antics," the "grotesque parody of youthful abandon," and Mick's "consummate naffness" (dweebishness).

Seeing and listening to the Stones as old men makes *me* feel old. My god, I think, have I aged as much as Charlie? Do I look as bad as Keith? When I dance do I look as ridiculous as Mick? I'm sure I look worse. But I do it once or twice a year, at a wedding or New Year's party, and nobody's looking. I don't embarrass my entire generation in front of tens of thousands of pairs of eyes. *Voodoo Lounge*? It was more like a zombie jamboree up there.

Listening to *young* bands doesn't make me feel old. It makes me feel young. Young*ish*. Even when they're repeating dumb rock tropes I was playing twenty-five years before they were born, if they've got the excitement, the energy, the sense of freshness and discovery, and they convey that to me, I'm happy. That's rock 'n' roll. The Jagger of 1965 is very rock 'n' roll. The Jagger of 1995 is a nightmare, precisely a "grotesque parody of youthful abandon."

Yes, I know: Old Mick would not be up there if there weren't tens of thousands of boomers (and their younger siblings, and their kids) willing to pay millions of dollars to watch him shake that old ass of his. We're as much to blame as he is. How low we have fallen, to so willingly overlay the excitement of seeing the Stones in our youth with the empty nostalgia of seeing these senior citizens pretend to recreate those days thirty years later. There's a line in The Who's "The Seeker" about how people want to shake the narrator's hand even as he's ransacking their houses.

Giorgio Gomelsky says that the Stones of the big stadium tours "became what we rebelled against, which was the soporific, bland, characterless, repetitive—*lifeless* music. It's everything we were against in the '50s and '60s, with the jazz and blues. We wanted authenticity, where music reflects from the audience, *with* the audience. They had no business going into the arenas. They're really not made for music. . . . The Beatles knew it was no good, and thank God they stopped. Forget it. Might as well have hired mimes and put records on. . . ."

Of course, one could chalk this attitude up to sour grapes from an old, largely forgotten, and not wealthy man whom the Stones left behind on their way to fame and fortune. But he's right. Listen to Keith Richards reminiscing about the band's earliest days:

"We were sort of evangelists. It was a very pure, idealistic drive that did it. The money we needed to live on, we didn't give a damn about. That wasn't the point. The point was to spread the music. We were doing what we wanted. We had all these kids coming to clubs, and we were spreading the music and doing what we wanted to do. It wasn't to make money."

Compare that to any rationale, any excuse Keith Richards could possibly give for the Stones' nostalgia extravaganzas of the 1980s and '90s. What was it the young Mick said? Oh yes:

*I hope they don't think we're a rock 'n' roll outfit. . . .*

Don't worry about it, Mick. We did once, but that was a long time ago.

# (3)

## Up Against the Wall, Mother Hubbard
### Rock and the Gestural Revolution

Rebellion's the only thing that keeps you alive. Why
don't they rebel—especially the young?
  —Marianne Faithfull in *Girl on a Motorcycle* (1967)

Now, I am doing my level best as a saboteur of values,
as an aider of change, but when it comes down to blood
and gore in the streets I'm taking off and goin' fishin'.
  —David Crosby, in *The Rolling Stone Interviews*

SIXTIES ROCK 'N' ROLL developed in a context of social upheaval on a scale that would not be revisited for the rest of the twentieth century. The Vietnam War was being fought against the backdrop of the superpowers' Cold War and nuclear standoff; the antiwar, antinuke, and student protest movements fused with a hippie dropout drug culture to create a "counterculture" also known as the "youth movement." The Black Power movement and the sexual revolution added to the sense of social turmoil.

Although Nixon was right that a "silent majority" of Americans remained pro-military and held to traditional social values throughout this turbulent period, the protesters, activists, dissidents, and dropouts represented a very visible minority. Few Americans then living had experienced such levels of domestic dissension and strife as roiled the nation from the 1960s up to the mid-'70s. It was a time when a serious-minded person could believe that revolution was not just possible, but imminent.

81

The year 1968 was a watershed. The Tet Offensive dealt a serious blow to U.S. war-making moxie and spread antiwar sentiment well beyond the peaceniks. There were student uprisings throughout the West. In Eastern Europe, there was rebellion within the Soviet empire. Lyndon Johnson announced that he would not seek another presidential term. U.S. Olympians gave the world the Black Power fist. The assassinations of Martin Luther King and Robert Kennedy, the urban riots that attended the former, and the police riot at the Chicago Democratic Convention all seemed to portend an impending apocalypse. Revolution, as a cliché of the moment went, was in the air.

But in the end, nothing much came of all the turbulence. Having sparked widespread uprisings, the leaders of the student revolt had very little idea of how to translate their movement into real political change. The New Left, unable to forge links with blacks or the unions, remained isolated. The SDS sent shock troops out to get jobs in factories, where they hoped to organize the proletariat the old-fashioned Marxist way, but they just got beaten up by their fellow workers, having failed to recognize the patriotism and deep personal commitment many working-class Americans felt toward winning the war. Notions of "armed revolt" engaged only a very tiny minority: Weatherman's "Days of Rage" street actions in Chicago in 1969 drew less than a thousand protesters, and the Weather Underground itself, after blowing up their Greenwich Village townhouse in 1970, reputedly numbered fewer than a dozen active members. Black radicals similarly failed to capitalize on the riots in their neighborhoods. The Panthers would soon succumb to dissension sown among their leadership by the FBI's COINTELPRO infiltration, and to local wars waged against them by constabularies in cities from New York and Philadelphia to L.A.—as well as their own weaknesses for gangsterism and drugs. The Vietnam War dragged on for another seven years. Richard Nixon became president, in an election in which the racist George Wallace, running as an independent, polled 14 percent and took five states. As the then-antiwar and later anti-political correctness scholar Frederick Crews memorably put it, 1968 turned out to be little more than a "gestural revolution" (*New York Review of Books*, June 25, 1998).

Political revolution, the violent overthrow of the established government, does not come easily to the privileged children of a capitalist democracy. Most of us hadn't the slightest idea what we meant when we said, "When the revolution comes . . ." Why should we have backed a revolution? As white, middle-class, educated Americans, we had every reason to buy into the establishment, not tear it down. "America's cultural revolution," conservative critic Roger Kimball has written, "was a capitalist, bourgeois revolution: a revolution of the privileged, by the privileged, and for the privileged." The manifesto of the May 2nd Movement, the student organization founded in 1965, complained: "The university offers no explanation of what's wrong, of what's happening in a world principally marked by revolution. Instead, it grooms us for places as technicians, managers and clerks within the giant corporations, or to be professional apologists for the status quo within the giant multiversities, or to fit some other cog-space that needs the special 'sensitivity' that only the polish of factory education can bring." It was a distinctly minority complaint. In 1965, as in 2001, the majority of students were quite content to be groomed for their future roles in the adult working world.

By the early 1970s, the politics that had once been a loosely integrating influence in the counterculture began to pull it apart. Many antiwar and anti-Nixon activists entered mainstream politics as supporters of Eugene McCarthy, George McGovern, or local progressive candidates. Frustrated, the few remaining radicals were convinced that the only way to bring about the revolution was through violent guerrilla action or domestic terrorism. This isolated them from the rest of the counterculture numbers, who, for all that they'd loved "Street Fighting Man" and punching the air with their fists at protest marches, were not ready to pick up a gun or a bomb to kick-start a violent rebellion. Despite making headlines through the 1970s, authentic revolutionary groups such as the Symbionese Liberation Army or the Baader-Meinhof group in Europe were tiny cells operating in the most profound isolation from the great mass of young people.

The Vietnam War was winding down. The economy that had supported the utopian pipe dreams of the 1960s was listing toward depression. I can clearly remember the ominous clouds of doubt and gloom that came on as early as 1970. For my friends and me, the melancholy wistfulness of Neil Young's *After the Goldrush* seemed the perfect soundtrack for the new era. Coming so soon after Woodstock, the next set of events, all downers—the deaths of Jimi

Hendrix and Janis Joplin, the ugly anti-Woodstock of Altamont, the shootings at Kent State, the Weather people blowing themselves up—filled us with a sense of foreboding. After the wild party of the previous decade, 1970 came on like a bad hangover. After the goldrush, indeed. For those of us with hippie/counter-cultural leanings, 1970 was when you either opted out of society and headed off to a commune or a cabin in the woods, or you gave up and opted in.

And so, Jerry Rubin famously segued from Yippie to yuppie. Tom Hayden stopped fighting the government and joined it. Black Panther Bobby Seale eventually sold barbecue sauce on the internet. Black Panther Eldridge Cleaver went from radical leftist presidential candidate to Reagan Republican to crack addict to environmental activist. Hanoi Jane became an exercise instructor, TV mogul's trophy wife, and Christian (though into the twenty-first century, she could still draw boos when she appeared on the TV in any working-class bar in America). Bernadine Dohrn, the Weatherman pinup girl who invented a "fork" hand gesture with which to salute the Manson Family's literally sticking it to Sharon Tate and the other little piggies, became director of the Children and Family Justice Center of the Northwestern University School of Law Legal Clinic. ("They all run daycare centers!" boomer filmmaker John Waters quipped in an interview in 2000. "Every ex-Weatherman runs a daycare center.")

All that was left was the "cultural revolution." When proponents such as Susan Sontag or Ellen Willis speak of cultural revolution, they mean nonviolent change in social values and power valences—equality for women and gays and ethnic minorities, a freeing up of gender roles and sexual attitudes. A conservative opponent like Roger Kimball sees it differently. "In a democratic society like ours, where free elections are guaranteed, political revolution is almost unthinkable in practical terms. Consequently, utopian efforts to transform society have been channeled into cultural and moral life. In America, scattered if much-publicized episodes of violence have wrought far less damage than the moral and intellectual assaults that do not destroy buildings but corrupt sensibilities and blight souls. The success of America's recent cultural revolution can be measured not in toppled governments but in shattered values."

Interestingly, both sides assume that the cultural revolution has been victorious in broad society. But an alternative theory can be argued: that 1970s radicals retreated back to the campus and became the ineffectual, marginalized campus leftists of the 1980s and '90s, arguing increasingly minute points of identity politics among themselves, almost entirely outside real-world concerns. The Left lost itself in the intracampus arcana of political correctness, the argumentative polemics of queer theory, the impenetrable obscurantism of poststructuralism, and the inanities of Cultural Studies. You can't Fight the Power and fight for a tenured position at the same time. Preaching received wisdom to smug converts in white educated enclaves from the East Village to Oberlin to San Francisco will never transform the masses into a revolutionary force. In the real world, the cultural revolution has been at best a symbolic resistance to the mainstream and establishment.

John Sinclair wrote in 1969: "We have to realize that the long-haired dope-smoking rock and roll street-fucking culture is a whole thing, a revolutionary international cultural movement which is absolutely legitimate and absolutely valid. There wouldn't even be a question about this matter if the honkies didn't attempt to deny our validity so that anybody can see and know that it exists as a force in the world." In *Steal This Book*, Abbie Hoffman put it succinctly and prophetically: "Don't let the pigs separate our culture from our politics." Poor Abbie. He needn't have worried about the pigs.

○

Rockers, being (mostly) young and (mostly) countercultural, naturally reflected aspects of all the change and turmoil of the 1960s in their music and in their personae. For the most part, rock's role was, as Danny Fields so dryly observes, to be the rhythm section, provide the soundtrack, "entertain the troops." (See below, where Tuli Kupferberg calls the Fugs "the USO of the Left.") Whenever there was an antiwar or anti-Nixon rally in the offing, you called up some bands and they would come play. In a more general way, rock was very good, then as now, at expressing anger, disillusionment, dismay, and rejection of authority on the one hand, and hippie-druggy-sexy utopianism on the other.

Only a very few bands presented themselves as rockin' revolutionaries. In this chapter I'll address three of the best-known—the MC5, Jefferson Airplane, and the Fugs.

In the winter of 2000 I found myself watching the Super Bowl in a bar/
restaurant in New Orleans, working my way through a big boat of crawfish,
while John Sinclair, former chairman of the White Panther Party, sat across the
table from me, eating raw oysters and making cracks about the commercials.
A big, bearish man with bad teeth and a gnarled goatee, he regularly rode his
rusty old bike around the French Quarter, wearing a baggy sweat suit, chatting
with everyone in a low, easy rumble that occasionally flared into flashes of an
old anger. It had been an unusual week for Sinclair. While he and his wife were
out of town, there had been a fire in the house they were renting on Rampart
Street, on the ragged fringe of the French Quarter. Their home wasn't totally
destroyed, but there was plenty of damage, and it would take the landlord a few
months to fix the place, which was boarded up by the time I checked into my
hotel across the street.

Sinclair was taking it all with a sort of old bluesman's resigned grace, which
suited the fifty-eight-year-old hepcat and former rock 'n' roll revolutionary.
The story of John Sinclair and the MC5 has been told many times, and told
quite well in two books of the 1990s, *The Mansion on the Hill* by Fred Goodman and *Please Kill Me* by Legs McNeil and Gillian McCain. At a time when
American rock's support of "the revolution" mostly came down to the bloated
posturing of David Crosby or Grace Slick—"Up against the wall, motherfucker! AND HAND OVER THAT LAST SLICE OF PIE!"—the least you
can say about Sinclair is that he was a true believer who literally put his ass on
the line.

John Sinclair was known as Detroit's "King of the Hippies" when the MC5
made a point of meeting him in 1967. A former high-school English teacher
from Flint, Michigan, Sinclair was the city's loudest, largest counterculture figure, openly advocating free sex and pot use in the uptight milieu of the Midwest industrial town, and drawing rather intense scrutiny from the local con-
stabulary. The MC5 showed up to play when Sinclair threw himself a party on
being released from jail after a six-month pot possession sentence. They played
so loudly that Sinclair's wife pulled the plugs on their amplifiers. Sinclair himself was not a big fan of rock music at that point—having been disappointed
when 1950s rock 'n' roll devolved into denatured pop in the early '60s, he'd
become a jazz snob. But he was impressed with the MC5's "high energy" and

believed he heard in them a way to mobilize the masses of young hippies and "freeks" into a revolutionary counterculture. So he agreed to become the band's manager, the band's members in turn became the radical chic stars of his commune, Trans-Love Energies. Germaine Greer was among the luminaries who would make the pilgrimage to pay their respects (and, in her case, reputedly shack up for a week with lead singer Rob Tyner).

Sinclair's next move was more hippie than revolutionary. Disturbed by the Detroit "race riots" of 1967, Sinclair moved his commune to the relative tranquillity of Ann Arbor, a small college town, where he installed his operation in a pair of large gingerbread mansions. There Sinclair was free to dream great visions of revolution and revolt. Trans-Love Energies became the White Panther Party, and everybody became a Minister of something. MC5 roadies prowled the grounds carrying rifles. Black Panthers from the neighborhood partied with them and took shooting practice in the woods behind the houses. (At their headquarters in L.A., the Black Panthers officially denounced the White Panthers as "psychedelic clowns.")

In August 1968, the MC5 were the only band who showed up to play the Yippies' "Festival of Life" in Lincoln Park outside the Chicago Democratic National Convention. ("Yippie Music Theater To Tune Up Viet Beefs During Dems' Chi Conv," *Variety* had announced in its inimitable way.) Everyone else, including the Grateful Dead and most of the Fugs, had been scared away by the prospect of police violence. Cops in riot gear surrounded the park as the band began its set. "When I saw all those cops, the only thing I could think was, Jesus Christ, if this is the revolution, we lost," drummer Dennis Thompson recalls in McNeal and McCain's *Please Kill Me.* After a handful of songs, Sinclair and the band leaped into their van and went bouncing out of the park. In later years they would make it sound as if truncheon-wielding cops were hot on their tails, but the police violence actually didn't erupt until after dark, hours after the band left. "Chicago was supposed to be the show of solidarity, goddamn it," Thompson says. "No one showed up but us. . . . I knew the revolution was over at that moment—I looked over my shoulder, and no one was there."

A guy calling himself "Brother" J. C. Crawford introduced the MC5 onstage and exhorted the audience: "Brothers and sisters, the time has come for you to decide whether you are gonna be the problem, or whether you are gonna be the solution. That's right. You must choose, brothers, you must choose." In Chicago, apparently, everyone chose to be the problem. But the concert did get the band their first national coverage, when Norman Mailer mentioned it in his *Harper's* piece on the convention.

Sinclair issued the first "White Panther Statement" that November:

Our program is Cultural Revolution through a total assault on the culture, which makes us use every tool, every energy and any media we can get our collective hands on. We take our program with us everywhere we go and use any means necessary to expose people to it.

Our culture, our art, the music, newspapers, books, posters, our clothing, our homes, the way we walk and talk, the way our hair grows, the way we smoke dope and fuck and eat and sleep—it is all one message, and the message is FREEDOM! We are the mother country madmen in charge of our own lives and we are taking this freedom to the people of America, in streets, in the ballrooms and teendubs, in their front rooms watching TV, in their bedrooms reading underground newspapers, or masturbating, or smoking secret dope, in their schools where we come and talk to them or make our music, in their weird gymnasiums—they love it—We represent the only contemporary life-style in America for its kids and it should be known that THESE KIDS ARE READY! They are ready to move but they don't know how, and all we do is show them that they can get away with it. BE FREE, goddamnit, and fuck them old dudes, is what we tell them, and they can see that we mean it. The only influences we have, the only thing that touches them, is that we are for real. We are FREE. We are a bunch of arrogant motherfuckers and we don't give a damn for any cop or any phony-ass authority control-addict creeps who want to put us down.

For the first time in America there is a generation of visionary maniac white motherfucker country dope fiend rock and roll freaks who are ready to get down and kick out the jams—ALL THE JAMS—break everything loose and free everybody from their very real and imaginary prisons—even the chumps and punks and honkies who are always fucking with us. We demand total freedom for everybody! And we will not be stopped until we get it.

We are bad. There's only two kinds of people on the planet: those who make up the problem and those who make up the solution. WE ARE THE SOLUTION We have no problems. Everything is free for everybody. Money sucks. Leaders suck. School sucks. The white honkie culture that has been handed to us on a silver platter is meaningless to us! We don't want it! Our program of rock and roll, dope and fucking in the streets is a program of total freedom for everyone. We are totally committed to carrying out our program. We breathe revolution. We are LSD driven total maniacs of the universe. We will do anything we can to drive people crazy out of their heads and into their bodies.

ROCK AND ROLL music is the spearhead of our attack because it is so effective and so much fun. We have developed organic high-energy guerrilla bands who are infiltrating the popular culture and destroying millions of minds in the process. With our music and our economic genius we plunder the unsuspecting straight world for money and the means to carry out our program, and revolutionize its children at the same time.

And with our entrance into the straight media we have demonstrated to the honkies that anything they do to fuck with us will be exposed to their children. We don't need to get rid of all the honkies, you just rob them of their replacements and let the breed atrophy and die out.

We don't have guns yet—not all of us anyway—because we have more powerful weapons—direct access to millions of teenagers is one of our most potent, and their belief in us is another. But we will use guns if we have to—we will do anything—if we have to.

We have no illusions. Knowing the power of symbols in the abstract world of Americans we have taken the White Panther as our mark to symbolize our strength and arrogance.

We're bad.

Well, you had to be there. It was rhetoric, Sinclair would later explain, consciously aimed at the "lumpen hippies," the disaffected Detroit kids, any of whom could easily appreciate that "program of rock and roll, dope and fucking in the streets," if not the White Panther Party's later, more fuzzily argumentative ten-point program. ("Free all prisoners everywhere—they are our brothers. . . . Free all soldiers at once—no more conscripted armies. . . . Free the people from their 'leaders'—leaders suck—all power to all the people freedom means free everyone!" You have to have some place in your heart for a "political party" that keeps declaring "leaders suck.") The closest the White Panther Party ever came to fomenting the violent overthrow of the status quo was when its "Minister of Defense" threw a bomb in the direction of a CIA recruitment office on the University of Michigan campus in Ann Arbor, damaging the sidewalk. Most of the MC5 say that they never took the revolutionary stance too seriously. Only singer Rob Tyner, who was a little older than the others and had been attracted to Sinclair's hippie scene early on, seems to have been a true believer—and even he would later recant before his untimely death in 1992. Still, interviewed by Sinclair for the underground paper *The Sun* in 1967, before Sinclair was managing the band, Tyner demonstrated a perfect competence in talking the talk:

> The thing is, people live inside the game structure, and they're just not involved. They can't be involved, man, because they get the world in a little picture tube. Everything happens in there. So if you haven't been in there, or if you haven't come out of a speaker box on the radio, then you don't exist. You dig. . . . And TV time—did you ever dig those Saturday morning cartoon shows? Some of them are so bogue, man, some of them are so senseless. Why couldn't we get some of that time and do something with it? I just wonder how possible that would be. Why don't some of our people get into that end of it, where we could see it and hear it on the media? I mean, our people are getting into the music thing, and really doing it, but you can't hear it on the radio. So we have to start taking over the mass media, because that's where it's at—that's where the consensus of the people's thinking comes from. It's part of their lives. We just have to show them that there's more than what they already know. What you can understand is limitless.

"Our people" did, in the end, "get some of that time" on TV, on radio, throughout the media, and . . . they made it hipper. They created "cool" sitcoms, and ones with major characters who were gay; they created MTV and lots of car commercials featuring classic-rock songs. But the "really together" cultural revolution Tyner thought was going to come out of their taking over the media failed to materialize. They just made the media look and sound more cool, the better to market their products and their advertisers.

Danny Fields, A&R man and "house hippie" at Jac Holzman's Elektra Records in New York City, flew out to see the MC5 and their friends the Stooges, led by the seventeen-year-old Iggy Pop, shortly after the Chicago convention. He was skeptical of the politics, but he liked the bands and convinced Holzman to sign both to record contracts. He also convinced Jon Landau, the influential *Rolling Stone* critic, to come hear them. Landau was suspicious of Sinclair and his ranting, but he, too, liked the MC5's energy. Fields paid him a consulting fee to write an assessment of the band for Holzman's attention. Landau then got the band—still without a record—a large spread and loving homage in *Rolling Stone* (January 4, 1969). He also mentioned them as one of the few authentically political rock bands in a nearby article about the Stones: "Politics has not been fashionable since Dylan left it among musicians. There have always been the few hold-outs left over from the folk period, but despite the mass media's continually mistaken references to rock and roll as 'protest music,' rock musicians have done remarkably little protesting. Protest is a hallmark of the liberal. It is an appeal to the conscience of the majority to remedy some injustice being done to the minority. It presupposes a belief that meaningful change can be worked out within the system. Rock and roll musicians, for the most part, don't buy that. They don't take the government seriously unless they are forced to. They find the whole political process something worthy of contempt. . . ."

It was Sinclair's idea to make the first MC5 album a live one, recorded on Halloween at the Grande (locals pronounced it "Grandee") Ballroom. If they were known for nothing else, the MC5 became internationally famous for their one-line slogan, "Kick out the jams, motherfuckers!" though Sinclair and the band agreed to censor it at their Elektra bosses' request. The single "Kick Out the Jams" came out with "Motherfuckers" replaced by "Brothers and Sisters." It was a number-one hit in the Detroit market, where it unseated Tommy Roe's dippy pop tune "Dizzy." Nationally, the album made it into the Top 30, a very respectable showing.

But politics kept getting the band in trouble. The MC5 was banned in

Boston after sharing the mic with a representative of the Motherfuckers, the notoriously bad-ass New York revolutionary cell. When the band came to play the Fillmore East in New York, the Motherfuckers showed up again, accused the MC5 of being sellouts, and started a riot. Consequently Bill Graham banned the band from both his Fillmores. And when the large Detroit retailer Hudson's refused to stock the incendiary *Kick Out the Jams*, the band took out an ad in the local underground newspaper declaring "Fuck Hudson's"—with Elektra's logo on it, as though the label had approved the ad.

Elektra dropped the band. Fields and Landau, working together, promptly convinced Atlantic to sign them. They also persuaded the MC5 to drop Sinclair and the politics and get down to the business of becoming rock stars. The band fired Sinclair just before he went to prison in July 1969 to serve an extraordinarily severe nine-and-a-half-year sentence for possession of two joints—his third pot bust, set up by his enemies in the local police.

Not a single member of the MC5, not even his old friend Tyner, came to visit Sinclair in prison. No one in the band lifted a finger to help his pregnant wife. "You guys wanted to be bigger than the Beatles, and I wanted you to be bigger than Chairman Mao," Sinclair famously complained in a letter to guitarist Wayne Kramer. He and Kramer would eventually patch up their differences and tour together again as old warhorses in the 1990s.

Life turns full circle. Wayne Kramer went on to struggle with and eventually beat heroin addiction. Years after the MC5 fell apart, he fled the drugs and other evils of the big city for the gentler environment of Key West, where he became one of the carpenters who built Jimmy Buffett's first Margaritaville club. Buffett would go on to expand the club into a successful franchise operation, a kind of McDonalds for adults who like to drink. He would grow rich as the living avatar of the kind of nonstop happy hour a guy like Kramer, struggling to remain clean and sober, could only dream about. Kramer, for his part, would continue playing rock 'n' roll and electric blues, touring with Sinclair as well as putting out records as a solo act. But he never made more than a fraction of what the insufferably goodtimey Buffett pulled in from his alcohol-fueled empire.

While Sinclair was languishing behind bars, Landau was producing the MC5's second LP, *Back in the USA*. It was very consciously the antithesis of what they'd sounded like under Sinclair's influence. Landau advised them not only to shuck the politics, but also to drop the long-format, free-ranging wildness. The result was the MC5 stripped down and tamed for the radio, squeaky clean; whereas they had originally thought of themselves as experimenting with a kind of rock Jazz, now they were assaying '50s-retro teenage rock 'n' roll. The sound was thin, flat, and featureless as a Stridex pad. While *Kick Out the Jams* was not by any means a great record—it was sloppy and gawky, not even a very good example of Detroit-style high-energy rock—*Back in the USA* was a *terrible* one. If Sinclair had goaded the band into acting like silly faux-Panthers, Landau's influence made them sound like fast-buck pop stars. The MC5 was a proving ground for what Landau would later help Springsteen accomplish: retro-rock as a means to self-commodification. But the '70s hadn't happened yet, and that level of '70s fakery wouldn't yet fly. *Back in the USA* flopped.

The band went into the studio one last time, self-producing the only good album they ever made, 1971's *High Time*. It came way too late to save them, let alone be recognized as the long-awaited apotheosis of what the MC5 had always promised: an *intelligently* kick-ass rock band, jamming and vamping but in control of their material and their energy. And if they were not "revolutionaries" anymore, maybe they were something better, or at least more true to themselves: real rock 'n' roll populists who, instead of pretending to be a People's Party, were intent on bringing the party to the people.

But the truth was that for better or worse, without Sinclair there to whomp up a lot of extramusical hype around the band, people quickly lost interest in them. Whereas *Kick Out the Jams* had shot into the Top 30, *USA* never scratched the Top 100, and *High Time* failed to chart at all before disappearing, utterly forgotten for twenty years or more, until the CD reissue. As Danny Fields cannily observes, it was Grand Funk Railroad who became what the MC5 could've been, the premiere kick-ass midwest slam-a-rama early-'70s rock 'n' roll band for working-class kids and the lumpen hippies.

Sinclair, meanwhile, was still behind bars. During his two and a half years of incarceration he became an icon of the Left, seen as just as much a political prisoner as the Chicago 7. Even mainstream media wondered if ten years wasn't a bit much for a pot sentence. In December 1971, no less figures than John Lennon and Yoko Ono headlined the John Sinclair Freedom Rally in Ann

Arbor's Chrysler Auditorium, an eight-hour event that drew over 15,000 people; Stevie Wonder volunteered to play, and Phil Ochs was there, along with Black Panther Bobby Seale and Allen Ginsberg. Sinclair was released four days later. But even this victory was bittersweet. Sinclair's original hope was that the Ann Arbor rally would be just the beginning of a national rock-and-revolution tour, the "Guitar Army" tour, headlined by John and Yoko, featuring local bands and speakers in every city it visited, raising money for local countercultural causes. Immediately on release from jail Sinclair flew to Manhattan to discuss the tour with John and Yoko. Later, he would angrily recall how they kept him waiting an entire weekend before granting him "an audience." The couple lounged on a big bed as was their wont at the time; he felt like a humble supplicant. Yoko, who did most of the talking, disabused Sinclair of any plans for their participation in any Guitar Army scheme. Their excuse was a good one—Lennon was in danger of being deported, and they didn't want to risk antagonizing the Nixon administration. But they made a lifelong enemy of Sinclair, who would always remember that meeting as "the most humiliating experience of my life."

Sinclair returned to Ann Arbor to find the world much changed since he had last seen it. It was increasingly clear that there wasn't going to be any revolution, that rock was going mainstream and the hippies were all getting jobs. Disgusted with rock, Sinclair retreated to jazz, R & B, the blues—genres in which he is an acknowledged expert. He founded the well-respected Ann Arbor Jazz & Blues Festival and continued some grassroots political activity, but in a reduced capacity.

In the early 1990s Sinclair moved to New Orleans, and the life fitted him so well it was hard to believe he ever lived anywhere else. His "Blues & Roots" radio show on WWOZ (90.7 FM New Orleans) made him a local celebrity. Today, if you walk the streets with him in the French Quarter or drop into a bar or club or diner, you'll see all the homies greeting him. When I visited him in the winter of 2000, fans were responding instantly to news of the fire in his home. He and his wife were given the use of an apartment over the legendary jazz club Snug Harbor on Frenchmen Street. Scores of New Orleans–based musicians (including Michelle Shocked, the Wild Magnolias, Coco Robicheaux, and members of the Radiators) threw a benefit concert at the House of Blues the Sunday after I met with him, and there were other benefits that winter in L.A. (organized by Wayne Kramer) and New York City.

I interviewed Sinclair with the help of Don Gilbert, a writer and rocker and mutual friend.

*Strausbaugh: What happened to "the revolution"? In the late '60s, everyone used to say, "When the revolution comes..." You didn't have to be political. Everybody just assumed that it was coming, a couple of years down the line there were going to be huge changes.*

We believed totally that it was coming. It was inevitable. You know, they put the rap on me and the MC5, we were the "radical" group. And it probably doesn't make any sense to them, but I'm always arguing, "We were pretty much like everybody else we knew." We were nothing like the SDS, we were a rock 'n' roll band. We were just—the beliefs were the same, everybody we knew, [even] the Stooges felt this way. They were the most apolitical bunch of people you could ever want to meet. Nobody went in the army. Everybody smoked pot and took whatever drugs they wanted to take. It was a mass thing.

*Strausbaugh: And then at some point in the early '70s, for, I think, a lot of reasons, it just dissipates and fades away and it's gone.*

By '75 it was gone.

*Strausbaugh: The war had been a piece of the motivation for a lot of guys...*

Big piece. It created the context.

*Strausbaugh: Now the war moved on and they got rid of the draft. Now it's only black guys and poor guys who are going, and the white guys aren't so interested in "the revolution" anymore.*

Don't forget the economic thing in the early '70s. That was a big factor, I think. The so-called oil crisis and the inflation of the early '70s, when gasoline went from 38 cents to a dollar. That's what set the pace for the modern world. . . . You know, there's all these subtle methodologies that are developed to keep people in line. [One is] you've got to scuffle so much harder to eat and to pay your rent. [T]hey just keep raising the price of everything without giving you any more. You buy a house and two years later it's worth $100,000 more. Well, somebody's got to pay that $100,000, but they're not getting any more—the house isn't getting any *bigger*. You're not getting any more rooms. . . .

William Burroughs really had his finger on what was going to happen as early as forty years ago. The idea of the junk pyramid. Algebra of need. The idea of simplifying and degrading both the consumer and the product. I mean, nothing fits more in terms of an analysis of today's world. You've got people who will wait all night in the snow to buy a ticket for $65 to see the Smashing Pumpkins in a hockey arena. I mean, Jesus Christ, you know? There it is. P. T. Barnum must be dancing in his grave. . . .

So many things in modern life, if you'd thought about this in the '60s, we would have killed ourselves. If you would have told me Ronald Reagan would be president, followed by the head of the CIA, phew. I would have been outta there, man. And the crazy thing is, we believed the opposite would happen. We believed it, man. I went to prison, you know, and it didn't faze me in the sense that this was just part of the things that had to happen for their shit to fall. So I wasn't there feeling sorry for myself, I didn't sit around and mope and all that, I just felt . . . Not that I enjoyed it, mind you, but I just felt this is what you had to do, our revolution meant that people had to go to prison, and that's what they had for me, and I took it. . . .

*Strausbaugh: Of course, the other explanation is that we all just grew up, started families, got jobs and straightened out.*

I guess that's what we hate about growing up. . . .

But see, ten years before that we were trying to demonstrate the difference, that you didn't have to do that. I remember electing to have children, to show that you could have children and didn't have a proper job. It was very important to me. I didn't know if you could or not. I mean, you really didn't know, because everything was so experimental in the early, mid-'60s. You'd take this acid, which had never been there before, and all of a sudden everything was different. You felt different, you saw everything differently, and then you tried to tell everybody about it. Before that we never cared to tell anybody about it. I remember this so well. In '63, '64, '65, everything transformed. Now you had the idea that you could change the shit.

Before that, in the beatnik era, it was still *beat*. "We're beat, man," and the best you could do was to get underground and find a place to live with some other weird dope fiends and musicians and poets and what-have-you. And no one gave a fuck about what you were doin'. If they found out they might try to stop you. But if they didn't find out, if you didn't pull their chains, they didn't even know you were there. There was never any idea of proselytizing."

*Gilbert: What made you think you could change the world then?*

It was the acid, man! [Sinclair laughs.] Whenever people ask me to talk about the '60s, [what] I have to say is, "Don't forget, we were on acid." That was what made all the difference. Before acid we didn't want to turn anybody on. When you were smokin' joints you wanted to smoke joints with other people who knew what a joint was. Or someone that you liked very much, that didn't know, you'd turn them on like this . . . [He holds an imaginary joint to Gilbert's lips.] Doin' that. But it wasn't no big deal, 'cause you really didn't have any hope that things could change.

The other big thing [was] the civil rights movement. You can't overestimate the effect of the civil rights movement in the early '60s. Here were the most downtrodden people in our society, and they were standing up and saying, "Fuck it. I'm not taking any, I'm not going to the back of the bus, I'm not gonna go drink out of this water fountain, kiss my ass. You have to put dogs and hoses on us and drag us out of here, we ain't going for it no more." And the moral example of that had such a tremendous impact on everybody. People like us, white people, when you saw this you just said, "Jesus Christ, these people." They set a moral example, an example of courage and an example of standing up to the fucking racist dog-eat-dog type society and said, "We want it to be different."

*Strausbaugh: And there's the influence of the music. There's jazz first, and then rock 'n' roll. Just by opening up an appreciation for this sexy music, it implicitly goes against the uptight Eisenhower-era mainstream.*

Right. Ain't no more Guy Mitchell and Eddie Page. It's Wynonie Harris. I had the privilege and the blessing of growing up in this. I bought "Maybellene" when it came out, "Tutti Frutti." These were landmark events in my youth, and for everybody I knew that was the least bit hip. The future farmers of America at our school [in Flint, Michigan] didn't want to go into Little Richard too deep. But there was a small group of people where this became the motivating force in their lives, this music. It was so exciting, and we didn't have any idea where it was coming from. When I first started hearing it, I didn't even know that they had Negroes, in a sense. You know what I mean, there was like one family in our little farm community way out in the country. We didn't know anything about anything, then all of a sudden you had a record by Amos Milburn, you said, "Jeez, this is the best shit I ever heard in my fuckin' life." The first record I remember hearing was "One Mint Julep" by the Clovers. "*Maaan*, this is the shit." My whole development was trying to find out where these records came from, who was making them. And why. And why wasn't the rest of the world like this? You know what I'm saying? That was one of my intellectual developments.

*Gilbert: Didn't you once write something like, "What's up with these jive rock 'n' rollers?"*

I just thought it was lame, you know. Someone came up to me with a Rolling Stones record. "Man, this shit is great." And you'd play it and it'd be these watered-down versions of Muddy Waters and Bo Diddley tunes and Chuck Berry, and you'd say, "Man, haven't you ever heard of Muddy Waters?" And they hadn't.

*Strausbaugh: But that's an important point, these pasty-faced little English guys . . .*

Listening to Howlin' Wolf.

*Strausbaugh: . . . and doing their imitations . . .*

They *were* totally different from the Beach Boys.

*Strausbaugh: . . . and that's the first time many of us ever heard . . .*

Absolutely. Ever. And when they went on *Shindig* they made them bring Howlin' Wolf on with them. Or they wouldn't go.

*Strausbaugh: You've got to give them credit for that. That was extremely important. They weren't very good at it . . .*

But they got much better. They weren't saying, "I Wanna Hold Your

Hand," they were saying, "I Wanna Make Love to You." "Let's Spend the Night Together."

*Strausbaugh: Though they made it "Let's Spend Some Time Together" for The Ed Sullivan Show.*

A way to bowdlerize it. Well, we did the same thing. [He shrugs, referring to the "Kick Out the Jams" single, and then chuckles.] Learned it from Mick.

*Strausbaugh: But that's another important strain, the self-censorship. If you want a hit record . . .*

And you do.

*Strausbaugh: . . . and you want to make a million dollars, it became clear that you can't do that and be, say, the MC5.*

They're not gonna allow it. You could be as debauched as you want. But if you want to say something . . . I mean, we were the whipping boys for that lesson, the MC5 . . . [To this day, people say,] "When are they gonna put the MC5 in the Rock and Roll Hall of Fame?" And I say, "They *aren't*. Those are the people who drummed them out of the business. You think they're gonna come back around and recognize them now? No, they represent everything that's wrong with rock 'n' roll."

*Gilbert: I was always curious about the Five's political commitment. On the one hand, it was fun going out back to take target practice with the Panthers. On the other, when things got heavy . . .*

Well, they were afraid it would impinge on their chance for success. Because first and foremost, they were rock 'n' rollers. Or else they wouldn't have been in a rock 'n' roll band. Basically, they wanted to buy their mom a new house. And a new Cadillac. Everybody wants to be Elvis. Buy new Cadillacs for your friends, you know. So here they were, they had a record contract, and there was the big chance that as rock 'n' rollers they had hoped for. They were on a major label, they had some success—and then the shit hit the fan because of the content of what they were doing. So they censored the album. Stores refused to sell it. Elektra fired us. . . .

*Strausbaugh: I know you agree with the Fred Goodman thesis that everything changed for rock in the early to mid-'70s. It became corporatized, market-segmented, made suitable for radio . . .*

Well, that's when they changed it all. Everything busted out in the mid-'60s, all these factors came together in about '65 and just exploded, and it took 'em until '72 [to regain control]. Woodstock was like the dawning of the idea that this was hip. Before that they just tried to say it was just these weirdos. And all of a sudden there was half a million of 'em there, and they just transformed the concert business. And of course the marketing forces also transformed the record companies. Transformed the whole approach to things. Within three years they had it all encompassed.

*Strausbaugh: The point is, it wasn't like "The Man stole our music." We were The Man. Richard Nixon didn't ruin rock radio. People my age who'd been smoking dope in college listening to rock got jobs as A&R men and radio station managers and figured out how to turn it into easy units of sales, discrete genres . . .*

And keep it the same.

*Strausbaugh: So in a sense it's a reiteration of what happened at the end of the '50s, when the rock 'n' roll rebellion was tamed and corporatized and morphed into Bobby Vee. By the early '70s, the wild hairs and rebels of '60s rock had either died or been tamed, and you had the Eagles, Dan Fogelberg, REO Speedwagon . . .*

*Gilbert: And then you had disco.*

Yeah, then Studio 54. Then the beautiful people started taking over . . .

I mean there was a period where it was really exciting, from the early to mid-'60s to '71, '72. I remember the end starting when ABC bought seven underground rock stations—back in the days before Reagan, when you could only own seven—in different markets [around the country]. . . . That was when they started to homogenize everything. The hegemony of rock. Because the thing was, the movement, the mass movement, in its various [incarnations] was fueled by rock 'n' roll. The popular movement. And once they got a grip on that, they put the Eagles and the Fleetwood Macs in place, they installed them in the leadership. Elton John and all this kind of horseshit. It's never gone anywhere since. They froze it.

*Gilbert: Putting Springsteen on their playlists. He was the guy that was gonna take rock back to the corporations.*

Well, he did, too. He did a great job. . . . I remember going to see Bruce Springsteen on his first tour when he came to Ann Arbor. Man, that was like a Broadway show about rock 'n' roll. I was just shocked. He'd go like this [he strikes a dramatic rock star pose]—and the spot would hit him, you know. And everything was all choreographed and staged, and the music was so lame. They quit rocking—or they quit *rolling*. They took the roll out. The roll is the African part.

*Strausbaugh: Goodman basically casts Jon Landau as the devil. He ruined the MC5, then he promoted Springsteen. Was Landau the devil?*

Him and Leon Russell. Don't forget Leon Russell. He was the devil to me. Because Leon Russell was the apotheosis of the studio musician taking over rock 'n' roll. Leon Russell was the bandleader on *Shindig*, the corniest, squarest shit imaginable when he was on. That was worse than *American Bandstand*. And then when he took over the Joe Cocker tour, Mad Dogs and Englishmen. That was Leon Russell, Carl Radle, and then they took over Eric Clapton and sent him on the Bonnie and Delaney ruse. And by then the standard in rock 'n' roll is studio players. You didn't have bands no more, you hired [session musicians]. They represented the rationalization of making music. Four sides in three hours. They used these guys because they could read and they could play the shit and they'd bring the wild man in and have him sing. . . .

(Our conversation reaches an impasse. Sinclair yanks on his goatee, sighs.)

Yeah, so what happened to the revolution? We got beat. And then we went home and took up our ploughshares, or typewriters or what-have-you. Licked our wounds and hoped that there weren't reprisals. Hoped that they wouldn't come after us and pummel us some more, even though we weren't causing them any more problems.

*Strausbaugh: It's hip to be square.*

Yeah, it's hip to be square, man. Amazing thing is, Huey Lewis was in a band called Clover. They opened for the MC5. [He laughs ruefully.] Fifteen years later it was hip to be square. That's heavy, huh? The nation's paradigm in a nutshell.

○

Joe Carducci didn't think much of the MC5 as a rock band, and he considered that "their best work was the extra-musical challenging of the California hippie rock scene to be as politically dangerous and irresponsible as they talked. . . ." He was speaking, of course, of the Jefferson Airplane. After the MC5, no other '60s rock band so branded themselves in the minds of their audiences as "revolutionary." The Airplane did this on the strength of one LP, 1969's *Volunteers*, and really only on two songs it contained, the title track and "We Can Be Together." In fact, when you come right down to it, they established their revolutionary credentials on the strength of a single line from the latter track, which instantly became ubiquitous in youth culture: "Up against the wall, motherfucker." It wasn't even their line. In American folklore, it was something holdup men said: "Up against the wall, motherfucker; this is a stickup." Black Panther Bobby Seale was probably the first to apply it as a '60s radical catchphrase. As Jon Savage noted in *England's Dreaming*, the Mother-fuckers had used it as well, in a handbill circulated in 1968. That the Airplane had ripped it off and used it, in effect, as an advertising slogan for a gold-selling Top 10 album was an irony largely lost on their primary market at the time. Seale, meanwhile, was in prison.

By 1969 the Jefferson Airplane were quite practiced in marketing revolutionary hipness to receptive youth. Despite what later generations like to think, the "commodification of cool" isn't something Madison Avenue learned only in the 1980s and 1990s, when the ponytailed boomers took over the ad agencies and introduced a '60s hipster attitude into that gray flannel world. From the Roaring Twenties onward, advertising closely monitored changing fashions in hipness, from the flappers and the Charlston through rap-metal and skatepunk, and tried (often with dismal effect) to incorporate those hip images into their advertisements.

The Airplane's first LP, 1967's *Surrealistic Pillow*, was hardly out when the band began commodifying its hip status with a series of radio advertisements for Levi's jeans that was a takeoff on the popular success of the single "White Rabbit" and on psychedelia in general. The catchy theme was "White Levi's in all colors." The ads became controversial among hipsters, and the band, inevitably accused of selling out, eventually withdrew from the campaign. Band leader Paul Kantner—sounding remarkably unrepentant—recounted it this way a few years later (1972) in a *Crawdaddy* interview:

"I liked the concept of those ads. We didn't make a whole lot of money from them. We did it mainly because they said we could do anything we wanted to. They gave us free reign but then that whole shit with the Levi factory came up. Graham sent a guy down to check out a rumor that the Levi people were scabbing or doing some shit and it was true. We were supposed to do another four commercials for them but we didn't do them. I'd do an ad for them today though. I like Levi's and I'll do an ad for anything I like. . . . We'd love to do a toilet paper ad."

Rock critic Lester Bangs was one hipster who saw through the Airplane's thin radical veneer. He wrote the band off as "radical dilettante capitalist pigs." The lukewarm review of *Volunteers* in *Rolling Stone* commented: "Some people are disturbed by the words. Well, they're certainly no more or less stupid than the average rock lyrics, and right about now lyrics about revolution are becoming about as trite as most of those about love have always been. Is 'We Can Be Together' a political statement? Listen to how the 'revolutionaries' sing the line 'And we are very proud of ourselves' before launching into the self-indulgent 'Up against the wall' part. If there's a political statement here, maybe it's get musically, if not politically radicalized."

Paul Kantner wrote "We Can Be Together" and co-wrote "Volunteers" with Marty Balin. Kantner was backing away from serious interpretations of the album's rhetoric as early as the following year, when he had a conversation with *Rolling Stone* interviewer Ben Fong-Torres:

*RS: People are calling you and the Stones the rock and roll bands most outwardly calling for violent revolution.*

Paul Kantner: Violent in terms of violently upsetting what's going on, not a violence of blowing buildings up or a violent "shoot policemen" or violent running down the street with an AR-18 shooting everything you can see. But violent shit, changing one set of values to another.

*RS: Or something violent in the eyes of the establishment . . .?*

Paul Kantner: Oh yeah, just a whole turn-around of values. That's violent to them. It's extreme.

*RS: I like: "It doesn't mean shit to a tree" [from "Eskimo Blue Day"].*

Paul Kantner: It doesn't. Don't get serious about it all. 'Cause it's not serious.

*RS: So this whole conversation is just a gag?*

Paul Kantner: There's no real importance to attach to it in the general scheme of the universe.

*RS: So what's the importance of what you do—rock and roll, live performing?*

Paul Kantner: Important's a shitty word.

Balin, who went on to write some awful, treacly pop love songs like "Miracles," also disavowed the implied revolutionary intent of "We Can Be Together" and "Volunteers," saying that if people interpreted them as political, it was a "misconception": they were meant to raise merely awareness, not arms. Indeed, he once claimed that "Volunteers" began as a song literally about the Volunteers of America, the charitable organization that collects and sells used goods, before Kantner radicalized and anthemized it.

Grace Slick later said, "We were very naive." In her 1998 autobiography she wrote: "The sixties were a time when people with electric guitars naively but nobly thought they could change the whole genetic code of aggression by writing a few good songs, and using volume to drown out the ever-present whistling arsenal." This rings more true than an equivocation the forty-seven-year-old Slick had made in 1987 to *New York Times* pop writer Stephen Holden:

Ms. Slick scoffed at the Jefferson Airplane's image as 60's political revolutionaries. "If you examine a song like 'Volunteers,' it doesn't make any sense, and it never did," she said. "All it says is, 'Look what's happening out on the street. Got a revolution.' It's a rhetorical comment. We never said what anybody should do or how things should change."

That was as disingenuous as Balin insisting "Volunteers" had been written about the VOA.

Two groups did take the Airplane's political sloganeering seriously: their fans and the government. Agencies including the DEA, FBI, military intelligence, and CIA kept surveillance tabs on this band and others, such as the Fugs—whom the FBI misidentified as "the Fags"—the Grateful Dead, and John Lennon, as well as rock music festivals generally. "We were pitiably easy to monitor," Ed Sanders later wrote. (As a high school senior, during the 1968–69 school year, I attended an SDS meeting at Johns Hopkins University. The government "infiltrator" made no effort to conceal himself as he stood to one side and photographed each young person in the room.) The Airplane did play at or lend their celebrity support to a number of antiwar and anti-Nixon rallies, well into the 1970s, and in the process developed an FBI dossier, some of which was later made public under the Freedom of Information Act. Like all classified government documents, it is fascinating to read. There's a memo marked "Urgent" from the FBI's Cleveland bureau to the director of the "Domestic Intelligence Division," discussing "possible disruption of Jefferson Airplane concert, Kent State University." A 1974 memo from the FBI's Cincinnati bureau to FBI headquarters warns "that YIP plans gathering on ellipse, Washington DC, April 27, 1974, for speeches and rock concert, possibly utilizing rock concert group known as Jefferson Airplane." The band has talked about often spotting poorly disguised undercover agents at their concerts, joking that with so many LSD-spiked beverages on hand, it's likely that some of these agents went on unscheduled trips.

Not unlike the White Panthers' antics, Grace Slick's most famous act as an agent of political disruption had a comic element. She brought Abbie Hoffman as her date to a White House "ladies' tea." Slick had been invited to this event for graduates of Finch College, the finishing school she attended between September 1957 and June 1958. She showed up with Hoffman, who, though he'd greased his hair back and put on a bad suit, insisted on draping a homemade peace flag over the White House fence. Secret service agents turned them away.

Slick had some powdered LSD in her pocket; given the opportunity, she'd intended to spike Tricia Nixon's tea. The FBI files suggests that the government only learned of this plot a couple of month's later, when she spoke about it in an interview in the *East Village Other*. "The article," the FBI memo notes, "dealing with the impact of rock and roll on the cultural scene and its connections with the revolutionary youth movement in the United States, quoted Slick as stating, 'I prefer not to kill people, but I'd like to destroy as much property as possible.'"

By which, of course, she did not mean her *own* property. By the fall of 1971, when Fong-Torres interviewed them again for *Rolling Stone*, the Jefferson Airplane had moved, as he put it, from "gotta revolution" to "gotta evolution." RCA had bought Kantner and Slick an expensive house outside of San Francisco, with a pool, a view of the Pacific Ocean, and a state-of-the-art recording studio. Here Kantner could make the lumbering space-opera fantasies that characterized his '70s output, released on the band's new record label, Grunt, funded and distributed by RCA. Slick, meanwhile, was abusing drink and drugs and crashed her Mercedes sedan into a bridge.

In the December 1972 issue of *Crawdaddy*, Patrick Snyder-Scumpy looked back on the Jefferson Airplane of *Volunteers* with a fond nostalgia that is surprising evidence of how, already by 1972, the Revolution was history. He begins describing a Jefferson Airplane concert at the Fillmore in 1970, some eight months after the release of *Volunteers*—the intense flow of energy between the band and the crowd making the event feel like "a tribal war dance." When the band struck up the song "Volunteers," "a thousand fists leaped into the air," and there was a sense that a revolutionary "jihad" was about to be launched against the Nixonian establishment.

But Snyder-Scumpy also records the "severe disillusionment" the fans subsequently felt when the Airplane turned out to be just posturing rock stars, and "*their* promised land was seen to be full of bilk and money." This, he decides, was an unfair criticism. "When our radically veering course of cultural evolution confronted the entrenched forces of the establishment and became by necessity a radical political revolution, we assumed that the shamans who had guided us in the former would become the field marshals for the latter with no thoughts of their abilities, qualifications or desires. Whether Paul Kantner saw himself in the role or not, millions of kids looked to him for political guidance. This was our mistake, our failing, our naivete, not his. He was but a medium to communicate and preserve the truths we had discovered and come to accept; a poet, the producer of an ethnic artform by and for white, middle class acid heads. . . . [A]s events have shown us, we were no more committed to a real revolution than they were. I never bought a gun or put my body on the tracks of a train loaded with napalm. It was all a rap, a take off on a bad Hollywood western where the good guys had long hair and the bad guys short."

Boomers often cite Grace Slick as one of the smart rockers who got out of the game before she got too old. But Slick went on singing rock and then pop music for twenty years longer than she should have. It would have been better for all if the Jefferson Airplane in its entirety had called it quits after *Volunteers;* the band's various later iterations and variations grew increasinngly tired and tiresome. The woozy, unwieldy Jefferson Starship of the '70s, reeling like a bad drunk from one stage to the next, became better known for its members' marital and drinking problems than the music. By the 1980s, Jefferson Starship, a collection of middle-aged, millionaire veterans with no meaningful connection to their '60s selves, was a mainstream, professional pop band. Only Slick and Kantner were left of the originals; the others had formed Hot Tuna or were practicing yoga. The new members of Starship were L.A. rock hacks and sessionmen such as Mickey Thomas, previously the vocalist on Elvin Bishop's hit "Fooled Around and Fell In Love."

"As we entered the eighties," Slick writes in her autobiography, "long songs about revolution and chaos were mostly in the past. . . ." Mostly? The band had stopped writing its own material and was recording tunes written by teams of professionals. Slick is candid: they weren't trying to express themselves anymore, just to make hit records. It was a business venture now.

The commercialism finally became too much for Kantner, who left in a huff when the band accepted a teen zit-cream manufacturer as a tour sponsor. The group shortened its name, symbolically cutting all ties to its past, and became simply Starship. With Slick the only surviving Jeffersonian, it went on to make some of the most embarrassing pop music and videos of the mid-to-late-'80s. Still more depressing was the Jefferson Airplane reunion tour and album in 1988–1989, at which point they were all hitting fifty years old.

But eventually Slick did finally get it, and by the '90s she realized that no one wants to see a fifty-five-year-old rock diva onstage. In her autobiography she is bluntly funny about her decision, finally, to quit:

"With classical music, it doesn't matter how old you are. . . . But hard rock? Picture spandex on Ted Koppel, or Newt Gingrich behind a drum set. Hideous, right?

"That doesn't mean I think everybody over the age of thirty ought to give up; it's just *my* take on the situation. If you don't mind geriatric rock, that's fabulous. It'll buy Grace Slick a home in Saint-Tropez if you continue to show up at concerts in throngs of thousands and give up your forty dollars a head to listen to a fifty-eight-year-old woman say, 'Up against the wall, motherfucker.'

"That was okay in 1969. But would you buy that now? Maybe I could be the first rocker to have a bedpan roadie, an oxygen unit onstage between songs, a change of Depends, and a Count the Liver Spots contest, or . . .

"Give rock and roll back to the kids, and make soundtrack instrumentals like a good old rascal."

It's a pity so few of her contemporaries took notice.

○

Danny Fields tells me a specific and pointed story about the Revolution. As the big May Day antiwar rally in Washington, D.C., approached in 1971, a highly unreliable rumor spread that Aretha Franklin would perform for the marchers. (Franklin was not known for her antiwar sympathies.) Fields, having been fired from Elektra for signing the MC5 and the equally label-embarrassing Stooges, was then serving as house hippie and talent scout at Atlantic Records, Franklin's label, and he used the rumor as an excuse to wangle himself an all-expense-account trip to the rally. Arguing to his bosses that if Ms. Franklin did attend the event she'd need someplace to stay, he booked a two-bedroom suite in the Holiday Inn on Virginia Avenue, just across from the not-yet-infamous Watergate.

Franklin did not show up, but the May Day organizers, including most of the biggest-name "radicals" of the day, did. For one weekend, Fields's hotel rooms became, as he puts it wryly, the "hospitality suite" for the Revolution.

Abbie Hoffman, Phil Ochs, Jerry Rubin, and a large cast of others crashed there, freely availing themselves of the room service, the bar, the restaurant—all on Atlantic Records' dime. Fields left D.C. on Sunday night, but he did not check out—he left the room available to the May Day crowd for one more night, with the tab still open. "And those revolutionaries went *berserk*," he recalls, racking up "thousands of dollars" on the final bill. The wild spending spree and lavish partying cost him his job when Atlantic saw the bill.

Fields relates another telling story. One night he was at Max's Kansas City with John Sinclair, who was eating a big, expensive steak on Elektra Records' dime. Steve Paul, impresario of the premiere late-'60s rock club The Scene, saw the wild-haired, bearded Sinclair happily devouring the steak. "What happened to the revolution?" he asked. Sinclair cut another piece of steak and held it up on his fork. "This *is* the revolution," he replied.

For Fields, looking back from the year 2000, those two anecdotes say a lot about what "the revolution" was and why it evaporated. The revolution was *eating a steak on The Man's dime*. Look at Sinclair's original definition of the revolution: rock 'n' roll, dope, and fucking in the streets. For a large contingent of youth, the kind of people Sinclair describes as lumpen hippies, the revolution didn't add up to much more than that, Fields insists. They wanted to play loud rock 'n' roll wherever and whenever, without The Man pulling the plug or sending in the cops. They wanted not to have jobs. They wanted to smoke dope and have a lot of sex. And they sure did not want to go get their asses shot off in Vietnam.

"There was nothing systematic about it," Fields suggests. "No philosophy—certainly not Marxist philosophy." He thinks the Beatles had it right. "You say you want a revolution? Yeah well, what else do you want?"

Most important, he notes, you didn't have to have a revolution to get those things you thought you needed it for—rock, dope, sex, and a draft deferment were all quite available without resorting to armed revolt.

If that sounds cynical—and self-serving, given Fields's central role in de-politicizing the MC5—what is undeniable is that *if* all you wanted from the revolution was sex, drugs, and rock 'n' roll, then Fields is right. For instance, I knew almost no one in my white, middle-class collegiate cohort who couldn't get a draft deferment if he really wanted one. All you had to do was stay in school full time. You could flunk out or voluntarily opt out of your college deferment—I did and I knew other guys who did. By the time I started college in the fall of 1969 they had tightened the restrictions on deferments. In the mid-'60s, you could pretty much stay a draft-deferred student indefinitely. In 1967, at least partly due to pressure from high-minded radicals who objected to the draft's class biases, deferments were ended for graduate students. But for full-time undergraduates, deferments were effectively automatic. It's also true that even with your deferment, the simple *threat* of the draft was always there, looming like the now-equally-forgotten, constant if remote threat of nuclear war. It wasn't until some years after the war that I fully realized how that war, like all wars, was predominantly fought by lower-class boys, who either volunteered or didn't have the wherewithal to evade conscription. Like all my friends, I was convinced that the draft was a serious potential threat to *my* health and well-being. If they tried to make me join the army I was going to escape to Canada. It never occurred to me that they probably wouldn't want me. Even after I gave up my deferment—and later, when they instituted the lottery and I came up with a very low number (the lower the number, the higher the likelihood that you would be called up)—the military never showed the slightest indication that they seriously considered me army material. They had plenty of other cannon fodder to choose from.

It is worth noting here that three-quarters of those who did fight in Vietnam were volunteers—a higher percentage than in their dads' World War II or the Korean War. The figure is a bit deceptive—clearly many of those guys were unwilling volunteers who signed up rather than be conscripted, because you had a better choice of assignments. Still, a 75 percent volunteer rate is a reminder that, beyond the college campuses and hippie neighborhoods where most of us antiwar types hung out, the Vietnam War, certainly in its early years, was a lot more popular with average young Americans than we thought at the time, or may care to recall now.

Sex and drugs and rock 'n' roll were also all in plentiful abundance. Everybody was getting laid, getting high, listening to rock. Who needed to off the pigs? Especially if you had money. The MC5 certainly discovered that. They didn't have "jobs," they were buying all the drugs they could take, they were playing really loud all the time, they had the groupies and the sex slaves—what did they need with armed insurrection? In a microcosmic example for the whole generation, they'd become what they had been supposed to rebel against. The only thing a revolution would do for them is take away their drugs and force them to go ladle potatoes at a People's Free Lunch Program somewhere in downtown Detroit—the very place they had fled.

But it wasn't just the MC5, Fields suggests. By the turn of 1970, the corporate music industry was pouring tremendous sums of money into the hands of rock bands. The whole notion of rock 'n' roll as a cultural wing of the revolution became, very quickly, very hard to take seriously. "I don't think the ethos could support the hypocrisy," Fields says. When he refers to the "Street-Fighting" Rolling Stones as "the rhythm section of the revolution," he means it with all due sarcasm. And if the Stones were the revolution's marching band, the Jefferson Airplane and the MC5 were the cheerleading squads.

People derided the 1970s at the time as the Me Decade—although in retrospect the hedonism, self-involvement, and hard partying of the time seem almost like community service compared to the following decades. But Fields is suggesting that the '60s, at least the later, rocking 'n' rolling '60s, was just as Me-oriented; that despite the brothers-and-sisters, power-to-the-people rhetoric, a lot of young people were really just as motivated by self-interest.

"It was Spring Break," he scoffs. "There was no revolution. It wasn't serious. It was fun. You got laid and got stoned." It was sexy and exciting to be running en masse from nightstick-wielding cops. It got your heart pounding and your nipples hard. Never underestimate the role sex played in the revolution, Fields insists. They didn't call it the "sexual revolution" for nothing.

○

I Saw the Best Minds of My Generation Rock

—The Fugs

Ellen Willis is a non-doctrinaire feminist and leftist, a veteran of the original New Left and antiwar movements in the 1960s, and still in many ways an unregenerate hippie politics-of-ecstasy communard. She was, arguably, the first important female rock critic—her first long critical essay, on Bob Dylan, appeared in *Commentary* in 1967, after which she wrote about rock and pop for the *New Yorker*, about books for *Ms.*, and about women's and other social issues for *Rolling Stone* and the *Village Voice*. In 1990 she joined the journalism faculty at New York University.

Interviewing Willis in 2000, I was not surprised when she argued against the image of defanged American leftists bickering among themselves on the fringes of society. She countered that social change always starts with radical outsiders and then moves toward the center, so that what were once radical ideas eventually become mainstream, and that this is what happened to the New Left after the '60s.

> I do think that there are some really good ideas that start out as minority ideas, like that black people are equal to white people. . . . I think that radical change, social change, always does start with minorities who are willing to stick up for their beliefs. I think there were all different strands of the New Left in the '60s, and the strand that I identified with was a cultural radical strand that you saw in the women's movement, where people were actually talking about the quality of their own lives, and what ways bureaucratic and hierarchical institutions were crushing their spirit. The criticism of sexual morality, the criticism of bureaucracy in the university, and so on. I think there was also a competing strain on the left which was moralist and altruistic, which is "We are doing this for people less fortunate than ourselves," which I always think is never a good basis for radicalism. The main impulse in that is to feel morally superior. Real change happens when you recognize your commonality with other people. When you start to be in touch with your own desires and what you want, that can be projected on the social, collective level—when you start to make a critique based on your own discontent. Which certainly doesn't mean that you are supposed to be insensitive to how other people are being suppressed, but finally radical movements come out of people organizing themselves and people making other groups organize themselves.
>
> What happened in the late '60s was that the feminist movement starting organizing itself, which was really an outgrowth of that

cultural, radical, and particularly a libertarian, stream. The idea that freedom was a core issue—not only equality, but freedom. I think a lot of men on the left simply freaked out about feminism—if this is what being a cultural radical meant, they couldn't deal with it at all. Part of the reason that the Left went off the deep end in the late '60s was not only frustration at not being able to end the war, which I think was a big part of it, but because feminism was challenging all of their suppositions and they just didn't know what to do about it. I think black nationalism, too, played a part in this, but among the men with whom I was most in touch, it was feminism. Feminism was affecting the ways they think about things and affected their most personal relationships in their own lives and they simply couldn't deal with it.

Then I think what happened in the '70s was that, first of all, men, who came out of this background and were very deeply wounded by these culture wars, became quite socially conservative. Whereas the feminist movement, the black movement, the gay movement, went from the radical understanding that in order to change anything you have to make your own voice heard and break the monopoly, in the case of feminism, of men telling women what they were, who they should be, what they should be doing. Demanding to be included in that conversation, women went from that to what I think is the fallacy of identity politics, which is that only women can speak about women's problems, and that feminism, which is really about a universalist movement for freedom and equality, is really the property of the group. You know, working-class women challenging middle-class women to speak, challenging black women to speak—a lot of the debate on social issues became who had the right to speak about what, who was more oppressed than whom and so on. Again, instead of being a political movement aimed at challenging the structures of society, an awful lot of energy got displaced on being a moral movement aimed at improving woman's character. It became a question of morality instead of a question of politics.

And so now what I see in a lot of the Left is an argument by socially conservative men, who are using the mistakes of identity politics to try and discredit cultural politics all together. One of my arguments is that cultural radicalism actually has a *critique* of identity politics. You know, cultural radicalism is really about putting freedom and pleasure right at the center of one's political goals.

*When did you get into rock 'n' roll?*

I was a rock 'n' roll fan in high school. Totally unself-consciously—this was just the music that I loved. But I totally accepted the adult view that this was not serious, this was trash, this had no larger import whatsoever. It never occurred to me that wasn't true. So I think there was this peculiar situation for all of us that one of the most important things in your life, that made us happy, that was a source of great energy, was somehow coded as not being "real life."

One of the things that happened in the '60s was the realization that rock 'n' roll was a really important cultural form. Our 'secret life' *was* real life. This in itself had many ramifications worth writing about, but it was also in the context of a larger conversation about mass culture. The dominant view among literary intellectuals at the time was that mass culture was shit and, as Dwight McDonald said, not art at all but merely a form of chewing gum.

At the same time, there was an argument beginning to percolate that not only could mass culture be vital art, but that the very mass qualities of it could be the source of a *distinctive* kind of art. I think those of us who were writing early rock criticism were really writing about that idea. I personally was very influenced by Tom Wolfe, by Andy Warhol, in terms of looking at mass culture in ways that were different from the way literary intellectuals looked at high culture. Of course, I and other people like Bob Christgau and Greil Marcus who were writing about rock 'n' roll also had high-culture educations. We were literary; it wasn't like we were rejecting high culture. We just saw that the way we experienced rock 'n' roll was not the same as the way we experienced Beethoven or whatever. And we wanted to write about that.

*How was it different?*

Mass culture, and rock 'n' roll in particular, was something you experienced very much in context. It had to do with how you were listening to it, who you were listening with, what your mood was    It was the extension of art outside the frame. The effect it had on you involved all those other things. Now, people who wrote that were always accused of not caring about content or form. Of course we cared about those things. It just wasn't the only thing.

Secondly, the reach of mass media had created the performer whose public persona became an extension of his work. So somebody like John Lennon or Bob Dylan becomes a star and is subjected to saturation publicity. Everybody who listens to his work is going to have this "star" superimposed over the work. Then the question becomes what do you do with that. If you're an artist, don't you want to try to shape your images in ways that really will enhance and complement your work? I think part of the genius of the Beatles and Dylan and the Stones, Janis Joplin in a different way, and of course Andy Warhol was to create very rich personas that themselves had an aesthetic value. It was a mixed-media art in a way—it wasn't only music.

*What was your first exposure to rock 'n' roll?*

The first rock 'n' roll record I remember hearing was, ironically, one my father brought home—"Shake, Rattle & Roll," by Bill Haley. The first one I ever bought may have been "Earth Angel," by the Penguins.

*Do you buy the notion that in the '60s rock became, or tried to become, a cultural wing of the broader revolution?*

Well, I thought it was a time when teen culture and the wider youth culture merged. The result of that was that rock 'n' roll became rock at a certain point, and there was rock that was countercultural. For better and worse.

*What about the conflict that the MC5 and Jefferson Airplane faced—that to get the "revolutionary" word out there you had to become a celebrity, rich, famous, and therefore corrupted. By the time the Airplane was hanging with Abbie Hoffman and chanting "Up against the wall, motherfucker," they were rich, famous, and therefore completely ineffectual as representatives of the real, brown-rice-eating, poverty-practicing counterculture.*

I think there was a lot more to the counterculture than the barefoot, brown-rice-eating [stereotype]. I was counterculture and not particularly a barefoot rice-eater. The counterculture was also about fun, and technology and mass media played a big part in that. And insofar as the counterculture was into mass media and mass culture, the kind of bohemianism that resulted was different from, say, the Beats. [The new breed] were negotiating the relationship between art and commerce. Part of what made the Beatles rebellious was this notion of, "My god, I have all this money and I can do whatever I want. Fuck you." It was like they were beating the system. The Beats had hated rock 'n' roll. The folk revival people hated rock 'n' roll. Because rock 'n' roll was commercial. What we were basically saying was, "Yes, it's commercial to its core, but it's also wonderful." It's like, I'm not a fan of the Catholic Church but I have to admit there's a lot of religious art that's wonderful. I may not be a fan of corporate capitalism, but nonetheless there were certain things about capitalism, its entrepreneurial vitality and its mass outreach and so on, that resulted in wonderful art, too.

*Including rock.*

Yes. And I don't think it made it any less rebellious. I think there was also always a confusion between "rebellious" and "revolutionary." I always thought it was hype that rock is revolutionary. What does that mean? Looking back on it, even in some of the things I wrote I tended to toss around that word "revolution" in a rather loose way.

*Didn't everybody.*

You know, ultimately rock 'n' roll was not about transforming society. It reflected rebellious currents in society. It was certainly about having more fun, about beating the system, about pleasure and ecstasy— which I think are fundamental ingredients of any kind of social transformation or revolution. But in itself, music is not going to change the world.

*And you'd make that case not just for rock but for the broader counterculture—that what we kept calling "revolution" was really just youthful rebellion?*

I do think you could call the '60s a "cultural revolution," all things considered. It effected major changes in personal and social life. I don't have a problem with calling it a cultural revolution, although you could also call it a cultural revolt, rebellion, whatever. But when people talked about rock being "revolutionary," they meant something more political than it actually was.

She cites her September 1969 *New Yorker* article on Woodstock, "Cultural Revolution Saved from Drowning," which contained an insightful and prescient passage about youth culture and politics. She noted the urge among radicals to politicize Woodstock. "The underground papers made a lot of noise about businessmen profiting from music that belonged to the community, and some movement people demanded and received money to bring political groups to the festival and set up an enclave called Movement City as a center for radical activity," Willis wrote. But the hippie, pacifist Hog Farm group had a larger presence and greater impact on the event. And when Abbie Hoffman attempted to appropriate the stage, Pete Townshend knocked him off.

"What cultural revolutionaries do not seem to grasp," Willis concluded in her article, "is that, far from being a grass-roots art form that has been taken over by businessmen, rock itself comes from the commercial exploitation of blues. It is bourgeois at its core, a mass-produced commodity, dependent on advanced technology and therefore on the money controlled by those in power. Its rebelliousness does not imply specific political content; it can be— and has been—criminal, fascistic, and coolly individualistic as well as revolutionary. Nor is bohemianism inherently radical. It can simply be a more pleasurable way of surviving within the system, which is what the pop sensibility has always been about. Certainly that was what Woodstock was about: ignore the bad, groove on the good, hang loose, and let things happen. The truth is that there can't be a revolutionary culture until there is a revolution. In the meantime, we should insist that the capitalists who produce rock concerts offer reasonable service at reasonable prices."

*Something happened in the early-through-mid-'70s to derail and dissipate "the revolution." You cite economic, political, and cultural factors.*

I think a lot of things happened. One of the really important ones was the economic contraction. 1973 was a watershed. I remember grasping the import of the oil crisis as a real representation that the United States was no longer going to have a free ride—that the kind of abundance we'd enjoyed was maybe not going to last forever. I wrote about this—realizing that my own casual talk about revolution was based on taking for granted that things *weren't* going to change. There was a sense of security that things weren't going to change. Suddenly, I realized things *could* change, but not necessarily in the direction I wanted them to.

Then there was the fact that a political backlash had already started as early as '68. So you have a wave of passionate political and cultural radicalism, it catches people's imaginations with a whole new vocabulary and vision, and it takes the opposition a while to figure out what's happening, regroup, and fight back. So that was [in full swing] by the early '70s.

Culturally, *Roe v. Wade* was really important in that it was a big feminist victory on the one hand, but at the same time it really galvanized the right-to-life movement.

And then I like to quote this line from a song by the Roche sisters: "We got so far out there everybody got scared." It's like we were testing, in all kinds of ways, the limits of relationships and our own psyches, and people really did start to get scared that they were going too far and would never be able to live any kind of normal life.

And I think the generation started to get older and having to worry about making a living, taking care of their kids.

*Also, things got scary when they got real—when the Weatherman started blowing themselves up, and the Panthers were shooting it out with cops, and the National Guard was shooting to kill at campus protests.*

Right. Being white and middle class wasn't going to protect you anymore.

*And then the politics got mainstreamed as well. If you were "serious" about it you abandoned the revolutionary rhetoric and went "Clean for Gene" in '68—certainly you went whole hog for McGovern in '72.*

In the United States, liberalism has been an extremely powerful ideology for most of my lifetime. Liberalism has a tendency to absorb things. People always worried about being "co-opted." But I always thought that when you get to the point where your idea or vision is powerful enough so that liberalism was co-opting you, you'd won something important. The disadvantage is that liberals always then want to write radicals out of history and pretend that they [the liberals] did everything. But since they don't really have ideas of their own, they can't defend against the conservative backlash when it comes. . . .

Nonetheless, I think the "mainstreaming" of the counterculture's simply freer way of life has really changed American culture in a good way. When I try to explain to my daughter, who's in high school now, what it was like to be in high school in the '50s, she can't fathom it. It's not that there's isn't still a lot of sexism, but the kind of naked, blatant degradation we had to put up with is just gone.

*What role did rock 'n' roll play in that loosening-up of American culture?*
First of all, it was the eruption of "blackness" out of invisibility and onto the American scene. Second, there was the readiness of American youth for a much more frank sexuality. And it was also like a generational language. You could play a song for somebody and they understood all sorts of things about you.

*Do you buy the classic boomer argument that rock "died" in the '70s?*
Oh no, I don't think it died at all. It certainly changed a lot and became a lot darker. What went out of it was the utopianism. There was still the rebellion, but it became extremely pessimistic and almost misanthropic by the time you got to punk rebellion. No, I think there was wonderful music in the '70s. That music is a lot more lasting in my life than music from the '60s. There's something sweet about '60s music, but you think this was definitely another time and another place.

*But I do believe rock is specifically a youth music. You may not get too old to appreciate it, but you sure get too old to play it. It's not rock anymore; it's a nostalgic recreation of rock.*

I think you're framing the problem backwards. The problem is that in American culture—and in the '60s we were able to combat this to a certain extent, maybe delay it as much as twenty years—there's this idea that grownup people are supposed to "settle down." We're supposed to be interested in work and family, period. We're not supposed to have any sort of communal culture beyond that. We're certainly not supposed to have any communal culture of which eroticism and intensity of feeling are really important. . . . It seems to me that any new music that could draw together a communal culture of people my age would have some reference to rock, because that was our formation. It wouldn't necessarily be rock 'n' roll. Who knows what it would be? But the cultural pressures are such that that never happened. There probably are still plenty of musicians who are wrestling with making music that's relevant to their lives and their friends' lives that I would probably find really moving. But what's missing is the community in which that music could be important. I really feel the lack of that, and anger at that. I'm not supposed to be interested in dancing, I'm not supposed to be interested in sex. Hey, I'm not dead yet!

O

In the end, my favorite "revolutionary rock band" of the era—even though they weren't quite a band, and parodied rock more than they played it, and probably weren't any more effective as motivators of social change than any of the others—is the Fugs. They were more committed to their antiwar, pro-drugs, pro-sex ideals than the Jefferson Airplane ever were to theirs, and much smarter than the MC5. Interviewed in the online music magazine *Perfect Sound Forever* in 1997, co-founder Tuli Kupferberg put it simply and straightfor-wardly: "Our goal was to make the revolution. That would have been a complete revolution, not just an economic or political one. We had utopian ideals and those are the best ideals."

The Fugs were formed by poets Kupferberg and Ed Sanders in 1964. Kupfer-berg was forty-two, roughly twenty years older than Sanders, and already a well-known Beat figure, publisher of the poetry magazine *Yeah*. Sanders was a pacifist and war protester, publisher of the hippie zine *Fuck You/A Journal of the Arts*, for which he would be arrested on obscenity charges. (The ACLU pleaded his case for him and won.) The two poets were joined by musicians including Peter Stampfel (also of the Holy Modal Rounders). Though they rejected the term, they started out as a jug band, closer to a slovenly version of the folkies' protest music than to anything resembling rock. And more than either folk or rock, it was like performance art or a Happening, an anarchic beatnik joke. Even later, when they became more proficient as singers and had professional rock musicians behind them—at one point, even hired-gun Atlantic Records session musicians—they were largely joking around with the form. For every pseudo-folk-rock ditty such as "Frenzy" or "Doin' All Right," their albums were carefully landmined with quasi-country protest jokes such as "Wide, Wide River" (a.k.a. "River of Shit") or the eleven-minute opus "Virgin Forest," a radio playlet in form, which offered a vulgar thumbnail sketch of human evolution. They stand in comparison to what the Mothers of Invention were doing at the time, except that Zappa was basically a conservative and the Mothers' music had no real politics, or to a filthy-minded Firesign Theater sketch. My three favorite Fugs songs, Kupferberg's epics "Nothing," "Defeated," and the jingle "The Ten Commandments," are among the purest, bleakest—and yet funniest—expressions of the spirit of nihilism and anarchism in the annals of pre-punk music.

The Fugs became a success so fast they surprised even themselves. They started out playing small gigs for audiences of fifty or so East Village hipsters in Sanders's Peace Eye Bookstore (a former kosher butcher shop), at the Bridge Theater, Izzy Young's Folklore Center on Sixth Avenue near Bleecker Street, and Jonas Mekas's Cinematheque on St. Marks Place. "We were an instant hit there," Kupferberg recalls. "The whole East Side hippie community attended. They came up alongside the stage to sing along, to laugh, to scream, to break furniture, and they even helped to write some of our early songs." This was followed by a period of over a year in which the Fugs were a regular act at the Players Theater on MacDougal Street in the Village, playing more than 700 concerts.

In 1965 the Fugs recorded their first album, *The Village Fugs*, in four hours, working with the legendary Harry Smith as producer. It was released on

Broadside/Folkways, the label of folk and protest music. Shortly afterward they signed a deal with a new, experimental label, ESP, which rereleased *The Village Fugs* as *The Fugs First Album*, soon followed by *The Fugs Second Album*. These two LPs contain what is to this day some of the silliest and most scandalous material that ever made it into the Top 100. The Fugs would later move on to Atlantic—which, prefiguring the Sex Pistols, dropped the Fugs without releasing a single record by them—and Reprise. They toured extensively; Fleetwood Mac opened for them in Europe. Sanders was on the cover of *Life* magazine.

It is perhaps their own fault that in the eye of the general public they were seen as little more than the "obscene" pranksters behind joke songs such as "I Feel Like Homemade Shit," "Slum Goddess," "Frenzy," "Group Grope," and the ineffable "Boobs A Lot." As a revolutionary force they were taken less than seriously. Nevertheless, "Doin' All Right," with lyrics by their friend, the poet Ted Berrigan, uses a salacious image to tremendous effect in quite possibly the finest antiwar couplet ever written:

I'm not ever gonna go to Vietnam
I prefer to stay right here and screw your mom

Other songs like "Kill For Peace," "War Kills Babies" (a wordless sound-collage of horror), and "CIA Man" speak for themselves. The band was actively involved in helping to organize and play protest rallies and similar events all over the country.

"We were sort of the USO for the Left," Kupferberg tells me. "We played more benefits than any band I know." They were in effect the house band for the 1967 "exorcism" of the Pentagon, personally paying for the sound system and recording the chant "Out Demons Out" (it appeared on their LP *Tenderness Junction*). In another of their most famous moments, while performing their piece "Spaghetti Death" one night, Ed Sanders threw spaghetti sauce on Andy Warhol's white suit. "It was during Vietnam. I guess it was symbolic," Kupferberg says with a sly grin.

It was Sanders, disillusioned with the grim turn political and social events were taking in 1968 and '69, who broke up the band just as the '60s became the '70s. Kupferberg has said he thought it was exactly the wrong time for the Fugs

David Bowie models menswear.

Johnny Rotten, middle-aged punk.

Crosby, Stills, Nash &
Young reunion, 2000.

Giorgio Gomelsky
with a young Eric
Clapton, 1963.

Mike Doughty at
Rock In New York.

Savoy Brown's Kim
Simmonds, 1999.

Revolutionary
nostalgia: Rage Against
the Machine.

Jefferson Airplane's
Marty Balin, 2000.

Sting rocks
the Rockettes.

George Tabb and "Mini-Me" (AKA Stevie Ramone).

Yes on tour, 2000.

The Fugs' Tuli Kupferberg at
Rock In New York, 2000.

John Sinclair's revolutionary
rock manifesto, 1972.

to disband. "We ended at a time when I think we were most needed," he tells me. The "USO of the Left" really could have helped morale "when things started going down."

In 2000, at seventy-six years old, Kupferberg remained a familiar figure on the streets of the Village. Spotted and baggy-eyed as an old hound, with a limp mop of gray hair and a snaggle-toothed grin, he was still raffish and playful as ever.

*You've said you became the world's oldest rock 'n' roll star at the age of forty-two. How did that come about? Had you listened to much rock 'n' roll in the '50s? What were your earlier musical influences?*

I grew up in mid-Manhattan, in Yorkville. I was not in a Jewish ghetto. That liberated me in many ways. There were kids from fifteen or twenty ethnicities in my grade-school class. Central Europe, mostly. This was in the middle, late '30s. There was even a Nazi in my class who persecuted me for being a Jew. So the music—we had a Victrola, so it was the records of the '20s and '30s. A lot of Yiddish music, because my father belonged to a Landsmanschaft [a Jewish benevolent association] and there was a marriage every week, a lot of wedding music. I loved that music. I listened to a lot of classical music. And then I listened to movie music. It was all courtship music, but of the highest quality. I was also a jazz enthusiast at Brooklyn College, but when bebop came in I couldn't make it.

So rock 'n' roll, I guess I was superior to that at the beginning. But it wasn't that interesting at the beginning. It was still too much courtship music. If you examine American popular music there's whole periods where it's more than courtship music. Country and western is as wide as life, and the English ballads range around.

*So it's the early '60s, you and Sanders are friends and poets and reading on the Lower East Side. How did you decide to become a band?*

Ed and I read at Le Metro, which was the primo poetry cafe, and afterward we would go to the Dom [on St. Marks Place]. They had a jukebox in there, and it had the Stones and the early Beatles. Ed said, "We can do better than that." The Stones were pretty advanced, but the

Beatles' early music was . . . It had something. They became major poets later. So Ed thought we should start a group, and I found the name Fugs in Mailer's book [*The Naked and the Dead*, where it was used as a fig leaf for the f-word]. There's an apocryphal story that I like—some of them are too good to be true, right?—Dorothy Parker meets Norman Mailer at a party and says, "Oh yes, Mr. Mailer. You're the young man who doesn't know how to spell 'fuck.'"

*You've said the Fugs' goal was revolution. What happened to the revolution?*

The revolution in America was a youth revolution, and it was driven by the Vietnam War, although there were all those things in the background like the problems of minorities and the woman problem. It never made any connection with mainstream America—with adults or the working class or the non–urban centers. And since it never made that connection, in that respect it didn't change the fundamentals. A lot of things *did* change that were valuable, but it certainly wasn't the revolution that was predicted by the ideologies of Marx and the anarchists—a basic economic revolution with really tied-in social, cultural, sexual, and religious changes.

*You've said that it was a revolution of young people and academics who had good ideas but didn't know how to put them into practice to build the new society you wanted to see.*

The other thing was the wonderful failure of the Soviet revolution, or so-called revolution. Everyone in America in my generation started out as a communist, a CP sympathizer. But I was disillusioned very early and went into Trotskyism and then into anarchism. A lot of people in the end found out they'd wasted their lives in support of an incredibly murderous regime. That was pretty disappointing.

*I'm of the opinion that for a lot of young people "the Revolution" was almost entirely the antiwar movement.*

The war was a very simple thing. You had to decide whether you wanted to go kill or be killed, whether you were for that or not. It was at the center of American consciousness at the time.

*And it took a lot of momentum out of the larger movement when the draft ended.*

Well, it was a slow decline. The '60s were really '65 to '75. When the war ended, that was the real end of the '60s.

But [he adds, echoing Ellen Willis] we shouldn't really forget the accomplishments. A good deal on the racial level and on the feminist level, and a general loosening up of America's Puritan sexuality.

*The Fugs were definitely cultural radicals. Who was responsible for the Fugs' political radicalism?*

I blame myself. Ed was a pacifist when I met him, an undeveloped radical. You know, the whole Beat movement, outside of Ginsberg, was not exactly political in any particular sense.

*John Sinclair has a theory that in the '60s people were making rock for the art or the revolution, and in the '70s it became about making money.*

Yeah. Well, it was fun [in the '60s]. People did it for fun. And then once there was money in it, everyone gets corrupted to a certain extent. Some get more corrupted than others. You know, there was a time when the record labels were supporting the alternative press. It was a slow decline. There was a key ad. It was one of the airlines. They used the song "This Land Is Your Land." Then it deteriorated further, and George Bush used it in one of his campaigns. Maybe the one he lost. They always use the first verse. They never get to the one that goes:

As I went walking, I saw a sign there,
And on the sign it said "No Trespassing"
But on the other side it didn't say nothing
That side was made for you and me

So the commercialism was only part of it. It's the whole culture. How do you become a more perfect or happy person in a culture that's very imperfect and unhappy? The music was a thrust in the right direction, but look what it was facing. Three hundred years of American history. Or all history since we came down out of the trees. Now, has there been progress? I don't know. I bet there have been societies that were more ideal than some that we find now, and some that have been worse. . . . The Enlightenment idea that there's a single, straight line of progress is for the birds. . . . We don't know where we came from, what we're doing here, or where we're going.—Wait, is that our motto? Should we inscribe that on the seal of the United States? We live in pessimistic times, but with optimism for the future.

○

Radical rock, naturally, went the way of the radical Left in the 1970s. Of later efforts to harness rock to political causes, two of the more notable examples are from the U.K.: the punk-rockers' Rock Against Racism, founded in 1976, and the lefty-liberals' Red Wedge, founded in 1986. RAR was goaded into being by an offhand, probably under-the-influence remark Eric Clapton reputedly made onstage in Birmingham in 1976, when he said that he wanted to "keep Britain white." RAR consisted of mostly punk bands, bonding with reggae and other black musicians, which were trying to counter efforts by the racist, neo-Nazi National Front to use punk to recruit young members. RAR's founders were '60s-bred Trotskyists of the Socialist Workers Party.

The National Front was then benefiting from and spurring on a rise in nationalist, racist, anti-immigrant feelings among white Britons, especially in the working class—including a number of punks and punk rockers. RAR and the Anti-Nazi League staged big concerts and marches in London in 1977–1978, with spin-off activities in cities and towns around Great Britain. It can be credibly claimed that RAR helped retard the growth of neo-Nazi popularity among young people, even if it did not end it.

Red Wedge was born in the wake of Live Aid. Bob Geldof's global fund-raiser was hardly revolutionary in either intent or execution; it was just a celebrity charity event, a benefit concert, a global telethon. But as a relatively painless way for a bunch of rock and pop stars to look good, sound good, feel good, and do good, it proved an attractive model, imitated numerous times in the next several years. Red Wedge was the Labour Party's adaptation: an attempt to use pop music to recruit new members in its struggle against the Thatcherite Tories. Red Wedge put on some decent concerts, but it failed to have the desired mobilizing effect on its young audience. Labour did poorly in the 1987 elections.

"The histories of RAR and Red Wedge suggest that attempts to use mass musics to forge mass movements will always face two problems," Simon Frith and John Street have written (in the collection *Rockin' the Boat*). The first is that "[t]he power of popular music is by its nature momentary" and "novelty wears off. . . . The declining 'buzz' of the big RAR concerts, for example, was apparent event by event." The popularity of any specific act is "inherently unstable." The second, and I'd argue insurmountable problem, is the one political rock bands have always faced: You may gather an audience, and your audience may feel a certain "collectivity," a sense of "shared experience and identity," but how do you turn that into a political movement? "The question," as Frith and Street put it, "is whether this identity has any political substance."

In the United States, the closest the music industry has come to anything resembling those organized attempts to use mass culture to move the masses is probably Rock the Vote. Whereas rockers once exhorted their young audiences to reject the system or seize control of it, they now limply advise them to buy into it as registered voters so that, as the hoary old fairy tale goes, they can "change the system from within." Even the Right has gotten into the act: the late Lee Atwater, a genuinely rock 'n' rolling Republican, was able to gather numerous rock and blues acts to play at George Bush's inauguration ceremonies: Joe Cocker, Stevie Ray Vaughn, the Stones' Ron Wood, Dr. John, and Bo Diddley were among them.

Bob Geldof's Live Aid echoed through rock in the 1980s and '90s, validating the rock-and-pop version of the celebrity charity telethon as an easy, visible, and tax-deductible way to do good deeds. As a result, rock stars, like any other species of celebrity, have come to represent the height of limousine liberalism. Rock stars can play a benefit concert or lend their famous names to the cause of their choice and then retire to their mansions feeling good about themselves. Bono preaches about releasing all third world nations from their international debt responsibilities; Bono could *pay off* the debt of several small third world nations. In 1999, Clapton auctioned off a brace of guitars—including "Brownie," on which he had played "Layla," which went for a stunning $450,000. The charity? Free treatment at the Crossroads Centre, his posh drug rehab facility on the island of Antigua.

And then there is Sting. The epitome of the smug, self-satisfied, self-righteous hipster capitalist, a creature invented by the boomer generation; if he weren't Sting, he would be some other type of New Age entrepreneur, a promoter of solar-powered hot tubs or organically grown hemp leisure wear. Sting also has a penchant for the easy charity gesture, such as allowing his guitars to be auctioned off for one good cause or another.

I read an interview with him in *Sky*, the Delta in-flight magazine, in December 1999, at which point Sting was forty-eight—my age. The interviewer, Rob Spitz, posited to him that rock "by definition, has always been edgy, daring, even subversive music—the natural expression of rebellion. Don't you," he asked, "desire to fit in that groove anymore?"

To which Sting replied: "They say it's the music of rebellion, but it's been co-opted by some very reactionary forces. Rock wears the clothes of rebellion, but it's about as rebellious as drinking Coca-Cola."

When we hear the normal, garden-variety zillionaire uttering bogus populist sentiment about dark financial or political forces co-opting our culture, we know to be skeptical. But let a zillionaire celebrity—Sting, Bono, Zack de la Rocha, Tim Robbins—make the same sort of pronouncement, and we're innocent and gullible as lambs. At the same time Sting was making this statement to Spitz, he was making a music video that doubled, with a few editing changes, as a commercial for the Jaguar S-Type luxury automobile. Not since Eva Peron was at her summit had celebrity demagoguery rung so hollow.

Rock after the 1970s was not, of course, completely devoid of its proselytizers, espousing both left- and right-wing politics. But while some of them have become famous and made themselves tidy fortunes doing it, what impact their political sloganeering had on anyone else's life is an open question. The most striking example in the 1990s was Rage Against the Machine. While their music was '90s rap-metal, everything else about the band was an ingenious manipulation of '60s nostalgia. They used '60s iconography, such as the Black Power Olympians, for their cover art. They covered classic '60s rebellion songs like "Kick Out the Jams." They had Michael Moore, that demigod of boomer rebellion, direct their music videos. The official RATM website saluted a "Freedom Fighter of the Month," then it offered the opportunity to purchase an official RATM T-shirt with Che Guevara's image on the front. In all their public statements, the band's frontmen, Zack de la Rocha and Tom Morello, uttered the most pure wave-the-red-diaper polemic since the early Billy Bragg. And they moved millions upon millions of units doing it.

At times, Rage's ability to speak only in old-style revolutionary dithyramb produced surreal results. In *Rolling Stone* number 825 (November 11, 1999), "Random Notes" offered an account of how Zack had bravely gone onstage at Roseland even though he had a bum tummy:

> I was lying in bed two hours before the show.... I had some kind of stomach flu. I was about to lose it up there. But you know, nothing can kick you out of a deep flu better than seeing Public Enemy elevate some minds and tear the roof off a place. And when you think about people in Chiapas, Mexico, sick to their stomachs and still getting up and fighting every day, the least I could do is give some of that energy back. So it was nothing.

As silly as he sounded, I hope Zack was serious. If not, it was the most cynical usurpation of youthful rebellion since Jagger sang "Street Fighting Man." You do have to wonder what sort of coverage *Rolling Stone*, or any other mainstream magazine, would have given Zack's rhetoric if the band were named, say, Rage Against ZOG, and if instead of Chiapas he had referenced the freedom fighters of Montana who've given their lives to keep the white man's homeland free of mongrel foreign Marxist Asiatic infiltrators and blacks.

In *Harper's* that same month, David Samuels, writing about Woodstock '99, noted of Rage's performance: "The cultural contradictions involved in playing agitprop to a $150-a-ticket crowd are evident from the band's first song, 'No Shelter,' a Marcusian anthem and also the band's contribution to the soundtrack for the movie *Godzilla*. It is at once an angry grad-student rant, denouncing the cultural myth that 'buyin' is rebellin',' and also proof of the near-infinite capacity of that culture to absorb any criticism as long as it features kick-ass guitars."

In the same issue of *Rolling Stone* in which Zack was keepin' it real for the workers in Chiapas, Neil Strauss was reviewing Rage's new album *The Battle of Los Angeles*, noting that "you don't have to understand everything on de la Rocha's cut-and-paste laundry list of political wrongdoing; just feel the crunch of the rhythm section, heed the machine-gun guitar attack, and catch a couple of random phrases—'I'm empty, please fill me . . . killing . . . I need you . . . now testify'—and the song works, whether it's about the news or the nooky."

Over at the *Village Voice*, Eric Weisbard rhapsodized about listening to Rage while "on the treadmill at the gym . . . Kicked my flagging flab forward . . . Revolutionary rockers with strong beats are a perfect way to motivate yourself to run in place." Rage "are activists," he affirmed. "They make me feel like each step I'm taking is a blow in somebody's face and scowl at the walls of my corner of the gym like a political prisoner steeling myself for years of captivity." One imagines he was joking, but in the earnestly '60s-nostalgic context of the *Voice*, one never knows.

*Los Angeles* was the top pick in the music section at kozmo.com that same week. The blurb weirdly declared, "*Look out local government! Zack De La Rocha and the crew bash out more of their politically charged hip-hop rock.*"

The Revolution will not be televised, but it is on sale at kozmo.com and will be delivered to your door within the hour.

*Los Angeles* went on to become the band's third double-platinum hit (meaning over two million copies shipped). Maybe it really has come to the point where people who think they're being progressive are most often exercising what might best be described as revolutionary nostalgia—a nostalgia for the romance of the revolutionary gesture, which in the end is the most decadent and counterrevolutionary impulse you could follow.

"We hear thy rocks & rolls," Kupferberg wrote in his parody version of "My Country 'Tis of Thee," "Jingled by them greedy souls."

○

Reflecting on all this, Don Gilbert wrote to me:

> The premise you're working with is the failed promise of the revolution that was instigated by rock. The real question, it seems to me, is whether that promise had any foundation whatsoever (certainly for Brian Epstein, Andrew Oldham and Danny Fields it didn't) or not, and if Lennon, the Airplane, the MC5 and Sly should ever have been considered anything but a decent soundtrack to a pipe

dream. Does the last true believer get to whack the final nail? Did the music really act as a beacon for those willing to step over racial and other boundaries, as it always has for hipsters, even now? Was it mostly about getting laid? Or was it just nice to be stoned and listen to tunes and imagine some different, better world? If so, the 70s was the revolution and it was quiet and happened in living rooms. Man, it's dirty and dangerous out in the streets.

# Rock Pravda

How *Rolling Stone* Turned Thirty, and Why You Didn't Care

"ROLLING STONE USED TO MATTER," former contributing editor Mark Herts-gaard said to me in the spring of 1998. "Now it doesn't."

That seems quite obvious on the face of it, but the point is, there was a time when *Rolling Stone* mattered *a lot*. Over several months stretching from the fall of 1997 to far into 1998, there was much polite pretending that it still did, as the magazine and its friends toasted its thirtieth anniversary. Which was followed by the Buffy the Vampire Slayer cover.

The pretense that *Rolling Stone* was still a major voice in popular culture—that, as former staffer Jon Pareles wrote in the *New York Times* during the birthday bash, it was still "the preeminent journal of popular music and the culture around it"—wasn't just nonsense, it obscured the historical fact that there really had been a time when that was true.

*Rolling Stone* "may be 'preeminent'" in terms of sheer size, replied Robert Draper, a contributing editor at *GQ*, who wrote the booklength analysis *Rolling*

*Stone Magazine: The Uncensored History* (1990). "The salient question, though, is 'Is it relevant?' It's like being the best cigar magazine in America. Just how prestigious is that accolade?

"The problem with [Pareles's] assessment is that it suggests that *Rolling Stone* is every bit as prestigious, and for that matter every bit the tastemaker it was, say, 10 years ago," he continued. "Neither is the case."

I'd have said twenty-five years ago, not ten, but never mind.

"I think historically it's one of the most important magazines published since the Second World War," said Bob Guccione, Jr., founder of competitor *Spin*. "Without question in the top ten, possibly in the top five. My impression of it at thirty is that it's not as great as it was, but it's still very, very good."

That was very kind and polite, and very inaccurate.

When the first issue of Jann Wenner's brainchild hit the newsstands—or more likely, the headshops—in November 1967, it represented one of the most important American magazine start-ups of the twentieth century, along with *Esquire, Time, The New Yorker, New York, Playboy, Spy*, and *People. Rolling Stone* wasn't the first publication devoted to taking rock music and rock culture seriously; the U.K.'s *Melody Maker* (for whom a young Wenner unsuccessfully tried to write) and New York's *Crawdaddy* were models. But it was without question the most successful. Lots of competitors and imitators—*Crawdaddy* itself, *Creem, Fusion, Scene, Eye, Cheetah*—never made it out of the hippie era. The "gonzo" political/social/cultural commentary for which the *Rolling Stone* of the 1970s is justly remembered also had direct antecedents, in venues such as Barney Rosset's *Evergreen Review* and Warren Hinckle's *Scanlan's Monthly* and *Ramparts;* both Wenner and Hunter S. Thompson wrote for Hinckle prior to *Rolling Stone*. But *Evergreen*'s influence didn't last, *Ramparts* never outgrew its limited left audience, and only a media wonk would recognize the name *Scanlan's* today.

When *Rolling Stone* was at its height and firing on all cylinders—politics, social commentary, music news, music reviews—it was arguably the best magazine in America, one of those rare magazines that both reflects and influences its culture and its moment. "From 1970 until 1977," Draper wrote in his book, "no magazine in America was as honest or as imaginative as what Jann Wenner called his 'little rock & roll newspaper from San Francisco.'"

That's media-wonk consensus, but I happen to think it's true. (Even *Spy* co-founder Kurt Andersen, while he likes to refer to that period as *Rolling Stone*'s "putative golden era," concedes that the assessment is essentially correct.) If you were young, white, and hip in the '70s, *Rolling Stone* was very likely your most important source of information on the world. All the "culture" tags that applied then to that sizable boomer generation—youth culture, rock culture, drug culture, hippie culture, counterculture—added up to *Rolling Stone* culture.

"You look at the guys who passed through the portals of *Rolling Stone* during that roughly six- or seven-year period," Draper says, "and it's a Who's Who of American magazine journalism. It's astonishing that any magazine had a masthead freighted with that kind of talent." In its day, *Rolling Stone* published news and political commentary from Hunter S. Thompson, Tom Wolfe, Tim Cahill, Tim Crouse, Joe Eszterhas, David Felton, David Weir, Howard Kohn. In music, Jon Landau, Greil Marcus, Lester Bangs, Dave Marsh, Ben Fong-Torres. And Richard Brautigan, and Annie Leibovitz's photography, and on and on.

"The thing about Jann is, he's got his peccadilloes and such, but he's done incredible things," I was told by novelist and screenwriter Lucian K. Truscott IV, who freelanced briefly for the magazine in the early '70s. "If all he ever did was publish Hunter Thompson and help to invent rock 'n' roll journalism, then let him just retire. He's made a huge contribution to journalism in this country."

It would just be silly to argue that *Rolling Stone* at the time of its thirtieth birthday and beyond is anything like the *Rolling Stone* of the '70s. It's more like one of those '70s rock bands that refuses to quit touring the state fairs, with members who just keep getting older and fatter and more hoarse as they shamble through their one or two hit singles from thirty years ago. The *Rolling Stone* that entered the twenty-first century was so much more timid, so much more pandering, so much more market-researched than its youthful self, and so very far behind the curve of contemporary music and culture that it was regularly being scooped by its competition.

"They so often get there last," John Burks said to me in 1998. He was *Rolling Stone*'s first managing editor, 1968–70. Too often, he said, stories appeared in competitors as lowly as *People* or *Entertainment Weekly* before you saw them in *Rolling Stone*. "It's almost as if they're waiting for verification." In his day, he said, "If we couldn't get there first, then the hell with it."

I'm looking at a random issue from that birthday period—number 785 (April 30, 1998). Sarah McLachlan's face was on the cover, looking post–facial money shot. "Flower Child with a Filthy Mind," the cover blurb vamped, just in case the target male reader missed the unsubliminal message of her life-size, ready-aim-fire, up-from-your-crotch head shot. There was a big interview inside with actor David Spade. "Is This His Must-See Moment?" the cover asked, ridiculously. As luck would have it, the lead record review was of a Jimmy Page and Robert Plant reunion; it was given a three-and-a-half-star homage by Anthony De Curtis, a reviewer who was at least as old, plodding, and played out as Page and Plant reunions were by then. It was followed by a very-hard-to-take-seriously four stars for Bonnie Raitt's latest, as judged by the impossible-to-take-seriously Robert Christgau: ". . . in a musical world where 'everything's carefully prearranged,' Raitt has thrown a Birkenstock in the works, and the clatter sounds like life itself." It makes your hair stand on end to read such mendacious drivel, but it must not have hurt her career any: two years later, in the spring of 2000, I would watch Raitt be inducted into the heavily *Rolling Stone*-sponsored Rock and Roll Hall of Fame.

And yet . . . and yet, in that same issue appeared Michael Paterniti's "Indonesia," a finely reported, respectably knee-jerk feature on the social and ecological consequences of Grasberg, the world's largest gold mine, where local tribesmen were helping a giant multinational literally dismantle a once-sacred mountain. Classic *Rolling Stone* nonmusic writing, it saved issue number 785 from *Rolling Stone*'s own worst impulses: the apparently irresistible urge to hype empty celebrities and grovel before rock's ancien regime of Jann Wenner cronies.

William Greider was still writing for *Rolling Stone* in the spring of 1998. He later gave up and moved on to the secure obscurity of *The Nation*. For years he was *Rolling Stone*'s last grownup, often single-handedly maintaining its long tradition of mixing some serious, left-liberal political commentary in with all the rock chatter. He was especially good at keeping up *Rolling Stone*'s honorable thirty-year tradition of making war on the war on drugs. But it must eventually have gotten awfully lonely being the only adult left in a magazine that in the 1990s was resolutely aimed at a college-guy good-time market.

The thirtieth anniversary issue itself, dated November 13, 1997, had been awful—a joke, really, placing *Rolling Stone* dead last among mainstream glossies to discover that there are, hold onto your jockstraps, "Women of Rock." Having reported on the fact of their existence, *Rolling Stone* could come up with absolutely nothing new (Tina Turner, who appeared on the cover, had been the magazine's regular token black female since volume 1, issue 2), interesting, or even entertaining to say about women in rock.

The trend continued. The December 30, 1999, "Millennium Special" issue— a.k.a. "The Party 2000"—sported a cover that evoked *Sgt. Pepper's*, a puzzling mass of famous faces attached to various bodies, except with a lot of nudes thrown in. It looked like one of those MTV Spring Break beach specials. The central editorial conceit was a poll of a lot of famous people for their views on the twentieth century and their predictions for the twenty-first. Because mostly rock stars and comedians were polled, the result was largely stupidity and vapidity—visions of the future from geniuses like Jewel, Ellen DeGeneres, Billy Joel, and the startlingly unavoidable-in-*Rolling Stone* Trent Reznor.

For me as a boomer, the most appalling fraudulence came from David Bowie, who declared, "Popular music is becoming a conveyance of information rather than a sparkling and vicious-toothed vocabulary of the new. Rock & roll is a dying religion. In terms of being a revolutionary force of any kind, I think it just doesn't have that clout anymore. . . ."

Like he would know. What a self-serving, egomaniacal, fifty-two-year-old creep, to conflate all of rock 'n' roll with his own way-past-prime career. Mr. davidbowie.com—he's not a rock star anymore, he's an ISP. If he had written, "*My* music is becoming a conveyance of information rather than . . . etc.," he'd have been closer to the truth. Meanwhile, he was running full-page ads for davidbowie.com in rival *Spin*. Never say the man wasn't a master of marketing and self-promotion.

(That same month, in its January 3 "Business Day" section, the *New York Times* ran an article on advertising trends by Patricia Winters Lauro: "The commercial opens on a car blasting the 1970's rock and roll hit, 'Rebel, Rebel.'"

Note to self: Good song, but was it really a "hit"? In the United States? I don't remember it burning up the *Billboard* charts, but maybe that's me. "The car spins out of a parking garage past a startled guard and into the night. 'There is the pressure to conform,' a voice-over says, 'and then there's the Mazda 626.'" The driver was revealed to be a trim young mother on her way to a PTA meeting. Lauro observed, "The point: Sally Suburan requires a four-door sedan for her 1.7 children, but Mazda understands that inside, she is still a rebel." The ad was developed based on market research that showed that boomers—especially married female boomers, and especially those in the trailing edge of the boom, the ones who hit their adolescence and teens in the 1970s—wanted to know that although they were married and raising children, they were also still "cool." Lauro cited a trade advertisement for *Parents* magazine that put it to potential advertisers this way: "Incredibly, 97 percent of our readers didn't feel any less hip after installing a baby seat." Of course, you couldn't use a *new* rock song to convey this message of hipness to boomer women, because—since of course they really *weren't* hip anymore, at least not to the new music—they wouldn't recognize the song and would attach no coolness nostalgia to it, and it would only make them feel old and out-of-it. So you reach back to an almost thirty-year-old Bowie "hit" to be your "conveyance of information." That was Bowie's value to the culture in the year 2000: lending a false sense of hipness to young mothers who saw middle age fast approaching and feared it. It's a role not unknown to matinee idols and pop stars of a certain age: the virtual gigolo for lonely housewives.)

*Rolling Stone* number 832, dated January 20, 2000, had the Backstreet Boys on the cover, with their pants down. What message was this meant to convey? That they were available to the readers? Or that they would do anything to get on the cover of *Rolling Stone?* They were the readers' pick for 1999 Artist of the Year. The critics, meanwhile, chose Rage Against the Machine—as clear an example as I've ever seen of the conceptual and aesthetic gulf separating rock critics from their audience. (Britney Spears was the readers' choice for Best Female Artist. The critics went with Mary J. Blige.)

In May of 1998 ABC aired a dismal *Rolling Stone* two-hour thirtieth anniversary TV special. With the lame and slightly self-parodying title *Where It's At: The Rolling Stone State of the Union,* the special was basically what *Rolling Stone* had been for some fifteen years by then: imitation MTV. There were some *Real World*ish chats with young people of various types and situations; at their best, these bits contrasted some very serious Naval Academy midshipmen with a very serious thrash-punk band who played naked and destroyed household appliances. This band, the most lively and interesting segment in the two-hour show, was, not surprisingly, given very short shrift; one saw far more of *Rolling Stone* cover pets and Wenner-approved stars such as Marilyn Manson, Jewel, Fiona Apple, Beck, Bruce Springsteen, and Keith Richards. Michael Douglas and Tom Wolfe also made out-of-nowhere showings that would be inexplicable to anyone who didn't know that Douglas was Wenner's good friend and Wolfe a loyal editorial contributor. Still, the connection of these two grizzled geezers to rock 'n' roll would have remained mysterious to the average viewer. Johnny Depp's appearance, also completely out of context, could be explained by his happening to be the star of *Fear and Loathing in Las Vegas*, the movie version of the Hunter S. Thompson book that began as a series of groundbreaking articles in *Rolling Stone;* the film opened (to disappointing reviews and box office) that May. The most bizarre guest turn in the entire two hours, though, was Walter Cronkite pontificating about how he once found a Dead concert sort of enjoyable.

So that was the state of *Rolling Stone*'s union in 1998: a handful of Wenner's starfucker friends, a few pet performers, and, oh yes, a bunch of nameless, unimportant young people scattered around.

Perhaps at this early juncture I should pause and concede that, in blithe disregard for my baleful opinions of *Rolling Stone*, the magazine, along with Jann Wenner and Wenner Media, is sailing on into the twenty-first century in what appears to be blooming financial health. Despite competition from other youth-music magazines—*Spin, Vibe, Blaze,* and *The Source* all fought for slices of its market share in the 1990s—*Rolling Stone* still moves over one million copies every two weeks as I write this in the year 2000. Every year, its ad revenues increase with bland regularity. Like the music industry it still, if only desultorily, covers, *Rolling Stone* has become an establishment behemoth and corporate money-machine as it has aged. Old boomer rock fans such as me may not like it, but advertisers and marketers still love it. Draper argues that the magazine's continuing success is "probably more a function of its positioning on Madison Avenue than its tastemaking expertise. Madison Avenue is very very slow to switch horses. It sees in *Rolling Stone* a magazine with staying power, a mag that's very fat, that still has a large readership and significant enough clout to have an ancillary luster to it. So it's an appropriate forum, so thinks Madison Avenue , for them to peddle their wares to the so-called younger culture."

Others counter that you still have to give *Rolling Stone* credit not just for surviving, but for its continued success. And the credit, everyone agrees, goes to Wenner.

"*Rolling Stone* is a mainstream centerpiece now as a magazine," Truscott said to me. "Why do *People* and *Time* and *Newsweek* and the *New York Times* all cover popular culture and rock 'n' roll? Because *Rolling Stone* and the *Voice* dragged them kicking and screaming into doing that. And Jann hung on with it far beyond anybody else. He's still there. He's still doing it."

And Robert Sam Anson, who wrote a book virtually declaring *Rolling Stone* dead twenty years ago, now says he has "tremendous respect for Jann. . . . He's always been able to reinvent himself. . . . He's had some long dry spells, but he always comes out of them with something new."

It's not much of an oversimplification to say that *Rolling Stone*'s changes have closely mirrored the stages in Wenner's life. The magazine has always been identified with its founder and editor to an unusually high degree. What Jann is interested in, *Rolling Stone* is interested in (or else he spins off a new magazine to cover it). As Jann has grown up and aged from hippie to yuppie, so has *Rolling Stone.* The one stage, it is interesting to note, that *Rolling Stone* has not mirrored is his 1995 public conversion to a gay lifestyle. Probably Wenner is aware that this would be the one change in focus the magazine's core market of male rock fans would not have been comfortable with. Nevertheless, the magazine's history traces an almost classically pure boomer life-arc. Draper characterizes it as "essentially the by-product of a bygone culture, and now emblematic of yuppie culture. This could account to some degree for its lack of vitality."

Its largely male audience has grown up with it. The reported median age of its readership in 1998 was twenty-eight, pretty high for a "youth culture" publication. Bob Guccione, Jr., who once characterized Wenner as "the Dr. Faustus of the yuppie generation," tells me that he started *Spin* in 1985 because he believed that *Rolling Stone* had abandoned younger readers by then.

"I stopped reading *Rolling Stone* in the '80s because it became really boring. ... I said to myself, 'They're holding onto the youth market by default, because there's nothing else out there—there's no intelligent magazine addressing young people.' There were silly ones like *Hit Parader* and *Circus* and a bunch of others that were just silly." He wanted *Spin* to be "a modern-day version of what it was that excited me as a sixteen-year-old reading *Rolling Stone* in 1971."

In his mid-fifties as I write this, Wenner continues to define the magazine's personality. He's characterized as a genius, a nutcase, or often both in the same sentence. As an editor, he has always used the pages of *Rolling Stone* to reward people he liked (or, in the early days, hoped to schmooze) and punish people he didn't like or felt had somehow dissed him. As a boss he's described as mercurial, unpredictable, erratic. Insiders say he'll pore over every caption and comma one issue, then virtually disappear for a couple of months. He's infamous for the legions of managing editors and music editors he's ploughed through over the years, and to this day you get the distinct impression that to hold a staff slot at the magazine is to be in an extremely tenuous position. Current and recent insiders spoke to me only on assurances of anonymity, or not at all.

I was surprised when, in the spring of 1998, Wenner agreed to be interviewed for the *New York Press* article that this chapter is based on. I was far less so when he blew off the interview the day before it was scheduled to occur. Wenner always masterminded his publicity, most impressively stage-managing his own "outing," with all attendant hand-wringing by hilariously guilt-ridden media, in 1995. Otherwise he could be as elusive as a loris. Like the celebrities he always loved to hang with, Wenner had for some time only granted interviews when he and his publicity people thought it might be of some advantage.

O

Wenner was a twenty-one-year-old UC-Berkeley dropout when he started *Rolling Stone* in 1967, with $7500 largely borrowed from the parents of his girlfriend, Jane Schindelheim, and office space donated by his printer, who was convinced that the hippie kids' rag would fold after a few issues. Born in New York in 1946 but raised in the Bay Area, Wenner is described by his prep school and college contemporaries as pushy, egotistical, arrogant, insecure—a wanna-be and a social climber from the start. When he told early staffers he had started *Rolling Stone* to meet John Lennon they thought he was at least half-kidding. It soon turned out he wasn't. A combination of the ultimate rock fan and the ultimate starfucker, Wenner always used the magazine as a vehicle for meeting and schmoozing heroes such as the Beatles, the Stones, and Dylan.

He was also the quintessential hippie capitalist, a high-roller from the magazine's earliest days. When staffers were slaving for pittance wages and creditors were at the door, Jann was driving a Porsche, jetting around, throwing big dinners and lunches, raiding the mail for subscription cash when he needed pocket money. The ethos he fostered, one of dope, rock, sex, and hedonism mixed with capitalism, brought inevitable and not altogether unfair charges that he was a next-generation Hugh Hefner (a scuttled 1970 plan to open a Rolling Stone Club didn't help).

Well, and so what? With some extremely well-chosen help—including the *San Francisco Chronicle*'s aging hipster Ralph Gleason, who had been mentoring him since 1965, and Greil Marcus, whom he had met at Berkeley in 1964— Wenner was perfecting (you have to say that Paul Williams's *Crawdaddy*, begun a year earlier, and the Hinckle publications came closer to "inventing") a new style of rock 'n' roll hippie counterculture journalism, and in short order *Rolling Stone* could have made a legitimate claim to be "the voice of its generation." (It's very telling, however, that Wenner never did make that claim— indeed, he specifically rejected it in several early editorials.)

At the *New York Press* offices we have a large stash of *Rolling Stones* that goes back to volume 1, number 2. Flipping—carefully—through the brown, crumbling pages of the first-year issues, I'm reminded how great, sloppy, vital, funny, and *new* the early *Rolling Stone* was. Sure, it was awful at first in many respects—band interviews were reprinted from *Melody Maker*, record-label press releases were run intact and without commentary. But it was also already covering the rock music industry—such as a financial scandal at Monterey Pop—as if it were worthy of a serious journalist's attention. This was something no one in America had done up until then. To counter the claims rival fans make for *Crawdaddy*, all you have to do is find and read a couple issues of it. In its early years, *Crawdaddy* leaned toward rock criticism for New York eggheads, featuring a lot of long, pseudo-academic jargonizing about the lat est LP from Bob Dylan or the Jefferson Airplane. It had its moments, but it was also a model for the genre of obfuscatory, pseudo-intellectual blather "rock scholars" such as Greil Marcus and Robert Christgau would soon be using to bedazzle and befuddle their readers. It was only after *Rolling Stone* blazed the way that *Crawdaddy* and other competitors began (in frankly imitative ways) to incorporate the kind of rock *news* that *Rolling Stone* regularly offered. Never mind that decades later this would devolve into the bland smirk of "MTV News." In 1967, '68, '69, when rock 'n' roll meant an awful lot to an awful lot of young people, yet the coverage in virtually all the "normal" media was so clueless and often condescending, there was something very exciting about getting your latest issue of *Rolling Stone* and reading in the "Random Notes" section that Bob Dylan and Johnny Cash were going to sing together, or that Arthur Lee's band Love was reorganizing for the third time and planning a residency at the Whisky-a-Go-Go, or that "Marty Balin got busted in his motel room in Bloomington, Minnesota, last weekend." (Okay, that's from 1970, but I couldn't resist citing it.) "Dope Notes" and "The Dope Page," meanwhile, treated this other extremely important facet of the average reader's life with similar gravity.

It's true that many of the music reviews in the early years were excruciatingly poorly written—to this day, the reviews are the magazine's weakest section. But it's also true that they didn't seem so then, or that one simply overlooked the terrible writing in the pure joy of learning about a new LP, and another and another and another. Greil Marcus, the first music editor, was not then the mind-blown gasbag he would become. And Lester Bangs, who was there from 1968 to 1973, helped keep *Rolling Stone* demotic *and* hip by championing "revolutionaries" such as the MC5 and Captain Beefheart over anything he thought arty or pretentious. Jon Landau helped bring the music writing out of its San Francisco–centric rut; he wrote, for instance, the legendary negative review that convinced Clapton to break up Cream, and, as previously noted, he was instrumental in getting the MC5 coverage in *Rolling Stone* before the band had even cut a record.

They printed 40,000 copies of the first issue and hand-distributed them to newsstands and head shops in the Bay Area. Some 36,000 copies were returned unsold. Wenner's undeniable genius for promotion and publicity soon turned that around. That first issue's cover photo was simply a publicity still of John Lennon in *How I Won the War*. A few weeks later, the movie's director, Richard Lester, was in San Francisco on a publicity junket. Wenner had someone hand Lester a copy of the first issue and got him to have his picture taken with it. And that was the cover of voume 1, number 3—*Rolling Stone*, the new and unknown hippie rag, apparently being endorsed by the famous movie director and, by extension, by John Lennon himself.

By the fifth issue they were giving away a free roach clip with every paid subscription, instantly legitimizing the magazine with its intended audience. For the first anniversary issue in 1968, with Jonathan Cott interviewing Lennon inside (a coup in its own right), Wenner got Apple Corp. to give him the soon-to-be-infamous *Two Virgins* photo of John and Yoko, naked, holding hands, their butts to the camera. He ran it on the cover. It made news around the country, especially after some fortuitous obscenity busts at newsstands. Before long, every major record label was buying ads in *Rolling Stone*. Atlantic's Jerry Wexler had already subscribed by the second issue. At Columbia, Clive Davis made *Rolling Stone* required reading for his staff.

John Burks was reading it, too. A young reporter for *Newsweek*'s San Francisco desk, he would offer some fairly blunt critiques to his friends on *Rolling Stone*'s staff, who included Gleason and former *Newsweek* writer Michael Lydon. One day, he recalls, Wenner called and said, "'I understand you think my magazine really sucks. I'm looking for a managing editor. When can you start?'" After some hesitation—"I liked the *idea* of *Rolling Stone* a whole lot better than the execution," he says, and Wenner could only pay half what he was making at *Newsweek*—Burks took the job, but only after getting *Newsweek* to give him a six-month leave of absence.

Credit Wenner's instincts: He and his music writers knew effectively nothing about news reporting or running a newspaper, so he sought out the talent. Burks was a few years older than Wenner and a lot more experienced in journalism. A number of other younger professionals—from the *San Francisco Chronicle* and the *Examiner*—were charmed by the new rag and wrote for it, often pseudonymously, so that "[n]o matter how much it looked like a hippie creation, it had experienced people writing for it," Burks says.

In the two years Burks was there, *Rolling Stone* rocketed from a claimed circulation of 25,000 to an audited 250,000. Despite certain persistent legends, Burks says doesn't remember tremendous levels of dope use at the office. Still, he does remember that the guy who stocked the office cigarette machine would occasionally throw in a pack—"and you never knew which brand it was going to be"—that was filled with joints instead of cigarettes. Sometimes a staffer would go to the cigarette machine and disappear for the rest of the day, and you knew they had hit the lucky pack. Other times they would share with the rest of the office, "and work would pretty much stop."

But generally, he says, "There was a real work ethic. It wasn't a bunch of hippies screwing around. The publications put out by a bunch of hippies screwing around are gone."

By 1969, Draper writes in his book, "Readership surveys showed that very few of *Rolling Stone*'s faithful read any other magazine, on any subject. Perhaps no other periodical in America enjoyed so captive an audience." Wenner was achieving his dream of hanging with his heroes. He conducted a rare Dylan interview for the second anniversary issue. He partied with Mick Jagger. John and Yoko, and Jann and Jane went to the movies together (John and Yoko would see *Let It Be* for the first time in Jann and Jane's company).

Wenner was already empire-building as well. In 1969, his newfound pal Mick Jagger put up the money for *British Rolling Stone*, which proved to be a short-lived disaster. Wenner also bought New York *Scenes* and started *Earth Times*, an environmental magazine. That was also the year of another brilliant publicity coup: the groupies issue. Burks wrote a lengthy insider account of the new and intriguing phenomenon of "backstage girls." Wenner spent $7000 for a full-page ad for the issue, which ran in the February 12, 1969, *New York Times* and "all but emptied *Rolling Stone*'s bank account," according to Draper. Legend has it that only three people tore out and sent in the ad's subscription coupon, but it woke up the New York media establishment to *Rolling Stone*'s presence and generated untold future revenues thereby. (Interesting side note: a version of Burks's groupies article ran first in *Newsweek*. He then expanded it to run in the more spacious *Rolling Stone*. Typically, it was the *Rolling Stone* version that generated all the buzz.)

In the fall of 1969, the Rolling Stones' tour crew used *Rolling Stone*'s offices to organize the Altamont concert for that December. When that concert turned into a fiasco, Wenner could easily have played down the coverage (as, oddly, most mainstream media did) and avoided pissing off his friend and business partner Jagger. Instead, he bravely told his staff to go for it, and the Burks-organized Altamont issue, "Let It Bleed" (January 21, 1970), though hastily patched together, was a stunning indictment of what rock culture had already by then become, as well as an unflinching kiss-off to the Love Decade. "What an enormous thrill it would be for an Angel to kick Mick Jagger's teeth down his throat . . ."; ". . . a nightmare of high-level money-grubbing . . ."; "Well, fuck Mel Belli. We don't need to hear from the Stones via a middle-aged jet-set attorney. We need to hear them directly. . . . A man died before their eyes. Do they give a shit? Yes or no?" One was used to seeing Richard Nixon or Richard Daley denounced so bluntly, but *Mick Jagger*? The Rolling Stones? One's jaw dropped.

○    ·

Politics was one area in which *Rolling Stone* only fitfully seemed to keep up with its readers. Always a mild liberal Democrat capitalist, Wenner was never really comfortable with the chic radicalism of the day. He urged his readers to stay away from the Chicago Democratic Convention in 1968 because there was going to be trouble. Pushed by his editors and writers, he reluctantly allowed the paper to adopt more of a rock-'n'-revolution tone in 1969—there was a "People's Park" issue that did a great job of exposing a police riot, and the then-famous up-against-the-wall "American Revolution" issue a little later that same year. Tellingly, however, "American Revolution" was followed by twenty-four issues with no politics on their covers at all. Jann was into peace, love, rock 'n' roll, and profits, not revolution, which scared off advertisers and angered patriotic newsstand distributors.

In 1970, editors and writers presented Wenner with a list of demands for the magazine to cover more serious news and politics. Wenner is said to have wept. *He* wanted the magazine to cover more pop culture.

Burks and some others quit. They would try, and fail, to start up a new and obliquely competitive magazine, *Flash*. "It didn't work, but it was a lot of fun trying to make it go," Burks recalls. He later became a professor of journalism at San Francisco State University.

Despite Wenner's resistance, more political awareness did become evident in the magazine's editorial voice. In 1970, with Nixon bombing Cambodia and Wenner's old pals Crosby, Stills, Nash, and Young going on about "four dead in Ohio," a little political awareness was unavoidable. Before Burks left, he edited the June 11 special issue with the cover banner "On America 1970: A Pitiful Helpless Giant." It was a magnificent document for its time, more like an issue of *Ramparts* than *Rolling Stone*, with twenty-five pages of reports from around the country on the state of the antiwar movement, the Black Power movement, the killings of students at Kent State and Jackson State (less remembered today, sadly; two black student protesters were killed in a hail of police bullets), the patriotic hard-hats' famous "Love It or Leave It" march through the streets of Manhattan to protest the protesters. There was a full-page advertorial from Elektra Records, with the enigmatic theme "Violence wounds us all," making the meretricious point that "[t]he music of our time is perhaps the only medium through which we can come to recognize and understand these ideas and feelings. . . . We are the communicators." (More evidence that the co-optation of hip did not wait until the 1980s to begin.) In one humorous bit, a *Rolling Stone* writer got someone on the line at the White House:

> Voice: Hello.
> Rolling Stone: Hello, Mr. Ziegler?
> V: No, this is Tim Elborn. Can I help you?
> RS: . . . My name is Jon Carroll and I work for ROLLING STONE magazine.
> V: Who?
> RS: ROLLING STONE. It's a music newspaper. 300,000 people read it.
> V: Yes?

As an indication of the enormous gulf of ignorance isolating Richard Nixon's White House from youth culture and American pop culture in general, this tiny anecdote is as priceless as Nixon's own (well-documented) failure to know who Elvis was when, that following December, the King also came calling.

Looking back on it now, of course much of the right-on hippie palaver in the "Helpless Giant" issue must strike us as silly. On one notably doofy page, a short report with the apparently unironic headline "Kesey Calls for Sanity" is followed by "Warren Says It Looks Pretty Bad," which begins:

> WASHINGTON, D.C.— Former Supreme Court Chief Justice Earl Warren said here that the United States is currently in a crisis graver than any in the memory of living Americans. Warren said the crisis was mainly due to the government's failure to enforce adequately the due process and equal protection sections of the 14th Amendment.
>
> In other words, lots of people still can't get fair treatment from the cops or a fair trial. Earl knows where it's at. . . .

As laughable as that second paragraph is now, you have to remember that notice of Warren's having made any such statement most likely would not have appeared in any venue outside *Rolling Stone* or the underground press. And that the gulf between the straight and the counterculture at that point was (or at least was perceived to be) so broad that the hipster gloss/explanation that seems so silly to us now was a necessary translation. There was much other political coverage in that very political year of 1970, including reports on the trial of the Chicago Seven one could not have read elsewhere. Meanwhile, on another front, David Felton and David Dalton co-wrote the best reportage anyone anywhere was doing on Charles Manson and his followers. In fact, 1970 was the start of *Rolling Stone*'s golden era, and it was precisely because of the editorial mix of music and nonmusic writing. It was the beginning of the Fear and Loathing years, the great age of Hunter Thompson, who wrote the cover story "Freak Power in the Rockies" that October and went on to write exclusively for *Rolling Stone* from 1970–1975. Joe Eszterhas came aboard in 1970 and wrote great reports about drugs, dealing, and the government's war on it all— cover stories with titles such as "Nark, a Tale of Terror" (February 17, 1972) and "Death in the Wilderness: The Justice Department's Killer Nark Strike Force" (May 24, 1973). These were pressing news issues to *Rolling Stone* readers back then. Even Wenner himself stunned the world with his two-part breakup-of-the-Beatles interview, with a bitter and unrepentant John Lennon. Annie Leibovitz's first cover photos appeared in '70.

Wenner started his book division in 1971 with the publication of his extensive interview with Lennon. Lennon, who had not authorized a book, was pissed. That year Straight Arrow turned its first profit.

Tom Wolfe wrote an enormous story in 1972 that became *The Right Stuff*. Tim Crouse, who accompanied Thompson on the '72 campaign trail, later wrote a great book about it, *The Boys on the Bus*. The teenage Cameron Crowe brought new energy to the music writing in 1973. (He would later quit to write *Fast Times at Ridgemont High*.)

But those first few years of the '70s belonged to Hunter Thompson. "Fear and Loathing in Las Vegas," which appeared in two issues in November 1971, changed American journalism forever. Thompson's campaign-trail missives in the following year were equally magnificent monstrosities—and in some ways more important historically, because they were about the political figures of the day, not just about Thompson himself.

Lucian Truscott hung out with Thompson at the 1972 Republican Convention in Miami. He was covering it for *Saturday Review*, Thompson and Crouse for *Rolling Stone*. Truscott had met Thompson a few years earlier in Colorado, where Thompson was living in writer's poverty with his wife, and Truscott, an unhappy young army lieutenant who had already done a little writing for the *Village Voice*, was stationed nearby. He would bring the Thompsons cheap groceries from the Fort Carlson commissary and hang out with them on weekends.

In Miami there was a press conference for celebrities who supported Nixon, including Jay of Jay and the Americans, John Wayne, and Glenn Ford. "The whole press corps was there," Truscott recalls. "Thompson and I were in the back, sort of chortling at everything. He and I had just been down in an encampment for Vietnam veterans against the war, who were all camped out. They had all marched down from Washington or something and were going to demonstrate. . . . They were the biggest thing happening" at the convention. "The Yippies were there, Abbie and Jerry and all them, but the vets coming out against Nixon was the big thing."

At the press conference, Thompson asked if Wayne would walk down to the encampment with him and meet the vets. "And John Wayne said, '*Waal sure Ah would, young fella.*'" When the press conference ended and Thompson met up with him, Wayne simply scoffed, "'You didn't really think I met that, did ya?' And he just brushed past us. In my story I think I said he kicked us aside like a couple of tumbleweeds. Then he turned to Glenn Ford and said, 'C'mon, Glenn, I need a martini.' And they ambled off."

On the day Nixon was to be nominated, Truscott was in Thompson's room at the Fontainebleau, up Collins Avenue from the Miami Convention Center. "We were looking out his window at this enormous traffic jam and wondering how we were going to get down to the convention." The hotel had a dock on the canal behind it. "The Republicans had one party boat lined up after another. RJR, all these cigarette manufacturers were wining and dining jolly Republican schlemiels from Ohio. So Thompson looks out there and says, 'Of course. The water. We must have a boat.' He talked like that, these little bursts of words. I got the Yellow Pages and started calling boat charter places and got us a speedboat. The guy says, 'Where are you?' I say, 'The Fontainebleau. Pull up outside and wave.'"

After years of miserly living, Thompson took a perverse joy in running up his *Rolling Stone* expense account. "Hunter always kind of abused Jann, and I think Jann liked it. Hunter was a neat guy to be around. There was always a lot of fun."

Truscott remembers that Thompson "always ordered two or three huge ice buckets stuffed with Heinekens. He instructed them over the phone how to build a Heineken bucket. They would stuff Heinekens in ice in these buckets and bring them up on big rolling carts. In his room he'd have two, three buckets of Heinekens and huge piles of room service grapefruit he'd just slice open and squeeze into his mouth. He liked vitamin C a lot. He'd squeeze it into his mouth and then drink a beer."

Despite all the gonzo stuff, Truscott insists that Thompson was "a fully functioning journalist"—and furthermore, that the political reporting Thompson was doing for *Rolling Stone* at that point, what became the book *Fear and Loathing: On the Campaign Trail, '72*, is "the best political writing in the past thirty or forty years in this country. It's smart, it's to the point, he's correct 95 percent of the time, his portraits of the people in the various campaigns are right on the money. Nobody has ever hit it like that again. . . . It makes Teddy White [who wrote *The Making of the President*] look like a piker."

Thompson was the superstar of the '70s, but there were other great reporters at *Rolling Stone*. Howard Kohn, who had come from the *Detroit Free Press*, wrote two groundbreaking stories in 1975. One was the definitive coverage of the Karen Silkwood story (the basis for the movie a decade later). The other, co-written with David Weir, was "The Inside Story" on Patty Hearst and her days in the Symbionese Liberation Army, which appeared in *Rolling Stone* scant days after the FBI picked her up. *Rolling Stone* scooped the world with that one, and inconsequential as the story may seem today, it earned the magazine incredible street cred with other journalists.

"Those were the glory days," Kohn said to me in 1998, by telephone from suburban D.C. "It was an easy time to be at the magazine." Partly, he believed, the magazine's tremendous impact in the 1970s was simply a product of "the demographics. We were dominating popular culture like crazy. *Rolling Stone* was the most vivid expression of popular culture at that time."—Still, I say, it's unlikely anyone else would have run, for instance, his Silkwood piece.

"Or even printed that many words," he laughs. "All those pieces were horribly long. Jann's idea was when you handed a piece in, 'Well, why don't you give me another thousand words on this angle or that angle?' . . . That opportunity to orate at length on some subject was just amazing." That considered, he says, "I think the writing was pretty decent."

Robert Draper believes that Wenner had "a really good sense of how writing could be like rock 'n' roll, expressive and urgent and vital. Some of the best writing in America during the period of 1971 to 1976 or so took place in the pages of *Rolling Stone*. It was an unlikely fete, but one for which you have to give Jann his due."

"You have to start and end with Jann," Kohn concurs. "He's a genius. Especially in those days, he ran the story meetings, he did the cover headlines, chose the covers—he had a lot of hands-on involvement. He's always been so frenetic and somewhat crazy. He stirred the pot every few weeks, dramatically, so that any idea that may have sunk to the bottom quickly came back up. Jann was primarily a writer himself, and then an entrepreneur, but he didn't have an M.B.A. or anything like that. It was a writers' magazine of a type I don't think exists anymore. . . . The writers ran the show with Jann sort of as the head cowboy. That changed over the course of the '70s, so that by the end of the '70s, when the magazine was in New York, some fairly serious business people established their influence over the magazine. They made it more like a regular magazine."

○

As part of its thirtieth birthday celebrations that spanned 1997–98, *Rolling Stone* produced a big, shiny coffee-table tome called *The 70s*. One morning I read two pieces from it in one sitting: one was Tom Wolfe on "Funky Chic," the other Joe Eszterhas on Evel Knievel. Both were vintage pieces from 1974, when the magazine was at its indisputable peak. Reading them again a quarter-century later was a bracing reminder of how far from its glory days *Rolling Stone* had by then slid.

After reading them I went to the gym, being a stereotypical middle-aged American white man in 1998. The gym's sound system usually played hiphop and '90s dance music appropriate to the pumping of iron. This morning, however, for unknown reasons, they were blasting some local classic-rock station that was in the throes of a promotion with the catchy, if natural-history-challenged, title "The Evolution of the Rock." As coincidence and ill luck would have it, they were doing the '70s, a soundtrack-to-my-nightmare compilation of relentlessly, ubiquitously awful pop and faux-rock tunes from that decade— "Venus," "Barracuda," the Carpenters, that Jackson Browne thing about the Great Pretender, and a string of those squeaky-clean, smiley-face, multivoiced puffy things that clotted the airwaves back then, by faceless one-hit anonymous fake-bands with names like the Friday Sunshine Conspiracy and Dennim.

I was surprised to discover that this stuff still had the power to make me want to drill out my eyeteeth with a dull three-quarter-inch masonry bit to drown out the noise and the pain of hearing it again, even after all those years. Meanwhile, a fortysomething Woody Allen type doing pretend Tai Chi near me was singing along. To all the songs. *He knew all the words.* I wondered if he was Robert A. Hull, who had a silly piece in *The 70s* trying to make a case for exactly this kind of pop being so fecklessly unhip and unreservedly mainstream in its day that by the very earnestness of its phoniness it was somehow alchemically transmuted from dross to pure crypto-subversive, proto-trans-gressive gold. Hull pitched '70s tripe such as "Brandy" and "Hitchin' a Ride" and "Me and You and a Dog Named Boo" as "but a handful of pop master-pieces" from the era. At least he had the decency to record that back when this crap was actually happening—all over every radio, jukebox, TV dance show, and in-store sound system that together made up the soupy aural environment of the day—Richard Meltzer, writing in *Rolling Stone*, correctly dismissed it as "limbo plus filler."

Hull's piece presented the classic history-nostalgia dialectic. Nostalgia mis-remembers the past, investing it with misguided fondness. And because nos-talgia's handmaiden is cheap irony, it inverts an era's worst aspects as some-thing air-quote *good!* air-quote. Thus *The Brady Bunch* as retro-chic and "Brandy" as a pop masterpiece, when history records them as the teeth-grind-ing, life-saturating horrors they actually were. The average *Rolling Stone*–read-ing hipster in the 1970s rightfully and righteously despised mainstream pop-culture glorp like "Me and You and a Dog Named Boo" with a ferocious animus before which Hull's twinky nostalgia must wither and die.

So, do you remember the '70s? Or just the '70s nostalgia? Either way, wasn't it just like the *Rolling Stone* of 1998 to come in absolutely dead last in the '70s nostalgia heat with a book like *The 70s*?

That said, it was not an altogether terrible book. The poorly thought and badly written parts heavily outweighed the good, but what *was* good was the way the book took the '70s seriously, treating the decade to the dose of straight-up, old-fashioned *Life*-style photojournalism it sorely needed after all the high-irony treatment it had received in the 1990s. (The 1990s will be remembered as the decade that made fun of the 1970s. How lame is that?) In reading any book like *The 70s*, it's best to start by conceding that there was, really, no such thing as "the '70s" (or "the '60s" or "the '90s"), convenient as it is for us all to speak and write in these handy terms. In reality, there is endless variety in what peo-ple think they mean when they name any decade. For ironic nostalgists who don't, won't, or can't really remember the decade, "the '70s" is all about the pop culture and mass marketing of that time, a period during which those of us then living suffered what was undeniably the apotheosis and simultaneously the nadir of kitsch in the twentieth century. The apotheosis *and* nadir because kitsch's goal is always to seek the lowest possible level of cultural expression. And *you* couldn't get any lower than it did during the '70s. People who think mass culture has been in straight decline through the '80s and '90s and '00s are not correctly remembering the TV of the '70s, or the radio, or the movies, or the smiley faces, the polyester, the platform shoes, the giant 'fros, Plato's Retreat, or "Brandy" on every jukebox.

There are other '70s for other memories. For '60s hipsters, the '70s are the anti-'60s, much as the '60s had been the anti-'50s. Politically, it's the Watergate decade. Economically, the decade of recession. There's the '70s as the decade of the Sexual Revolution and porn chic; the '70s as the gay-is-okay decade; the '70s as the disco decade, or the punk-rock decade, or the glam decade, depending on which of those scenes most appeal to you.

But most pertinently for our discussion here, there's the '70s as *Rolling Stone*'s glory decade. (What Hull failed to understand is that this *Rolling Stone* '70s and the one in which "Brandy" was a hit tune were entirely separate cultures. That's why we called them by different names. One was straight culture, the other was the counterculture. Does he think we were joking?) If any magazine of the late 1990s had a right to put out a big coffee-table book called *The 70s*, it was *Rolling Stone*, even granting that the *Rolling Stone* of 1998 was but a pale, exhausted, long-sold-out senior citizen compared to its youth. Maybe, in typical *Rolling Stone* fashion, part of the reason it could still take the '70s seriously was because it still takes *itself* so seriously. I could see corpulent old King Jann lolling on his throne. "The '70s? C'est moi." And in some ways he'd be right. Despite how far off the cultural beam his magazine had rolled since, back then, in the *Fear and Loathing* days, the Karen Silkwood days, *Rolling Stone* helped define and shape events rather than just report them (or, as it has increasingly in the 1990s and beyond, simply waddle along behind all the other media's reporting).

So part of the reason *The 70s* was not an altogether awful book was that it gave you some glimpses of that former glory, by way of direct reprints and excerpts from the magazine when it was great.

There was Mikal Gilmore's famous piece on being Gary Gilmore's brother. Excerpts from the Silkwood and Patty Hearst stories. Chet Flippo on Elvis. Tim

Cahill on Jonestown. The requisite snippet of Hunter Thompson. Yes, there were too many paeans to the likes of "Brandy" and Fleetwood Mac and *Star Wars* and the miniskirt, and the dopey pop-culture fluff did outweigh the good, serious entries by three to one. But then, it always had, even in *Rolling Stone*'s glory years. It was, after all, a rock 'n' roll magazine, not *The Economist*. The unintentionally sad effect of this '70s collection was to remind you how much more adroitly it had managed that balance in the old days than it did in its dotage.

○

When Robert Sam Anson, later a contributing editor at *Vanity Fair*, wrote *Gone Crazy and Back Again: The Rise and Fall of the Rolling Stone Generation* (1981), he was clearly convinced that when the magazine moved from San Francisco to Manhattan in 1977 something of the original *Rolling Stone* spirit died. The Woodstock Nation's paper of record, the gonzo-hippie-freewheelin' *Rolling Stone* of the '60s and '70s, was already by 1980 the corporate, glitzy, celebrity-driven, mass-marketed advertising-and-promotions machine we know it as today. You might well say that, like the entire boomer generation, Wenner was entering his third phase. He'd had his hippie rock-and-drugs phase, and his (however reticent) flirtation with a radical antiwar up-against-the-wall phase. Now the war was over, he had entered his thirties, and it was time to settle down to the serious business of making money.

For Anson, the writing was on the wall in the summer of 1976, when Wenner took over a townhouse on Manhattan's upper-crusty Upper East Side and threw a gala bash for Jimmy Carter's campaign staff, one night before the Democratic National Convention would anoint Carter as its presidential candidate. *Rolling Stone* had endorsed Carter in a big way—*this* was the kind of mainstream political game Wenner had always wanted to play, not that revolutionary stuff—and to hold this party in the heart of the East Coast media's game preserve was an obvious bid to be taken as a serious player, an insider.

Anson, who used the party as the opening scene for *Gone Crazy and Back Again* ("Terrible title," he muttered, when I got him on the phone in 1998. Well, it sounded better back then, I tell him), described it as a mad crush of celebrities, media types, politicos, and a few glum *Rolling Stone* stalwarts, jamming the rooms, spilling out into the street, blocking traffic, cursing the cops. Walter Cronkite (ah, so *there's* the connection!) and Carter adviser Hamilton Jordan, actresses Jane Fonda and Lauren Bacall (whom Anson has growling "This is a fuck-up" and storming off), Paul Newman, feminist politician Bella Abzug, journalists Harrison Salisbury and Seymour Hersh, Cyrus Vance (who would become Carter's secretary of state), a morose-looking Hunter Thompson ... all reduced to an unseemly mob, pushing and shouting, with the thirty-one-year-old Wenner beaming down from a balcony above, proud and pleased with himself.

The party was talked about for years after. To both New York society and media it was another of Wenner's publicity coups, announcing his arrival, but to Carter's prim wonks it had been a fiasco. The Wenners were later snubbed with terrible seats for Carter's convention acceptance speech, and they made only one visit to the White House during Carter's entire four years there. Wenner would back Ted Kennedy over Carter for the Democratic nomination in 1980. And when Kennedy failed to receive that nomination, Wenner went full-on yuppie and backed Ronald Reagan against Carter in the general election. He would back Reagan again in 1984, and not return to the Democrats' camp and good graces until Bill Clinton came along, who was in every way the fulfillment of what Wenner had wanted from Carter years earlier: a real rock 'n' rolling boomer president, a crypto-conservative "centrist" and friend of yuppie entrepreneurs, a true *Rolling Stone* kind of guy. Wenner would stump for Clinton with an unabashed enthusiasm that was downright smarmy at times, and he stuck with him loyally through all his Monicagate travails. Wenner would spend the '90s exhorting young Americans to get out and Rock the Vote, by which he meant Vote for Bill. During the 2000 presidential campaign, Wenner would run a flattering cover photo and interview with Vice President Al Gore, who hoped to follow Clinton into the presidency. Then, as Clinton was preparing to leave office, Wenner ran a fawning interview with him, in which the departing president was given much space to explain away or offer excuses for his many evident shortcomings and foibles. It was a far cry from the "Helpless Giant" years.

Wenner moved *Rolling Stone* to New York the year after that party for

Carter, taking big offices on Fifth Aveue with a view of Central Park and escon-
sing himself and Jane in a lavish townhouse on East Sixty-Sixth Street (later
a $4 million townhouse on Central Park West, and a Hamptons mansion, with
his own Gulfstream). The move put him in starfucker heaven, rubbing elbows
with the crème—Jackie O. and John Kennedy, Jr., Andy Warhol and Truman
Capote, Richard Gere, the so called "Velvet Mafia" of gay millionaires and
entertainment or fashion insiders, such as David Geffen and Ross Bleckner.

Howard Kohn made the move with the magazine, but only lived in New
York briefly before deciding he "couldn't handle it" and returning to San Francisco, where he and Ben Fong-Torres staffed the magazine's de facto West Coast
office.

"The big change coming to New York was, first of all, overhead went up dramatically," he recalls. "It became a serious business to meet the monthly bills.
So making money was truly a huge priority." Also, he admits, "Maybe Jann's
focus wasn't as specific anymore, because he was waylaid by a lot of other com-
mitments. Or [he adds with a chuckle], other parties."

Draper agrees. "It happened that the magazine suffered all kinds of changes
that look like decline" after moving to New York, and the city certainly did distract Wenner with "a host of temptations to which not only Jann but a number of his editors and writers succumbed." But then again, he argues, whether
it moved to New York "or Zimbabwe, the fact is the magazine was getting older,
the industry was changing, and *Rolling Stone*'s position was going to erode" no
matter what. "No one could have predicted in 1977 that less than ten years later
MTV would poach on *Rolling Stone*'s turf, or that magazines like *The New
Yorker, Vanity Fair, Details, Entertainment Weekly, Esquire,* and *GQ* would be
able to step right in and scoop *Rolling Stone* in a feature profile on a rock star
who ten years prior would have been covered only by *Rolling Stone*."

Truscott was on staff at the *Village Voice* when Wenner showed interest in
New York as early as 1972, testing the waters with a small office in the East
Fifties, in a building owned by Robert Redford. "So it was part of Jann's star-
fucking, you know," Truscott says. "It was a big surprise when Jann opened an
office in New York, because the last five years had been one long anti–New York
screed in *Rolling Stone*. 'We're San Francisco, our music is better than Lou Reed,
we have people who are mellow.' I think he was testing how difficult it was

going to be to get into New York and start to swing. He wasn't going to come to New York if when he got there everybody laughed at him and nobody invited him to parties."

Wenner started calling around to New York writers to see if they would write for him. Truscott remembers hanging out in the reception area when Ron Rosenbaum, who was also then a *Voice* writer, came out of Wenner's office. "I asked him what it was like and he just goes, '*Weird*.'"

Truscott remembers Wenner's room as a bizarrely theatrical power-office setup, with "this big round oak table" and Wenner enthroned behind it in a high-backed rattan "Huey Newton" chair. "He leans back, puts his feet up on the table and goes, 'So tell me about yourself.'" After brief pleasantries, Wenner asked if Truscott wanted to freelance for *Rolling Stone*. Truscott agreed, with the caveat that his first loyalty would be to the *Voice*, where he was on staff.

"And Jann gets this big grin on his face and laces his fingers behind his head and says, 'So how much does your loyalty cost?' That was when I got up and leaned over the table and grabbed him by the shirt and yanked him prostrate on the table so he was looking right at me on his belly. I said something to the effect of 'My loyalty is way too fucking expensive for you, Jann.'"

Not much later, Truscott was freelancing for *Rolling Stone*. He jokes that far from fazing Wenner, the little show of violence "was probably the biggest thrill he'd had in five years. He had the meaty little military-trained hands of a West Point killer on him. He was probably panting for the next four hours. I mean, none of us knew Jann's 'proclivities' back then, although there were rumors about him and various rock 'n' roll stars who were, shall we say, light in their Lucchesis."

With the move to New York, *Rolling Stone* irrevocably lost a good bit of its charmed outsider status, becoming, in effect, just another in a New York magazine publishing culture already crowded with the big, expensive, ad-fat glossies put out by combines such as Conde-Nast, a giant outfit (run by what are known in Manhattan publishing slang as "Conde-Nasties") in comparison to Jann Wenner's little hippie mag. To compete in that world, Wenner and his top aides set about recasting *Rolling Stone*, emphasizing the music again over the political and social commentary, increasing the coverage in other pop-culture areas such as movies and TV, all in an attempt to deliver "a more high-quality reader," as it was put at the time by Wenner's new number-two man, Kent Brownridge (who remains the second-biggest power at Wenner Media to this day).

It was with the move to New York that Wenner and Brownridge became addicted to market research and focus groups to determine the cover photos and feature stories that would best move copies off the newsstands. (Newsstand sales accounted for a relatively small percentage of total sales—generally speaking, 80 percent of copies sold were through subscriptions—but magazine publishers and editors pay strict attention to them as their best regular barometer of what attracts or puts off readers.) Although it didn't go to a glossy cover until 1985, *Rolling Stone* became slicker and more upscale in tone the instant the offices moved to Manhattan—more celebrity-conscious than ever, falling increasingly behind the curve of the music scene and of current events as well.

Kohn left the magazine in 1981 to start up the D.C. office of the Center for Investigative Reporting. William Greider "took over my slot and did a fabulous job with it," Kohn says, and he insists that "Jann and I have remained friends." At Wenner's invitation, he reappeared in the magazine with a half-dozen or so large articles in the late 1980s, including one major piece on the Medellin drug cartel. "I have to say, Jann has always been extremely good to me. Personally, I never had anything bad to say about him. . . . We've had a minimum of argument, ever."

○

Through the late 1970s and into the '80s, Wenner rolled on. He started *Outside* in 1977, just before the Manhattan move, ran it for a year, lost interest, and sold it. *College Papers*, edited by his sister Kate, lasted for a few weak issues in 1979. Also in '79, French publisher Daniel Filipacchi resuscitated *Look*, which had died of exhaustion and old age. In a brilliant stroke, he asked Wenner to come on as editor-in-chief and publisher, and Wenner agreed. In six weeks, Wenner knocked out three biweekly issues that everyone concurred were great successes; then Filipacchi inexplicably folded it. It was said to be the one time anyone had pulled the rug out from under *him*.

Greider, who came on in 1982, persistently pummeled the major media for their fawning coverage of the Reagan administration through the 1980s. Dave Black's two-part AIDS story in 1983 was a shocker and award-winner—though it's noteworthy that Wenner resisted putting it on the cover for fear of scaring off newsstand buyers. (The affable mugs of Richard Gere and Don Johnson brought them in instead.) Annie Leibovitz, whose photos had defined *Rolling Stone*'s image, left in 1983 in a bad breakup to go to *Vanity Fair*.

When *Rolling Stone* serialized *Bonfire of the Vanities* in 1984–85, some media observers wondered how many *Rolling Stone* readers would even know who Tom Wolfe was. It was rumored that he had ended up in *Rolling Stone* only because no one else would pay the $200,000 asking price for the serialization. Circulation was approaching one million copies by then, and Wenner could well afford to be generous to an old friend. (In the late '90s, *Rolling Stone* would serialize yet another Wolfe novel, *A Man in Full*, but by then both the magazine and writer seemed to be going through the motions, like two old lovers, and it stirred little interest outside media-wonk circles.)

Wenner bought *US*, the premiere newsstand expression of yuppie self-absorption, in 1985. The first issue under his ownership ran an upbeat review of *Perfect*, the Travolta–Jamie Lee Curtis movie about the fitness craze in which third-billed Wenner effectively played himself.

It was also the year of another self-promotional coup, the brilliant—though to some, terribly depressing—"Perception/Reality" ad campaign, which contrasted old hippie stereotypes still attached to *Rolling Stone* to the new "reality" of *Rolling Stone*.

Perception: a roach clip. Reality: a money clip.

Perception: VW bus. Reality: sports car.

Perception "All You Need Is Love." Reality: "What's Love Got to Do With It?" And so on.

The campaign was said to have greatly expanded the types of advertisers interested in *Rolling Stone*, ending the magazine's dependence on record-industry ads. Along with a new glossy cover and standard magazine format, these ads unrepentantly declared that *Rolling Stone* was now entering middle age, a full-on boomer-yuppie product—as David Blum put it in *New York* at the time, "a slick, mainstream magazine that bears almost no resemblance to the alternative rock 'n' roll fortnightly Wenner started. . . ."

To old fans and staffers who weren't into growing up with it, *Rolling Stone* died in 1985. *Spin* would spoof it with a campaign design of its own: *Rolling Stone* was the Perception, *Spin* the new Reality. Wenner's music writers and editors bitched, but he didn't seem to care; advertisers loved the "new" *Rolling Stone*. Ad revenues ballooned as much as 34 percent annually through the early 1980s.

This was also the year that Bob Guccione, Jr. saw the opportunity to, as he infamously put it at the time, "kick *Rolling Stone*'s ass." Which he still believes he went on to do. "Yeah, absolutely. In the young market, under thirty, absolutely." He cites market-research studies that put *Spin* number one among readers eighteen to thirty years old. Though *Spin* never sold anything like *Rolling Stone*'s million-plus copies, Guccione argues that with that younger market, "We literally did kick their ass. . . . I'd always liked and respected *Rolling Stone*, I just think they left the door wide open. . . . We flew in under the radar. They didn't see us for a long time. By the time they saw us, we were entrenched. . . . It was Jann Wenner's genius to keep it prominent" with its generation, and it had aged with that generation. "I knew that when *Spin* came out it was a second generation, with all of the sociological ramifications."

Fatter, sleeker, and puffier, *Rolling Stone* rolled on through the '80s and into the '90s. Wenner, along with the rest of his generation, was aging as well, turning fifty in 1996. He began to slow down. In the '60s and '70s it had been pot and speed and LSD; in the '80s it was coke and swigging vodka from the bottle at editorial meetings; in the early '90s he announced that he was clean and sober. He trimmed down, shaped up, and started *Men's Journal*, the outdoorsy fitness-and-adventure magazine, the idea for which he said came to him while backpacking in Arizona. He and Jane had adopted one child in the mid-'80s and had two more later. In 1993 he started *Family Life* (because "the generation that once raised hell is now raising kids"), telling interviewers that he was into staying home more, reading to the kids. The Wenners had become nesting boomers.

Jann's next incarnation, then, was a shocker. In January 1995, at the age of forty-nine, he left Jane and the kids to take up with a man, former Calvin Klein model Matt Nye.

After the first coy hints that something was up were floated in *Ad Age* and the *New York Post* gossip column "Page Six," it took weeks for the media to deal with the issue openly. The *Wall Street Journal*, of all places, finally "outed" Wenner in February, with a front-page story about the business implications of his leaving Jane, which were substantial: she and Wenner jointly owned Wenner Media in toto.

It's still hard not to see it all as yet another Jann Wenner publicity coup, staged and timed for maximum impact. The announcement that he was gay seems not to have stunned anyone who knew him or worked for him. Off the record, I was told stories to that effect—such as a joke that supposedly made the rounds at Wenner Media offices that Wenner was so out of touch with current music he thought Boyz II Men was a dating service. Wenner effectively outed himself by appearing in public with Nye. The media reticence and hand-wringing that followed were indicative of his clout—and of the conflicted state the media were in at the time about the whole issue of outing. The conservative high-society writer Taki (who would later come over to write for us at *New York Press*) suggested in print that publishers were terrified the Velvet Mafia would pull movie and fashion ads if publications covered the story. At the *Village Voice*, Michael Musto conceded he had held off on reporting the item, worried about possible legal repercussions. Kurt Andersen, then editing *New York*, says Wenner called and asked him not to go ahead with a planned article on the affair. To Andersen's credit, the story ran.

By March, in a classic move, Wenner was selling *Family Life*. He wasn't exactly a family man anymore.

Wenner closed out the century in relatively—for him—quiet style. There was the protracted year of *Rolling Stone* birthday hoopla, but since all of that was generated by *Rolling Stone* or former *Rolling Stone* minions, the impact was limited, the gaiety among the masses muted. In 1998 into '99 there was a period of no doubt unwanted comedy when a handyman laying a driveway on Wenner's ranch in Sun Valley, Idaho, uncovered a "buried treasure" in the form of ninety-six gold doubloons, worth up to a million dollars. Both Wenner and the finder claimed the treasure, and they went to court over it. Witty headline writers were quick to label the dispute "96 Tears." Otherwise, Wenner's big news as the millennium turned was mostly business news. He took *Rolling Stone* online. In an expensive and highly risky (some said crazy) move, in the spring of 2000 he took the struggling *US* from a monthly to a weekly publishing schedule to compete directly with the giants of the dentist's-office market such as *People*. "Realizing much too late that the *Stone* has become the Gray Lady of the boomer generation," the online satire magazine *Suck* opined, "Wenner has no comfortable way to do the fawning, sycophantic, weekly biopics he and the American public crave. Indeed, Wenner Media can't survive much longer on *Rolling Stone*'s brilliantly puerile, biweekly covers. One or two nudies per issue barely distracts readers from that sassily senile 'All the news that fits' tag. . . ."

○

If Wenner and *Rolling Stone* survived the changing of the millennial guard, the same can't be said for his relationships with a couple generations of staff. When someone has been around as long and successfully as he has, horror stories from disgruntled former staff come cheap and easy. But Wenner has ejected a lot of people for a lot of dubious, highly personal reasons over the years; his erratic management style can turn vicious in a second, as evidenced as early as 1970, when he fired his old pal and stalwart Greil Marcus for daring to pan Dylan's *Self-Portrait*.

And that's the point: Wenner always meddled with his editors' and writers' work, changing or censoring what you read in *Rolling Stone* to suit his personal interests and whims. Burks remembers Wenner coming along behind a music critic and rewriting a favorable Cream cover story into a pan "because he thought it would move better off the newsstands. I don't know about you, but I found that suspect."

Mark Hertsgaard, a journalist and book author, ran afoul of Wenner's mercurial style in the early 1990s. Hertsgaard had earned serious attention in the late '80s for his book *On Bended Knee: The Press and the Reagan Presidency*. William Greider was going on leave to write a book of his own, and Hertsgaard was brought on as a contributing editor, contracted to write fill-in columns and one large project of investigative journalism that he proposed: a two-part, twelve-to fifteen-thousand word, behind-the-scenes look at *60 Minutes*.

"Jann, to his credit, agreed" that it was a story worth pursuing, Hertsgaard recalls. Say what you will, Hertsgaard insists, "the guy was an inspired editor and publisher. He can have very good instincts . . . when he focuses."

As Hertsgaard went to work on the story (on and off, it took about six months), he was soon collecting female workers' tales of sexual harassment in the offices of *60 Minutes*—allegations of Mike Wallace snapping their bra straps, of Don Hewitt pressing them to the wall and sticking his tongue down their throats, things like that. Wenner continued to be supportive, at first. "I remember being in his office once," Hertsgaard says, "just shooting the shit, and he said, 'Well, Don called me.'" Hewitt knew Wenner from the Manhattan cocktail-party circuit. Wenner told Hertsgaard he had stood firm, adding, "'And [Don] knows that's the last time he can call me about that.' I thought, 'Bravo, Jann.' Little did I know . . ." Hertsgaard laughs ruefully. He says he made it clear to Wenner that he was coming up with some pretty dirty stuff on the *60 Minutes* team, and Wenner "didn't seem troubled by it."

Hertsgaard continued the investigation. There was a confrontation with Mike Wallace. "Wallace . . . well, 'panicked' is probably not too strong a word," he chuckles. For Hertsgaard, the kicker was an enraged phone call he got from Hewitt, complaining about and denying the sexual material Hertsgaard had collected. When Hertsgaard asked him how he knew what was in the story, Hewitt said he had spoke to an editor at *Rolling Stone*. When Hertsgaard asked him if he meant Wenner, Hewitt "vociferously denied it was Jann. 'I said I spoke to *an* editor, not *the* editor.'"

But of course it was Wenner. He called Hertsgaard a few days later, saying that he had run into Hewitt at a party, that Hewitt had badgered him to know what was in the story and he had spilled the beans. He apologized to Hertsgaard for this total breach of editor-reporter trust, which Hertsgaard regarded as a "decent" gesture, "but a little late." The saving grace was that Wenner still hadn't actually read the story at this point, so he didn't know how damning it truly was. If he had, it might have died right then. As it was, Hertsgaard turned it in and then, as he later told the online magazine *Salon*, "it sat and it sat and it sat. The piece didn't run for another twelve months. . . ."

Hertsgaard likes to think that some of that delay was simply a bureaucratic muddle—the magazine was going through one of its periodic editorial cleansings, and the editors who had originally worked with him on the story were purged. But it's hard not to conclude that *Rolling Stone*, which had made its bones off fearless investigative journalism in its heyday, now sat on a story for a year out of fear of pissing off a powerful media type whom Wenner would keep running into at cocktail parties. And remember, too, that a few years later, Wenner would hit the tabloid headlines with his gay midlife crisis; you have to wonder if he was hoping not to make an enemy of Hewitt because he feared being outed by one of those *60 Minutes* no-holds-barred investigative pieces. (I'm just speculating here. Remember, Jann turned me down for an interview.)

Hertsgaard adds that there was one more bizarre encounter with Hewitt during the delay. They had a breakfast meeting at the Plaza, and when the allegations of harassment came up, he recalls, Hewitt began shouting his denials so loudly the heads of all the power-breakfasters in the room turned. He remembers Hewitt's left hand quivering with rage during a thirty-minute tirade that included "everything from threatening to sue me to trying to hire me."

When the story, "60 Minute Man: How Don Hewitt Keeps His Ratings Up," finally did run in the May 1991 *Rolling Stone*—and then, Hertsgaard believes, only because the *Wall Street Journal* was about to break its own version—it was seriously "emasculated," cut down to a one-part, eight-thousand-word piece with many of the juiciest allegations removed. At about that time, Wenner "informed me they were not going to renew my contract," Hertsgaard recalls. By then, his big story bowdlerized and only five of his eight political columns having run, "I wasn't too terribly sad about not continuing." He went off to report on the Gulf War, then wrote a book on the global environment.

"At the end of the day," Hertsgaard sighs, "I love rock 'n' roll. I think it's important. I wrote one of my books about it [*A Day in the Life: The Music and Artistry of the Beatles*]. But it's a discrete slice of life." He concurs that what made *Rolling Stone* great in its heyday—potentially the greatest American magazine of them all, he agrees—was its unique mix of top music and cultural coverage with great political writing and gutsy investigative journalism. That mix has been conspicuously absent from its pages for some time now.

Music critic Jim DeRogatis lost his job at *Rolling Stone* under similar circumstances a few years after Hertsgaard did. He was brought in from the *Chicago Sun-Times* in the fall of 1995 as part of what was going to be a new, younger, harder-hitting music staff under new music editor Keith Moerer. In May 1996, he handed in a negative review of Hootie and the Blowfish's *Fair-*

*weather Johnson.* Wenner saw it, spiked it, and had the magazine run a kinder one in its stead. Wenner happens to be pals with Ahmet Ertegun, chairman of Atlantic, Hootie's label; among other things, they had together masterminded the Rock and Roll Hall of Fame, which opened in Cleveland that year.

The weekly *New York Observer* "Off the Record" column covered the incident in its June 3 issue: "When asked if he thought Mr. Wenner was a big Hootie fan, Mr. DeRogatis replied, 'No, I think he's just a fan of bands which sell eight and a half million copies.'"

DeRogatis was fired the next day. (By July, Moerer was out, too, having lasted just under a year. Mark Kemp, whom he had hired, stepped up to replace him. Kemp would be replaced soon enough by Joe Levy, a lifer in the rock-critic establishment and not likely to steer things in any radical new direction. Kemp moved on to MTV.)

DeRogatis says his eight-month career at *Rolling Stone* "was probably six months longer than it should have been." One insider I spoke to said that DeRogatis "was doomed from the day he showed up," partly because he's a feisty writer who fights for his opinions, and partly because he is a short, fat man who didn't have the sleek, hip look Wenner prefers to see in the people around the office. DeRogatis went back to the *Sun-Times* and in 2000 published *Let It Blurt,* a biography of Lester Bangs—whom, he pointedly notes, was fired by Jann Wenner in 1973 for panning Canned Heat, a band Wenner liked. "And what was Hootie if not the Canned Heat of 1996?" DeRogatis quips.

Understandably cranky on the subject, DeRogatis contends that there has *never* been a "golden era" as far as the music writing in *Rolling Stone* is concerned, that it has always been "mediocre and arbitrary, because it's always been determined by one man, Jann Wenner."

While I think that's a bit harsh, it's true that *Rolling Stone*'s music reviews have always been a problem. And surely that has something to do with the way every insider I spoke to, past or present, agreed that Wenner's music writers and editors all operate with, as one of them put it, "a certain amount of fear" that they might express an opinion that will piss him off. It's not an aesthetic thing with Wenner, they say, so much as schmooze control. One writer told Draper back in the late 1980s, "It is always a risk to rate too low anyone that Jann's had lunch with." That certainly doesn't mean that Wenner still reads every article, review, and caption the way he once did, but every writer knows he *may* read their piece, and disagree with it. They're always "second- and third-guessing themselves" to write what Wenner wants, "so the mediocrity permeates," DeRogatis says. "It was like being handed the keys to a Ferrari and then told you can only drive five miles an hour," he complains. "You have the most powerful tool in music journalism but you can't use it, because all the music journalism that appears in *Rolling Stone* is dictated by one man's whims."

Draper writes that Wenner's musical tastes were never very near to the cutting edge. Very early on he was at odds with Bangs, with Richard Meltzer—all the more "gonzo" of his music critics, the "reckless romantics," as Draper dubs them, who had a view of rock's importance Wenner never really shared. Wenner's view of rock "is more banal and has to do with celebrity culture," Draper argues. "This explains why Jann could be so taken with a John Lennon or a Mick Jagger and so repulsed by a Sid Vicious . . . [who was] sort of the antithesis of Jann's primal yearnings" for fame and glamour. Wenner stuck with "the group of musicians who were roughly around his age and began to achieve wealth and prestige, which was what Jann coveted himself." Already by 1970, '71, "Jann was furiously backpedaling from any pretense of being the standard-bearer of underground music." Everybody's favorite example: the article on the Stooges in a 1970 issue that starts with a kind of proto-parental warning label: "*Warning: The following article does not constitute an endorsement of current phonographic products.—Editor.*" One would like to think this was a joke, but I doubt it. Editor Wenner most certainly would not have approved of Iggy or any of the chaotic, anarchic, proto-punk impulses Iggy represented. "And the truth was, to be fair, Jann was never about that," Draper says to me. "Jann always had capitalist impulses the other underground magazine editors lacked."

Wenner seems to have stopped liking or understanding the music by the mid-'70s. He ignored disco (but then, so did pretty much the entire field of rock criticism). It's noteworthy that when Jon Landau declared Bruce Springsteen the future of rock 'n' roll, it wasn't in *Rolling Stone* but in Boston's *Real Paper;* at the very least, that was symbolic of the way the nation's music paper of record was consistently missing the boat on new acts and trends. In his mid-thirties by the time punk arrived, Wenner was notoriously unable to get the point of it. Charles M. Young's famous 1977 cover story on the Sex Pistols effectively ran over Jann's dead body—and when it tanked on the newsstands, punk's fate was sealed as far as *Rolling Stone* was concerned. One saw very little in *Rolling Stone* about punk over the next few years, and legend has it that Wenner has never listened to a Sex Pistols record to this day.

MTV, which started up in 1981 to general skepticism, was soon happily vamping a new style of music-video star (Madonna, Michael Jackson) for a new generation of consumers. By the time *Spin* debuted in 1985, all sorts of mainstream magazines were covering music. Most embarrassingly, *Rolling Stone* woke up to U2 and Talking Heads only after they had been in *Time* and *Newsweek*. *Rolling Stone* was so distanced from music at that point that Wenner went so far as to create a whole new entity, a (weak) "sister magazine" called *Record*, that would take over the bulk of the music coverage. It was short-lived.

When *Rolling Stone* published its infamous "100 Best Albums" list in 1987, with *Sgt. Pepper's* coming in first and *Never Mind the Bollocks* second, Wenner hit the roof. Draper reports him complaining, "Where's Loggins and Messina on this poll? Where's *Hotel California?*" A year later, he made sure his pals Billy Joel ("Uptown Girl") and Foreigner made the extremely jiggered "100 Best Singles" list. By 1989, *Rolling Stone*'s relationship to rock music was so flaccid and laissez-faire that Axl Rose could demand his official biographer rather than a *Rolling Stone* staffer do his interview, and the magazine agreed. Successive waves of editorial regimes struggled to reconnect *Rolling Stone* to the music of the day, with negligible results. In its unseemly desperation to identify and break the Next Big Thing before MTV (or *Details*, or *People*, or *Readers Digest*), the magazine fell all over grunge, then hiphop, then grrl rock, electronica, California pop-punk, and rap-metal during the 1990s, overcompensating for the general lack of interest of the guy at the top. A few individual performers became new pets of the magazine: Trent Reznor, Beck, Marilyn Manson, Kid Rock, Rage Against the Machine's Zack de la Rocha, and, of course, Hootie. Did the championing of those harder-edged rap-metalists mean that Wenner in the later 1990s was finally losing interest and loosening his grip? Maybe. But meanwhile, Wenner's old pals continued to roam the magazine's pages and covers, aging but apparently undying specimens of what George Tabb has dubbed "Jurassic Rock."

For a quick measure of how unchanging *Rolling Stone*'s view of the landscape has been, simply thumb through another thirtieth-birthday coffee-table tome, *Rolling Stone: The Complete Covers 1976–1997*. Start in 1970 or so and clock the stupefying regularity and frequency with which a certain small herd of Wenner's faves appear on the cover again and again and again and *again* and *AGAIN*. Bob Dylan, Mick and Keith, John and Yoko, Paul, Bruce, Jim Morrison, Linda Ronstadt, Neil Young, Jackson Browne, James Taylor, The Who, Rod Stewart, Carly Simon, Fleetwood Mac, Billy Joel. Several of them continued to make numerous appearances in *Rolling Stone* years after their music had any semblance of relevance to anyone besides Wenner and his put-upon staff. "Carly: Life Without James" was a cover story *in 1981*. The latest Crosby, Stills, Nash, & Young reunion would earn cover placement *in April 2000*. And when the Rock and Roll Hall of Fame came fully on stream in the 1990s, it joined the magazine in mutually reaffirming the status of this galaxy of increasingly aged and most often has-been rock stars. Clapton, Fleetwood, Billy Joel would be inducted into the Hall of Fame and appear yet again in *Rolling Stone* to mark the occasion. It became something worse than "self-fulfilling prophecy." It was more like a self-replicating virus. (And let's not forget Wenner's movie star friends who graced the cover of *Rolling Stone* innumerable times over the eons—Jack Nicholson, John Travolta, Michael Douglas, Robin Williams, John Belushi.)

It's hard to argue with DeRogatis's assessment that Wenner single-handedly made and unnaturally preserved the careers, or at the very least the images, of some of these beyond-has-beens. Where would Linda Ronstadt or Browne or Joel have been without *Rolling Stone* and the Hall of Fame? DeRogatis calls *Rolling Stone* "the *Pravda* of rock" and rails against the "insidious influence" of its "Wennercentric" version of rock history. In its magazines, its books, its website and TV specials, and at the Rock and Roll Hall of Fame, *Rolling Stone* and the Hall of Fame blank out all other versions of how rock and pop developed.

○

Kurt Andersen says he hears it all the time: that the late 1980s was the only time when you could have pulled off a magazine like *Spy*, just as the late 1960s was the only time Wenner could have successfully launched *Rolling Stone*. "I don't think that, and I didn't think that at the time," he counters, though he will admit that the late '80s was "a perfect moment to be influential" with a publication such as *Spy*.

It's a tempting comparison: *Rolling Stone*, the voice of its generation, enjoys a prolonged golden era of dominance, then survives to go on into a long, comfortable decline. Twenty years later, *Spy*, more briefly but no less influentially the magazine of its moment, quickly flames out when that moment passes.

Why did one keep going and the other not?

"I think there is a plausible scenario under which *Spy* could have achieved orbital velocity and gone on to be successful," Andersen replies, "and of diminishing importance." A big difference, he argues, is that "the wave *Rolling Stone* was catching was a giant, generational one," as opposed to "whatever little wave we were catching." The sheer numbers of young boomers, the sheer impetus of the drugs and sex and rock 'n' roll culture, "That was a pretty large set of stars to hitch yourself to."

Besides, times—and media—changed. "In the modern dynamic, it's hard for any magazine to have that salience in the culture for longer than a single-digit number of years. . . . It is hard in this balkanized culture to have that impact any longer."

Insiders defend *Rolling Stone*'s celebrity-consciousness, saying that there just aren't so many big stories coming out of music these days. Music doesn't sell the magazine anymore, they say. Movie stars and TV stars, especially if they're pretty females, especially nude or in bikinis, sell.

"The market has changed," Draper says. With seemingly every magazine, daily newspaper, and a thousand websites and TV channels covering popular music, "everyone has now taken bites out of Jann Wenner's apple." *Rolling Stone* is a victim of its own success in that way, he contends. Wenner and his colleagues "showed the world that readers were interested in this sort of thing. It should come as no surprise that others would poach on their turf."

"I know it's not cool to say you like *Rolling Stone*," muses Andersen (who notes that Wenner was "a very generous adviser" to *Spy* in its early days). But he adds that you have to be impressed that *Rolling Stone* still at least *tries* to be relevant, and has not become one of "the egregious examples of magazines and journals absolutely staying in one place,"

That's very kind and polite—and, I'd argue, very inaccurate.

# The Hall of Lame

## Why There Shouldn't Be Rock Museums

"LOOK, ROCK AND ROLL is above all an expression of the frustrations of youth," Pete Townshend once said. "Well, this is 1969, I'm an adult, I don't have the same frustrations anymore. My concerns now are mainly spiritual."

He also once said, "Rock 'n' roll is very, very important and very, very ridiculous."

I went to the fifteenth annual Rock and Roll Hall of Fame induction ceremony at the Waldorf Astoria in Manhattan on March 6, 2000. It struck me as the very precise and complete antithesis of rock 'n' roll.

The Rock and Roll Hall of Fame Foundation was started by Jann Wenner, Ahmet Ertegun, and other industry figures in 1985. (The museum, in Cleveland, opened in 1995. Townshend had been there for the groundbreaking in '93.) The board at the time of the 2000 ceremony was a panoply of big industry names, including chairman Ertegun, vice-chairman Wenner, president Seymour Stein, vice-president Jon Landau, and Chris Blackwell, Clive Davis,

David Geffen, Danny Goldberg, Jimmy Iovine, Quincy Jones, Antonio "L.A." Reid, Lenny Waronker, and BMG's Strauss Zelnick. A musician or band is eligible for induction twenty-five years after their first record. Landau and Seymour Stein chaired the 2000 inductee-nominating committee, which included board members as well as Phil Spector, Jerry Wexler, Danny Fields, Lenny Kaye, and rock journalists such as Anthony DeCurtis, Peter Guralnick, Chet Flippo, Dave Marsh, and Lisa Robinson. Ballots were "then sent to an international voting body of about 1,000 rock experts," according to the hall's literature.

Except for the Cleveland museum itself (discussed below), I would be hard-pressed to think of a building with less rock 'n' roll resonance than the Waldorf-Astoria. The hotel is a cavernous marble-and-chintz faux-luxe grandiosity that looks like an interior set for a 1950s Hollywood epic about the last of the czars; the only way rock 'n' roll should have been entering such a place would be to storm it in a rock 'n' roll peasants' revolt worthy of Led Zeppelin's hotel-trashing days. Instead, aging rock gods in tuxes and evening gowns pulled up front in limos, sweeping past the paparazzi and autograph seekers (the real peasantry were, of course, kept out on the sidewalk).

With its black-tie tedium of endlessly droned speeches occasionally interrupted by seizures of dubious "entertainment," its absolutely phony pretense of celebration, its hollow evocations of youth, and its grinning, back-slapping, fascistic suppression of anything resembling authentic joy (God how I wished George Grosz were alive to document the moment), the ceremony produced a sense of alienated boredom that was like being at a wedding where you don't know either family; only the music at most weddings would be more rockin'. Seen from above, the aged entertainers and impresarios arranged at their tables for the formal dinner were a sea of heads that if not gray were bald as stegosaurus eggs. It looked like the final House of Lords scene in *The Ruling Class*, all cobwebs and applauding corpses.

Not that I was actually in attendance. The press—except, I suppose, for a few heavy hitters close to Jann Wenner—was relegated to a backstage holding pen. We watched the ceremonies on TV monitors, just as anyone else might have on VH1 two nights later, except no one edited out all the dull segments for us. As I walked in, middle-aged local TV figure Penny Crone fired an unwelcome image into my brain, doing a standup in front of hot TV lights about how rock 'n' roll reminds her of heavy petting in the backseat of a Chevy.

A kind of bleachers section filled most of the room—definitely the cheap seats for the press—with a phalanx of TV cameras along the top row aimed like artillery at a low stage, where some inductees and presenters would be trotted out for photo ops and brief rounds of dopey "entertainment media" questions of a how-does-it-feel-to-be-inducted? nature. Flanking the stage were two widescreen monitors wherein the real action took place; I'm no expert on giant TV appliances, but these looked slightly smaller and lower-quality than the one my brother-in-law has in his rec room in Pacific Palisades.

Radio and Internet types were crammed into the far corners. Throughout the evening, a fat, lank-haired DJ doing live radio feeds to somewhere out in cow-patty country periodically erupted into outbursts of "mhm hmm mhm BIG APPLE! mnmn hmhm hmhmhm ROCK AND ROOOOLLLLL, BABY!" By 9 p.m., I'd estimate, roughly half the assembly was willing to strangle the mofo with his headphones cord. Other, meeker media types found themselves brushed off and pushed around all evening by some officious dick with a Hall of Fame employee laminate hanging from his neck. By contrast, the hired security guys were unfailingly polite and mannerly, in that slightly menacing mafioso-in-relax-mode way. And there were *a lot* of them, speaking into their cufflinks all over the building; I wondered for a while if Bill Clinton was coming with his sax.

In one sense, this fifteenth annual ceremony was an historical watershed. Within a couple of months, Microsoft zillionaire Paul Allen, a man who could buy and sell Jann Wenner before breakfast, would open his Experience Music Project in Seattle, the first competing vision of what a rock and roll museum should be. But that was about the only significance—a rather negative one—the 2000 ceremony could claim. Whereas past inductions had occasionally managed to stir up a glimmer of rock 'n' roll spirit, at fifteen years into it this one seemed particularly exhausted and offhand. Compared to, say, 1992, when the list of inductees included Hendrix, the Yardbirds, the Isleys, Booker T., Sam & Dave, Elmore James, Doc Pomus, and Leo Fender, the year 2000's crop seemed uninspired at best. One got the impression that the bottom of the barrel of rock talents Jann Wenner was willing to sanction had by then been scraped very, very clean. (As the Gen-X online satire magazine *Bully* put it after the 1999 induction ceremony, that Wenner-approved short list of rock peerage has come to resemble "elitist Country Club members as they perform for music industry snobs.") Eric Clapton was inducted for the third time; I think at that point they should have just declared him God and retired him to his own niche in Cleveland. Other inductees included Bonnie Raitt (another Wenner favorite, and a regular participant in Hall of Fame ceremonies years before being inducted herself), Earth, Wind & Fire, the Moonglows, and the Lovin' Spoonful; a new category honored relatively unsung session men such as Elvis's guitarist Scotty Moore and Motown bassist James Jameson; Billie Holiday and Nat King Cole were recognized as early influences. In one of the evening's rare moments of candor, Natalie Cole, when asked by the press how her father—who hated rock 'n' roll—would have felt about being inducted, admitted, "He would die. I think he'd be slightly mortified." Standing next to her in an extremely shiny jacket, Ray Charles grinned and grinned.

It would be hard to say which speakers were the more tedious, those presenting or those receiving induction. Paul Simon, introducing the Moonglows, looked ancient and out of it; at one point he seemed to be hallucinating, mumbling some nuttiness about how great it is to be an adolescent, "before the imagination has been dulled by cultural pollutants." Melissa Etheridge, another regular at these affairs, hamboned interminably and with incredible phoniness about what a great musician, feminist, sex symbol, and humanitarian Bonnie Raitt is. John Mellencamp, an absurd little fellow with a basted-on booth tan and a practiced faux-rock insouciance that would earn him a smackdown in most corners of the real world—he blew smoke rings at the press as if he had been practicing it since he was fourteen, despite a recent heart attack—insisted on singing half the Lovin' Spoonful's song catalog while introducing them.

Patti Smith introduced Clive Davis. She looked ashen and paralyzed with stage fright. I was told she was a late replacement for Whitney Houston, who was said to be having a problem with certain personal habits that could render her suddenly unavailable for public speaking. Patti sang, with no show of irony, "The People Have the Power." The power to what? Lick the floor in Clive Davis's office? Purchase another 12.5 million units of Santana, Davis's latest pet project?

Smith's choice of the fist-waving anthem was intended as a show of support for the sixty-six-year-old record mogul who had founded Arista a quarter-century earlier. All that winter and spring Davis had been in the process of being forced into retirement by the boomers of the German megacorporation BMG, Arista's parent company. Smith, Aretha Franklin, and other rock and pop artists who felt they owed their success and fortunes to Clive Davis had been very vocal in expressing their "outrage" at the way BMG was treating him. Ironically, that May, Davis would finally be ousted and replaced as CEO of Arista by a forty-two-year-old former drummer, Antonio "L.A." Reid—who happened to be a black man, making him one of the very few blacks to reach the executive level in the recording industry.

Something seemed not only meretricious but also counterrevolutionary in Smith's tit-for-tat support for her millionaire boss. Then, to make things worse, at the end of her song she reminded us all, as if we had forgotten, that 2000 was an election year, and she urged us to go out and exercise our people's power of the vote. Thus yet another aged former punk rocker reveals her utterly conventional and bourgeois roots.

The inductees themselves barely dragged a rock 'n' roll spirit into the oddly stuffy Waldorf hall. After each member had thanked every sentient being in the known universe, the group would toddle over to their equipment and stumble through a couple of signature hits they hadn't played together in twenty years. You can hardly blame them for being rusty, but what was the point of embarrassing everyone that way?

The answer, of course, is that that is the whole point of the Rock and Roll Hall of Fame induction ceremony. Like the Academy Awards, the Grammys, your local chamber of commerce's annual citizen-of-the-year award, Hall of Fame induction is a business award. It exists as a back-patting exercise for the business side of things, for those moguls, producers, impresarios, and highest-level sycophants who had what they consider the genius to recognize talent when they heard it and knew how to make a buck off it. The actual performers and artists in attendance were quite evidently enjoying themselves a whole lot less than Ahmet Ertegun, Clive Davis, Seymour Stein, and Jann Wenner, beaming into the spotlights.

After the 1999 ceremony, *Bully*'s Ken Wohlrob had reminded his readers of

"some pretty horrifying and yet hilarious incidents" from previous ceremonies. These included "John Fogerty refusing to play with the rest of Creedence Clearwater Revival"; the time "the surviving members of the Doors"
praised a drug-free life "while Pearl Jam's Eddie Vedder, who filled in for the
deceased Jim Morrison, said 'I don't know what they're talking about. I was on
acid the whole time'"; and "Led Zeppelin bassist John Paul Jones insulting his
former bandmates by saying 'I'd like to thank Robert and Jimmy for remembering my phone number this time.'" (They had been playing around a lot
together without him. Then again, on the basis of the 100-percent unlistenable
solo record he released, to absolutely no public or critical response, in 2000,
one could say they had some reason. Almost all bassists' solo records are unlistenable, as are almost all drummers' solo projects, but this one was doubly so.)

Sadly, there were few such moments of comic relief in 2000 to alleviate the
drone of geriatric tedium. Like all awards ceremonies, this one went on two
hours longer than it should have. Press was made to arrive between 4 and 7
p.m.—I aimed for 7. The event got rolling maybe 8:30. At around 12:30, by
which time everyone in the press room was hot, bored senseless, hungry,
thirsty, and cranky, Paul McCartney, who has become another Hall of Fame
regular, appeared on the monitors and began the induction speech for James
Taylor.

At James Taylor I draw the line. Still to come were a video about him, his
speech, his playing a couple of tunes I loathed thirty years ago, and then the
spectacle of the big all-star jam. I got up and left. As I passed in front of the
still-packed press bleachers, a couple of reporters gave me dirty hey-where-
you-think-you're-going? looks, as if I were violating the newsman's code by
abandoning this ship without them. A couple of others applauded.

○

A few months later I went to Cleveland to visit the actual Rock and Roll Hall
of Fame and Museum. Cleveland, as many have remarked, is a funny sort of
place to have sited what is the unofficial national museum of rock 'n' roll. A
connection to Alan Freed is the primary stated reason; it is also true that for a
not-so-big city Cleveland can claim (or plausibly hijack from its smaller neigh-

bor Akron, or sponge off its surrounding state of Ohio) connections to more than its share of famous folkies and rockers, from Phil Ochs to Pere Ubu, Joe Walsh, Chrissie Hynde, Devo, the Dead Boys, and Trent Reznor. Then again, it has often been noted that a number of these stars had to leave Cleveland, or Ohio, or even—in the case of Hynde—the United States to find true success. But never mind. A crumbling Lake Erie waterfront in desperate need of reviving provided Cleveland's civic and business community with the financial rationale. Also, I suspect that for Jann Wenner there could have been a compelling marketing argument for siting the heavily *Rolling Stone*–sponsored museum in the heart of the American Heartland, which in the 1990s was perceived as the last great reservoir of an audience for straight-up, old-fashioned rock. Call it Reznorland—a big, flat, obstructionless market of white guys still pumping their fists in the air when the Journey revival concert comes to the state fair. And finally, while New York or L.A., Detroit or Memphis or San Francisco, might have seemed a more logical home for a rock 'n' roll museum, you only build an attraction like this as a tourist magnet, and Cleveland sure needs the tourists.

The hall stands on the shore of Lake Erie, a vast inland sea that stretches off, flat and the color of lead, to the horizon. I had been told it's the ugliest building in Cleveland, and it certainly is an eyesore (designed by I. M. Pei), but I'm not sure it's *the* ugliest. Cleveland, like most other big-little cities in America, has had a number of modern and postmodern monstrosities inflicted on its skyline, in a fit of urban "renaissance" that was utterly disrespectful of the crumbling charm of its stately beaux-arts downtown. But yes, it sure is an ugly building. And the lakeshore site, next door to a working pier (I watched a big rusty tanker called, romantically, the *Millenium* [sic] *Hawk* being offloaded) and near one of the city's two big sports stadiums, makes no sense as a place to celebrate rock 'n' roll. A maritime museum or city aquarium would be more appropriate. Why put the hall there, instead of, say, somewhere on Euclid Avenue, which still has a few working rock clubs on it, or over in the fake-river-front bars-and-restaurants area called the Flats, which gathers crowds of people looking to have a good time? Sticking it on the lakeshore, off to one side from the rest of the city's downtown life, is just the first of many unsettlingly decontextualizing decisions.

It was rainy the Saturday I went, and the high-ceilinged, glass-walled entrance hall did in fact feel like an aquarium, damp and echoing. Staff with boomingly amplified voices split visitors into tour groups (busloads of Midwest high school students, big heiffer-kids from the heartland of white America, milk-fed, mostly blonde, glowingly pale) and individual ticket-buyers. It was a most un-rock-'n'-roll-looking crowd. Lots of gray-headed retirees and middle-aged beer bellies, lots of strollers getting in traffic jams with wheel-chaired grannies. I saw exactly one couple, in their early thirties I would say, that I could visually identify as "hipsters." All the rest were indistinguishable from a crowd amassed for a baseball or football game. No, I'm not saying that only hipsters are allowed to appreciate rock. But if you went to someplace where you were going to encounter real rock—a club, say—you would see a lot more hip-looking young people and a lot less Farmer Brown old folks. It gave me the distinct impression that many of the visitors weren't there out of an intrinsic interest in rock 'n' roll history, but simply because it was another attraction on the extremely limited itinerary of things to do in Cleveland.

Luckily for them, the Hall of Fame does a terrible job of evoking anything remotely like an authentic rock 'n' roll experience. It's just a popular-culture museum, like any other. It has the same distancing effect upon the viewer, drops your energy to the same low-key, keep-shuffling boredom level. It could hold antique farm equipment or Civil War battle scenes or hot rods or textiles or NASA space vehicles. It's as true to the spirit of rock 'n' roll as a Hard Rock Cafe—one in which there are way too many children and you can't get a drink.

As it happened, when I was there they had just installed (in the "Ahmet M. Ertegun Exhibition Hall") the dismal Tommy Hilfiger–sponsored "Rock Style" show, a collection of stage outfits worn by dozens of rock, pop, soul, and rap performers over the years. I had already seen it a few months earlier at the Metropolitan Museum of Art in New York. To coincide with the New York opening, the December *Vanity Fair* had carried a Tommy Hilfiger advertorial insert called "Icons of Rock: Fifty Years of Rock 'n' Roll." There's no nostalgia worse than rock nostalgia. This supplement managed in a very few words (by boomer rock journalist Lisa Robinson, who really should have known better) and many shopworn images to convey every insipid, fatuous cliché ever invented about rock as "style" and "fashion," along with ads that suggested if you shopped the right boutique for Tommy gear you could be a rock star, too. (Except for rock females, who, the photos suggest, preferred to be naked, even Janis Joplin and Patti Smith.) The most glaring signal of cluelessness was the insert's promoting Lenny Kravitz as the "rock icon" of today. Kravitz is possibly the lamest man in rock 'n' roll, and positively the least funky black Jew in the world.

A sham and a dispiriting bore, "Rock Style" had absolutely nothing to do with rock 'n' roll and everything to do with promoting Tommy Hilfiger and fashion-consciousness in general. It was the history of rock as a runway show, drawing absurd inferences about the cultural weight of Kiss's platform boots or a Jagger jumpsuit from one of the Stones' terrible late-'70s stadium tours. But at least it made more sense in the context of the Rock Hall than it had in an art museum.

Not surprisingly, rock's fashion plates were prominently featured, which made it a rather Steve Tyler–centric view of rock; somehow worse, though, than staring through glass at David Byrne's big suit or Madonna's bullet-tit bra were the unextraordinary items that were only on view by virtue of their having touched the flesh of some rock star and thus been transmuted from, say, a black T-shirt to a black T-shirt *worn by Lou Reed*, or a common flannel shirt to one that had belonged to *Bruce Springsteen*. It reminded me of Elvis memorabilia auctions I had been to.

I frankly don't get the impulse my fellow boomers have to authenticate what they once felt was hip and cool by making a movie or a museum exhibit about it. I felt a hundred years old shuffling along with the crowd ogling silly costumes hanging on mannequins representing Blondie and Jimi and Bowie and Bono—figures this show made seem more ancient and distant than the pharaohs, their former outfits older than the ancient Egyptian artifacts on view in another wing of the Met. I felt like it was the year 3000 and we were People of the Future filing past antique remnants from the Age of Rock.

*Salon* culture writer Stephanie Zachwerek wrote about the show when it was at the Metropolitan, effusively buying into the message that "a big part of what foments [cultural] change is not just how rock 'n' roll is played, but how it's presented, and for that reason alone, the superbly put-together 'Rock Style' . . . needs to exist."

This is, of course, complete nonsense, as the very show she was describing documented. Seeing "rock styles" change from the 1960s through the 1990s, one could clearly see how they had followed, not set, the fashions of the larger hipster culture to which they were trying to appeal. The Beatles dressed like Mods, Jimi and Janice dressed like hippies, and so on. Only the more extreme costumes stood out as some sort of boldly individual fashion statement—Kiss's ridiculous superhero gear, Madonna's equally ridiculous superslut attire, Bowie's hyperdrag outfits of the early '70s—and even in those cases it would be a big stretch to argue that those costumes in themselves somehow fomented "cultural change."

Zachwerek went on to muse: "[S]omehow just about every piece of clothing chosen, even when it's uninhabited, captures some inexplicable something about the wearer." Could she have been any more vague? Then she made the history of rock sound like a Disney animated feature:

"When I think of the musicians I've loved best over the years . . . it's always, of course, the sound that comes first. But oh, the look of them! How is it that creatures who sound so good can look so heavenly as well? . . . I still believe that it has more to do with the transformative power of rock 'n' roll—its ability to work magic both on the people who make it and on the people who listen to it. By making them feel different, it also makes them look different, as if by a spell. . .

"If the essence of rock comes from inside, do the clothes have anything to do with it at all? That's a question that would be asked only by someone who doesn't understand the talismanic quality of certain garments—and we're talking about something as simple as a flannel shirt."

Judith Shulevitz, a wiser and I'm presuming older head, wrote more calmly and accurately about the show for *Salon*'s rival *Slate*. She dismissed it as "the boldest display of corporate muscle and easy museological virtue to appear at a respected New York art institution. . . ." Whereas Zachwerek thought the show had "plenty of intelligence," Shulevitz found it "stunningly fatuous." It was, she correctly noted, nothing more than "a Hilfiger commercial, legitimating as art the marketing strategy embraced so successfully by Hilfiger in the past few years, which mainly consists of turning rock musicians into fashion models. What's notable is that the show's exhibition strategy is essentially the same—reducing rockers to clothes horses, and without adding an iota of critical perspective."

In the year 2000, rock style is Birkenstock running ads in *Rolling Stone* touting the "J. Garcia limited edition sandal (quantities while supplies last)." It's David Bowie appearing on the cover of *Men's Fashions of the Times*, the *New York Times*' glossy spring couture supplement, modeling a brown tweed sport coat—a sport coat designed for accountants, insurance salesmen, hog-feed merchants. Jann Wenner wouldn't be caught dead in such a sport coat. Ahmet Ertegun would die first. But there was Bowie, with that chameleonic boyish grin that had carried him so far, wearing his hair long again, not hippie long but '70s pop star long—David Cassidy long. I guess it was supposed to make him look twenty, thirty years younger. It didn't. He looked exactly like the fiftysomething zillionaire entrepreneur geek he'd become.

The attempt to totemize clothes and objects associated with hundreds of rockers is, of course, the chief modus operandi of the Rock Hall and Museum. What the Hilfiger display attempted to do for rockers' clothing the rest of the hall attempts with a variety of other exhausted-looking ephemera and effluvia. It's like a walk-through eBay, or a bad natural history museum, in which random artifacts from unrelated lost civilizations are thrown together in a meaningless jumble. Decontextualized and wantonly aggregated, they're just objects, drained of any use-value, meaning, or emotional resonance. Ultimately, such collections say nothing about the objects or the cultures they were stolen from; they speak only of the collection itself, the acquiring and cataloguing and labeling of objects.

Here's a tom-tom Keith Moon once played. It's a drum, like any other drum. Without the identifying placard, you wouldn't have the foggiest idea it's supposed to be a *special* drum. And even when you know it's a drum Keith Moon played, the drum itself just sits there behind its security perimeter, powerless to move you, to instruct. The spirit of rock 'n' roll cannot reside in a tom-tom drum once touched by Keith Moon, like a wood nymph in a hollow log, and it's the most infantile form of magical thinking to pretend that it does. The visitor has to accept the museum's word that Keith Moon did in fact touch this very drum, thereby transferring to it some sort of ineluctable rock 'n' roll mojo; as with many collections of artifacts, it's the label itself that has the juice here, not that undistinguished tom-tom.

Here's a pair of big black boots worn by someone in Alice in Chains. Here's a gym bag filled with hotel keys collected on the road by one of the Eagles.

Here's a mic stand the Temptations used. The spirit of rock 'n' roll inhabits none of these things. They're just things. The best that can be said is that the museum does contain a nice assortment of used guitars, played by everyone from old bluesmen to contemporary rockers. But they look sad and mistreated hanging on the walls behind glass. Guitars are musical instruments, they cry out to be *played*, not stared at like . . . well, like a bag of hotel keys. If there's any spirit of rock 'n' roll inhabiting those guitars, it's begging you to smash the glass, pull that ax down off the wall, strap it on, plug it into a big stack of Marshalls, and fucking *play* the thing. It's a key to how wrong-headed, how *nonmusical* the Rock Hall is, that no one associated with the institution understood what an anti–rock 'n' roll gesture it is to crucify all those instruments like that.

At the most absurd, one case displays a Jim Morrison Boy Scout patch. At the most ghoulish, on one wall are mounted some twisted remains of the plane in which Otis Redding was killed. Wrenched out of context, simply stuck on a wall in a hallway between more flashy multimedia exhibits, even those scarred remains, which should be a frightful or sad reminder of the mortality of pop stars, lose all emotional impact. Again, it's the lack of context that drains all the juice from these things. Rock 'n' roll is all about context, as Ellen Willis said to me (and as Joe Strummer says in one of the hall's several film and video presentations). Removed from its place and time, it crumbles; it withers and fades away. The visitors push their strollers and their wheelchairs past rows and rows of this junk, pausing briefly, staring blankly, and then stroll on, obediently, following the signs, traveling the chutes-and-ladders system of escalators and stairs that eventually dumps them, with a terrible inevitability, in the gift shop. And even the gift shop is a lousy gift shop, just an HMV outlet where you can buy the same CDs you already have at home, and tacky Rock Hall keychains. Just more objects, and none of them remotely close to evoking real rock 'n' roll. At least the garish surfeit of gift shops across the street from Graceland in Memphis is totally in the spirit of Elvisness.

Does the Rock Hall do *anything* right? Well, I liked the video and film installations. Because they feature interviews with and live performance footage of actual rock 'n' rollers, they give you a better feeling for the history than any of the objects displayed. Still, you could stay home and see the same footage— and much more—on your TV. No need to trek to Cleveland to see it.

When I walked out of the Rock Hall I wandered along the lakefront down to that area called the Flats, where the Cuyahoga River meets the lake. It's a small area of fish restaurants and frat-boy bars, and a couple of rock clubs. In the middle of a Saturday afternoon, one of these clubs was housing an all-ages hardcore show. Just standing on the sidewalk at the open door I got more rock in five minutes than I had in three hours inside the Rock Hall.

○

Having said all that, I find myself needing to admit one thing: I *like* natural history museums, the dustier and more old-fashioned the better. I love to paw over things at flea markets and garage sales and antique stores, trying to pick up the faint resonance of the past, the echoes of other people's lives that are left behind, like fingerprints, on their tools and jewelry and books and records. I *do* believe that mere objects can transmit, to the imaginative viewer, some ineluctable sense-trace of where they've been, who handled them and why. If I stumbled across one of those old bluesmen's battered old guitars in a flea market I'd be thrilled to touch it.

So why did the same approach in the Rock Hall offend me so? Could it be simply that the Rock Hall strikes too close to home for me? After all, it's *my* past they've put on display there; I don't mean mine alone, just that it's not a museum dedicated to, as they usually are, something remote, like the history of British royalty or of steam engines. The hall is supposed to present the history of rock. It's depressing as hell to see it laid out looking so bland and drained of its magic. I feel violated, perhaps a little like the way an American Indian feels seeing the bones of an ancestor on display.

So maybe that's some of it. But it's not all of it.

*I do not believe the Rock and Roll Hall of Fame should exist.* To its very core, I believe, it is antithetical to the spirit of rock 'n' roll, a multimillion-dollar monument to the sad fact that my generation has completely forgotten what makes rock cool or fun or even "important." It therefore has to resort to the cheap, old-fashioned, and inherently conservative "hall of fame" sham—a trope most associated in America with baseball—as a very imperfect way of reminding itself of what it once loved. But the Rock Hall is a completely inaccurate representation of what that was. If there are two adjectives that most definitely do not apply to this building or the concept behind it, they are "cool" and "fun."

The Hall of Fame is about old and dead people; rock 'n' roll is about the young and living. The Hall of Fame tries to reform rock 'n' roll, tame it, reduce it to bland, middle-American family entertainment; it drains all the sexiness and danger and rebelliousness out of it. Rock 'n' roll is *not* just any other American pastime, equivalent to a sport, though many players and promoters of '70s-style stadium rock have tried hard to make it that; anyone who appreciates rock 'n' roll must want to resist the athletic idioms inevitably employed by a rock "hall of fame," the implied notions that Rock Hall inductees are somehow rock's "champions," who were quantifiably better at the sport of rock than other rockers were because they "scored" more "hits" or some such nonsense.

The Hall of Fame operates according to the tastes and diktats of powerful industry figures and "experts"; but rock 'n' roll is, at its best, a grassroots, out-of-the-garage, populist music, maybe not "democratic" in spirit (obviously, no one believes that all bands are created equal) but certainly anarchic. Anarchic both in the true sociopolitical sense of self-organizing and anti-establishmentarian, and in its vernacular meaning—"all fucked up." The Hall of Fame violates this spirit with its soul-deadening bureaucracy working for a thinly disguised oligarchy.

The Hall of Fame is about rock that happened at least twenty-five years ago; rock 'n' roll is the music of here and now. I don't mean that rock 'n' roll can't, shouldn't have a history. You want to remember a great song from twenty-five years ago? Play the original. You don't "honor" some great band from your youth by dragging their old butts out onto a stage now, forcing them to go through the motions one more time like Ahmet Ertegun's trained circus animals, pretending to still feel a song they sang and/or wrote back when they were kids. Listen, I was there when the fiftysomethings of the Lovin' Spoonful got out on that Waldorf stage and croaked and creaked their way through "Do You Believe in Magic?" And I don't believe there's enough "magic" in the world to have transformed those old men into the Lovin' Spoonful again. Couldn't we have just spun the record instead? You want to "honor" the Moonglows, Jimi Hendrix, Cream? Buy the records. Play the records. Enjoy the records. Cherish the memories. Don't make old musicians try to recreate their youth. Don't hang up their old shirts in an ugly building on the waterfront in Cleveland.

Besides all that, there are fundamental functional problems with having a "hall of fame," and they become more glaring with every passing year. One is, Who decides who gets in and who doesn't? By what criteria? How do you decide who was a truly great rock star, worthy of an eternal place in the great hall of heroes, and who was just an also-ran? Clearly, despite those thousand ballots sent out to a global network of "experts," the dominant criteria are the tastes and predilections of Jann Wenner and Wenner's cronies. Fleetwood Mac and James Taylor were shoo-ins, and I'm sure the Rock Hall could easily have gone on inducting Clapton every year as far as Wenner was concerned. Think the Cro-Mags are ever going to be inducted? The Dropkick Murphys? Manitoba's Wild Kingdom, Mighty Sphincter, the Sick F*cks, Furious George, that little no-name hardcore band I heard in the Flats that afternoon? At the time of this writing, the MC5, Iggy and the Stooges, and Ozzie Osborne still haven't been inducted. Overwhelmingly, if not exclusively, the Rock Hall preserves a vision of rock as Jann Wenner likes it: mainstream, commercially successful, and, whenever possible, bland and nonaggressive. Yes, of course it gives its nods to punk rock and rap and heavy metal, but such outré forms of rock music are presented very much as adjuncts and addenda to the main story, and the main story is Beatles–Stones–Bowie–Springsteen–Billy Joel. Even Elvis, and '50s rockers in general, seem downplayed—they're treated as a kind of dimly recalled, prehistoric prologue to the rock we Wenner-aged boomers know best, which begins with the Beatles. And with the Stones. Jann's old friend Mick seems to pop up in every corner of the hall.

The Rock Hall sanctifies that elitist, top-down view of rock we saw before in James Miller's book, here codified and given the mock authority of a quasi-official national rock 'n' roll museum. Where are the grass roots, the little-knowns, the thousands of bands and performers who made rock 'n' roll the ubiquitous cultural factor it was and yet never made it to the level of fame and celebrity that makes a Jann Wenner want to meet them? When I visited in May 2000, the only nod the museum gave to such lesser-knowns was a condescending and ultimately insulting wall of plaques commemorating "one-hit wonders." Characteristically, the museum's experts had singled out maybe a dozen of "the best" of the one-hit wonders, allowing hundreds, nay, thousands of others to keep languishing in (implicitly deserved) obscurity. A good argument could be made that rock 'n' roll—and *certainly* pop music, chart-topping singles music—is an industry built on the backs and dreams of one-hit/two-hit/three-hit wonders. Even an elitist has to admit that many of the most successful artists in the history of the form are not *much* more than one-hitters. What do you call a pop sensation such as Britney Spears? What, in the end—be honest—do you call Chuck Berry or Little Richard? Four-hit, five-hit wonders? Does that make them four, five times more "important" than, oh, ? & the Mysterians or Jay and the Americans? They may be more important—but surely that's not quantifiable by the relative number of "hits" they had. How many "hits" did Nirvana have? I mean in terms of songs that the average visitor to the Rock Hall could name? One, maybe two, at best three? Does that mean Britney's more important than Nirvana? How about ABBA, Cher, Billy Joel, Backstreet Boys?

Oh, but wait—by my own definition, they're not rock, they're pop. They're specifically built to crank out hit singles. Nirvana was a rock band. The hit singles were icing. But the Rock Hall isn't just about rock anyway. As Wenner et al. run out of real rockers who meet their criteria for greatness, they've been casting their net wide, inducting extremely not-rock performers such as Billie Holiday and James Taylor, and even *anti*-rock types such as Nat King Cole. At the 2000 induction ceremony, Paul McCartney noted, correctly, that it's becoming no longer accurate to call the hall a rock 'n' roll institution at all; with all the blues, R & B, and other not-rock styles it has been "honoring," it would really be more appropriate to rename it the Popular Music Hall of Fame. It would open vast new fields of music to exploit—I mean, honor. When her time comes, Britney will be inducted. Billy Joel was.

○

In June 2000, just a few weeks after my visit to Cleveland, Paul Allen opened his new, high-tech version of the Rock Hall, the Experience Music Project, in

Seattle. My cynical next-generation pal Doughty referred to it as "a second attempt by searching, tormented baby boomers worried that their youthful passion might not be remembered by the ages as the world-changing force they believe it to have been."

Allen, who co-founded Microsoft with Bill Gates, was one of the five richest men in the world. He was also a lifelong amateur rock guitarist, which makes complete sense, since he was right in the middle of the boomer pipeline—forty-seven the year the Experience opened, a year younger than me. An avid collector of rock memorabilia, he had originally envisioned the EMP as a place to house his Jimi Hendrix collection, which included the guitar I heard Jimi play at Woodstock. When relations with the Hendrix family broke down, he expanded his vision to something more like a Silicon Valley challenge to Wenner's Hall of Fame. Built with $240 million of Allen's own money, the EMP was designed by superstar architect Frank Gehry and, not surprisingly, is filled to the brim with computer-generated spectacle and interactive displays.

Reflecting Allen's guitar-duffer background, the EMP represents a more playful and hands-on idea of a rock 'n' roll museum than does Wenner and Ertegun's pantheon of heroes in Cleveland—but it still is a rock 'n' roll museum, still an attempt to reduce rock to a collection of artifacts assembled to promote good, clean, nostalgic, Microsoft-enabled family fun. I don't approve. If you really insist on having a museum of rock 'n' roll, I say, you don't get I. M. Pei or Gehry to design it, and you certainly don't let the Jann Wenners and Ahmet Erteguns dominate it as a museum devoted to themselves, and you don't let it become a whited sepulcher of a mausoleum to a popular art form that is implicitly dead. Nobody asked my advice, but if they had I would have told them to buy a working rock club somewhere, a place that's already a living piece of rock 'n' roll history. Buy CBGB from Hilly Kristal if he'll sell it. Or buy a club that's gone bust—wasn't there, in fact, a failed last-minute effort to transform the Fillmore East into a rock history museum to preserve it? You put your museum on one floor—preferably down in the basement—and keep the performance space open. Bring in all sorts of rock acts, new and old, subsidizing them as necessary. Make it a *living* museum to the spirit of rock 'n' roll.

And for Christ's sake, at least serve beer.

# Punk

## Not the Death of Rock, Just the Decline of Western Civ

Penelope Spheeris: "Why don't you put something on
it to make it not qet infected?"
Punk Girl: "Because I'm lazy and I don't want to."
—The Decline of Western Civilization III

'Anarchy in the UK.' What the fuck's that? What good is
that to those of us in Utah?
—Stevo, in SLC Punk

YOU KNOW WHY punk rock had to happen. It can be summed up in three words: classic '70s rock.

I suppose a man approaching fifty has absolutely no business discussing punk rock. Then again, punk was originally made by people of my generation (the Dolls, Ramones, Joe Strummer, Patti Smith) or just a few years younger (Johnny Rotten). Still, I was already twenty-five or twenty-six when punk rock finally made it to Baltimore in a big way, and that was too old. I liked punk, I had some younger friends who were into it, but I couldn't pretend to "be" punk: I was not included in that shared youth experience, having already had a shared youth experience of my own. Punk suddenly made it fun again to go into skanky little clubs full of art students and listen to really loud, bad rock— but that was who it was for in Baltimore, arty college kids, not guys my age. Punk was their reaction against the music people my age had been liking. I had no right, really, to get off on it, at least not right up in their faces. I couldn't

191

pretend to be punk—I had a day job; in another couple of years I was going to be married and buy a house.

I write about punk rock here in the context of my fellow boomers. We boomers make primary claim to all rock, and punk rock is definitely a genre of rock, created by tail-end boomers. In fact, boomers give punk rock a very honored place in rock history: To boomers, punk rock was the death of rock. As James Miller so handily outlined, 1977, the year Elvis died and the Sex Pistols rose internationally, is the terminus of the rock age. According to Miller, after 1977—after punk rock—rock is a fixed, "completed" art form, like jazz, and every supposedly new expression of it (hardcore, grunge, rap metal, etc.) has just been repetition and rehash of forms and idioms that were all originated and explored and established by the time punk came and went. That the supposed death of rock coincides so neatly with '60s boomers' becoming too old to appreciate rock anymore is just a happy coincidence.

I don't think rock died in the '70s, but it did (mirroring its '60s fans) grow up and get a job then. After the brief flowering of rockin' rebellion in the late '60s, all phases of what had been an often haphazard industry became organized and consolidated during the 1970s. The leading wild hairs and rebels of rock in the '60s either died off or got with the program. There was big money to be made, giant concerts to be played, endless lines of coke and groupies to be enjoyed. The commercial record labels, which had reached out feebly to the hipsters through a handful of "house hippies" such as Danny Fields, now began to field small armies of young, hip A&R men—former bong-hitting college-boy rock fans, now a few years older and out in the work world—whose sole job was to identify and sign new acts. At the same time, the programming of rock radio became more rigid and more tightly coordinated with the labels and with tour promotions. In the new era of huge arena and stadium concerts, rock tours mushroomed into a multimillion-dollar wing of the industry, with control of major venues gradually falling into the hands of a small number of giant promoters. (By the turn of the century, much of the tour business in the United States would be absorbed into a single entity, SFX Entertainment, which would itself be bought out by Clear Channel, owner of more than 800 radio stations throughout the U.S., giving the new conglomerate virtual monopoly control of the acts, the venues—with giant TV screens for showing corporate sponsors' commercials—*and* the radio promotion of big rock tours in America.) As the entire industry became more corporate and consolidated, one effect was to drive the good rock that was being made out of the mass-marketplace, so that bad, prefabricated pop-rock such as "Joy to the World" (Three Dog Night, a definitive '70s MOR vocal group that somehow time-traveled a couple of years into the '60s to release preemptive tripe such as "One" and "Eli's Coming") and "Brandy" and "Fly Like an Eagle" achieved a ferocious, inescapable ubiquity on the radio, on TV, and on the Muzak at the mall and the burger joint.

Bruce Springsteen epitomized the triumph of the programmatic, corporate faux-rock spectacle John Sinclair railed against back then and ever since. What rankles about Springsteen's carefully manicured image as a regular guy, a man of the people, a working-class hero is that he is one of the most craftily marketed performers in rock, a millionaire many times over who is as close to the average member of his audience as Barbra Streisand to hers. One can't help noting the unironic use of his nickname, The Boss. Shades of Jagger's Mr. Turner.

In 1974, in Boston's *Real Paper*, Jon Landau wrote what became one of the most often-quoted lines in American rock criticism: "Last Thursday, at the Harvard Square theater, I saw my rock 'n' roll past flash before my eyes. And I saw something else: I saw rock and roll's future and its name is Bruce Springsteen." Landau was perhaps more right than he knew: Springsteen was both the past *and* the future, an instant nostalgia item. He had struck on a formula for producing a formulaic, choreographed, middle-of-the-road fake-rock with broad appeal. As Sinclair (who admittedly had good reason to despise Landau) wrote back in 1974, Springsteen's *Born to Run* sounds more like *West Side Story* than actual rock, and it has as much to do with actual rock as *West Side Story* had to do with actual teen gangs. Landau did not content himself with writing rave reviews of his discovery. He went on to become Springsteen's manager, adviser, confidant. He quit rock journalism and became a wealthy man riding the astronomical success Springsteen became.

By the mid-'70s, rockers had neatly segregated themselves into the subgenres of hard rock, soft rock, heavy metal, country rock, progressive rock, jazz rock, and so on. The cause may have been a natural urge on the part of the musicians to explore variations on what had by then become a predictable format. The effect was ease of market segmentation on the radio, at the record store, in the concert hall. You could market Jackson Browne *and* James Taylor to the soft rock fans, the Eagles *and* America to the cowboy-rock audience, Yes *and* Kansas to the prog-rockers, Bowie *and* Roxy to the dress-up crowd. This is not to say that there wasn't some good rock being made within some of those categories, but that the appearance of the categories themselves, the imposition, or re-imposition, of business sense and order after the wild ride of the late '60s, is a key indicator of what was happening not just to rock, but to the rock generation. We might even stretch a point and say that in its fragmentation, rock in the mid-'70s became a kind of "identity rock," oddly paralleling what was happening as the remnants of the radical political movement split up into the separate camps of identity politics—lesbians here, blacks there, black lesbian separatists trumping them all over here—each competing with all the others for maximum politically correct campus cred.

Without stretching any points, we can surely say that rock had been, for a while in the '60s, at least loosely aligned with the counterculture and the "freeks"—the rhythm section of the revolution. Now, with the freeks all settling down with jobs and families, rock too tamed its act. In the early '70s, rock returned to the "mainstream." They had a term for it: MOR, Middle of the Road rock. In the '70s, Carducci's distinctions between rock and pop (see Chapter 1) became hard to make, because so much rock was striving so hard to be pop. Was Three Dog Night rock or pop? Frampton? The Doobie Brothers, Queen, Electric Light Orchestra, Heart, Steve Miller, Billy Joel, Bay City Rollers, Wings, America, Bachman Turner Overdrive, REO Speedwagon, Boston, Fleetwood Mac?

Late boomers who had their formative rock years in the '70s go nuts when a '60s boomer says this, but the big mainstream rock acts of the decade were slim pickings. Led Zeppelin? Son of Yardbirds, with less taste and, until late in their game, less smarts. Tom Petty? A good Electric Dylan imitator. Aerosmith? A Stones tribute band who somehow lucked into the big time. J. Geils? A good bar band who somehow lucked into the big time. The '70s mainstream was also a comfortable home to a number of '60s holdovers—Clapton, Rod Stewart, the Allman Brothers, the Jefferson Airplane/Starship, the former Beatles—

variously on the descent, some falling faster and into deeper holes than others. Certainly there was good rock being made in the 70s, but as the industry grew more powerful and efficient at mass-marketing and promoting the mediocrity, the good stuff fought an uphill battle against the increasingly ubiquitous and all-pervasive schlock and pop. Put simply, it became harder and harder to hear the good stuff through the white noise of commercial muck. This condition of the marketplace was not new—the '60s had its Herman's Hermits and Gary Pucketts just as surely as the '70s its Elton Johns and Billy Joels—but it became more extreme.

The MORizing of so much rock meant that it temporarily lost its *meaning*. It's not mere boomer nostalgia to say that rock in the '60s meant something; the meaning may have been murky and ineffable, or mostly imputed to the music by its naive audience, the way some of us took "Street Fighting Man" seriously, but rock was still a social signifier of some large import. The nuances of rock's meaning shifted throughout the '60s, but certainly we can identify it as meaning "new," "change," "rebellion," "youth," "freedom," and, for a little while, "revolution," at least in the sense that it was closely identified with Ellen Willis's cultural revolution. Whether you were young or old, "for" it or "against" it, you understood that rock came bearing these messages. Can we hear these messages in the music of, say, Peter Frampton? Did Jeremiah the Bullfrog or Uncle Albert have any message for us at all? As rock mainstreamed itself in the '70s, it became not only vapid and formulaic but also meaningless, soulless, and, to paraphrase John Sinclair, roll-less.

Jackson Browne personified this trend. Musically, he was a leading avatar of the '70s electrified folk music that went by the oxymoronic term soft rock, a genre promoted by industry powers David Geffen and Jac Holzman (who had founded his Elektra label almost exclusively on folk music in the 1950s, dabbled in rock during the '60s, and returned to his softer roots in the '70s). Politically, Browne also represents a softening, from the rock rebelliousness of the 1960s into a more innocuous, MOR liberal do-gooderism. He came to epitomize the Live Aid model of conspicuous celebrity beneficence. He became famous less for his music than for his willingness to play it on the stage of any benefit, telethon, or charity fundraiser if the cause was a liberal one: No Nukes, Amnesty International, the rain forest and other ecology causes, Native

American causes, Central American causes (he visited Nicaragua to protest Reagan's funding of the Contras), arts education, low-power radio, anti–death penalty rallies, and so on. In late 1999, when the Stones called on a host of rock and pop celebrities to sing on a Christmas single to benefit children's charities, Browne was naturally there. In early 2000, when Robert F. Kennedy, Jr., together with family members and various star guests, gathered in the ski resort of Vail, Colorado, to raise money for environmental causes, one of Browne's guitars was auctioned off (to another Hollywood celebrity, as it happens, actress Julia Louis-Dreyfus) for $5000. (Roger Daltry was also on hand at the affair and sang, of course, a rendition of "My Generation.")

I do not wish to comment on any of Browne's causes *qua* causes. But if they were good causes, they were good to him as well. And although it would violate the nature of celebrity, it would be nice to see stars sometimes taking public positions that actually challenge their audiences' preconceptions, instead of safely preaching to the converted all the time. (Who among Browne's or Sting's audience is "against" the rain forest? Who among *Rolling Stone* readers isn't "for" a cure for AIDS? Who among Rage Against the Machine's young audience thinks, "Ah, the hell with it—*fry* Mumia.") In 2000, humorist Joe Queenan wrote a satire of this kind of celebrity do-gooding, *My Goodness: A Cynic's Short-Lived Search for Sainthood.* "The one thing I had learned over the years from watching the Susan Sarandons and Ben and Jerrys of the world was that there was no point in being a wonderful person unless everyone else knew about it," he wrote. "Believe you me, when I set out on the Road to Perfection, people were going to get all the facts and figures."

Perhaps, though, the charity grandstanding of Bob Geldof and Jackson Browne, or the nostalgic bumper sticker slogans of Rage Against the Machine, are as close as rock can ever be expected to get to genuine political activity. Karl Marx, as well as the Frankfurt School, would have treated the notion I raised back in Chapter 1—when I wondered if rock's mass-media status might not have been an effective way to spread rebellion to the greatest number of the disaffected—as a forlorn hope. They took a dim view of mass media as an arena for political struggle or consciousness-raising. A medium entirely controlled by capitalist interests, they argued, commodifying cultural output as a pacifying entertainment product for passive consumption by the masses, is not exactly a venue for teaching resistance to that same mass culture. Thus the down-with-capitalism provocations of Rage Against the Machine are neutered and nullified by the very media that broadcast them to the masses.

○

So, why did punk rock have to happen? Because somebody, as Alex Harvey put it, had to come along and say fuck you. Punk rock tried to give rock back its meaning. Now its meaning was "Fuck you." Time to get back to basics.

Since punk rock didn't penetrate the American mass consciousness until 1977, the year of *Never Mind the Bollocks*, some people have thought, then and since, that punk rock was a reaction to the disco music fad. This is a fallacy, product of an accident of history. Punk rock and disco both developed from the early '70s on, and in a way the two very different genres had at least one shared impulse: a desire to fashion a simple, straightforward, physical dance music. (They were also both dress-up musics.) Johnny Rotten writes in his memoirs that as young punks he and his mates very much enjoyed going to London discos and fashioning their own outlandish dances to the steady disco beat. That punks were wryly fond of disco is evident in the ease and enthusiasm with which bands such as Blondie incorporated punk rock into their sound.

No, punk rock was a reaction to and rejection of rock itself, the fat, mannered, pretentious, roll-less rock of the 1970s. When the Sex Pistols started playing in London in 1975, the older, established British rockers were as a rule not kind. Punk rock shamed and embarrassed them. It made what they had come to represent in the '70s—the riches, the decadence, the pompous music and spectacular stadium concerts—look monstrous, and they knew it. Johnny Rotten claims that when he went backstage one night to meet his hero Iggy Pop, Iggy's mentor David Bowie had him physically removed from the premises. Mick Jagger publicly said the Sex Pistols were poor musicians—as if that had anything to do with it. John Lydon responded years later in his memoir: "Shame on you, Mick. The Stones were one of the most notoriously inept bands in music, and here was this old coke hag pointing fingers and calling us disgusting." He derided '60s rockers as "shifty little businessmen doing their utmost to stifle the opposition. The lot of them deserved the name *dinosaurs*—too big, too pompous, elaborate, enormous amounts of equipment, only playing very large auditoriums or open-air festivals. Music became as remote from the general public as you could possibly get. . . . The system! They became it."

Punk rock was an attempt to reach back past those "coke hags" to an earlier, purer rock. That's something else people often later forgot about punk: how retro it was. Like Springsteen, punk rock was not a progressive impulse at all, but a *regressive* one, even a *conservative* one. A drive to strip rock back to its basics: three chords and a steady four-four beat, lots of energy and a guy shouting into the mic. And there was much for punks to look back to. Before there was punk rock there was a lot of rock that had punk*ness*. What was "My Generation" if not the first punk anthem—by a band that was not very punk at all? What was the sneering attitude powering a song such as Link Ray's "The Swag" or even "Louie, Louie," or any number of other early recordings by any number of '60s garage-bands like the Sonics, if not a "punky" attitude? Lenny Kaye, best known for his work with Patti Smith, put together the original *Nuggets* compilation of lost garage band "hits" specifically to acknowledge punk rock's indebtedness to those earlier bands. The Ramones were a conscious and sincere attempt to recreate classic girl-group and surf music. And so on. (Twenty years later, it all came full circle when Joey Ramone produced an album for Ronnie Spector of the Ronettes, and she sang a lovely cover of Johnny Thunders's "You Can't Put Your Arms Around a Memory.")

The neat boomer theory that punk rock rose with the Pistols in 1977 and ended with Sid in 1979 is, of course, another fallacy. For one thing, it's more of that elitist Great Men of History thinking, ignoring the hundreds of punk bands before, during, and after the Pistols. But even using the Pistols as the model, it's an inaccurate view. Once more for the record, a bit of chronology:

In 1969, the Stooges' eponymous first album is released (containing "1969," "I Wanna Be Your Dog," "No Fun"). Although little heard at first, it and the 1970 *Fun House* are seminal LPs for future punk rockers—a cover of "No Fun" will be a Sex Pistols staple, one of their handful of best songs—despite the fact that with *Fun House* Iggy thinks he is making something more like jazz, and the awful, long sax-squawking jams are the antithesis of the brevity punk rockers (and Iggy himself) will favor.

In 1972, the New York Dolls are on their disastrous first visit to London (drummer Billy Murcia ODs in a London bathtub and a *Melody Maker* reviewer calls their first London concert the worst set he's ever heard); they meet Malcolm McLaren in his shop, then a Teddy fashion place called Let It Rock (later Sex). Patti Smith is in New York reading her poetry on rock bills. Teenage future Sex Pistols Steve Jones and Paul Cook begin their campaign of stealing enough equipment from working bands (including Bowie) to have a band of their own.

In 1973, Iggy and a reformed Stooges (he had "retired" after *Fun House*) are brought to London under Bowie's wing to record the stripped-down redline *Raw Power*. If not "the first punk rock album," it is at any rate extremely influential on all punk and back-to-basics rock from that point on. Again, the Pistols openly acknowledge their indebtedness; Jones recalls sitting down with Iggy's and the New York Dolls' records and basically learning how to play guitar by playing along with them over and over. (Many years later, he would play guitar for Iggy's great 1988 comeback.)

Anyway, 1973 is the beginning of punk rock for other reasons: the Ramones and Television are both formed in New York City that year. This is where punk rock begins, in New York City, in 1973.

In February 1975, Malcolm McLaren visits New York City, sees Television's Richard Hell in a ripped T-shirt and chopped-up hair, and returns to London to "invent" punk fashion, which, again, the misinformed masses and mass media will forever after assume was a British fashion statement first, borrowed and imitated by American punks. (Alternatively, John Lydon claims that he first showed McLaren and McLaren's designer Vivienne Westwood the ripped-and-safety-pinned look. It would remain an issue ever after: Who was the first punk, Hell in New York or Rotten in London?)

By the middle of 1975, you can walk into CBGB and see the Ramones, Blondie, and Talking Heads all play on a single bill. Meanwhile, John Lydon is auditioning for the Sex Pistols. By the fall, the Ramones are starting to record demos of songs such as "I Wanna Be Your Boyfriend" and "Judy Is a Punk." Their first LP, *The Ramones*, will come out the following spring. When the Pistols go into the studio to record *Never Mind the Bollocks*, they will carry it with them, to demonstrate how they want to sound.

The Sex Pistols play their first gig in October 1975.

In November 1975, the first issue of the magazine *Punk* is published in New York. The Clash debut in mid-1976. They are major Ramones fans, heavily influenced by the Ramones' knack for getting it all down to two and a half minutes. Indeed, though Clash aficionados would always prefer the long, droning dub experiments and the multidisc *Sandanista!*, it could be argued that their best work was their singles, the short, bright, tightly knit, and closely played "hits" such as "White Riot," "London Calling," "Tommy Gun," "Hitsville UK," "Rock the Casbah."

The "Anarchy in the U.K." single is released on EMI in October 1976. In December, the Pistols make their infamous "dirty fucker" appearance on British TV. Punk rock as a media scandal arrives in full force in England, though its mass-media impact has yet to be felt outside the U.K.

EMI drops the Pistols, who sign with A&M in 1977. A&M drops them the same day they sign them, surely some kind of a record. They sign with Richard Branson's Virgin, where they become a smash, if brief, success. Meanwhile, the Clash sign with CBS in 1977. Punk's DIY purists are already crying sellout.

"God Save the Queen" comes out in May 1977. It goes to number one on U.K. charts despite efforts to suppress its sales and a virtual blackout on radio and TV. With this one song the Pistols polarize the British populace the way no band had since the early Stones. *Never Mind the Bollocks* comes out in the U.K. the following October. The Sex Pistols, who have been on the verge of becoming an international *succès de scandale* for a year, are sure there now. Some people will look back and see "punk rock" beginning at around this point. Others will say that this marks the end of its first, "underground" phase: From 1977 on, they sniff, it's part of the commercial rock mainstream.

The Pistols come to the States in January 1978 and fall apart by the end of the month. Their entire U.S. tour lasts twelve days.

They leave behind a handful of great songs and a huge media-image-myth gap no other punk rock band will begin to be able to fill. Which may be just as well, since what the Sex Pistols had become was arguably not punk rock anymore anyway. With all the hype and the chart-topping hits, the Pistols had moved very far very fast from their punk roots, become much more of a mass-media, pop-culture phenomenon, the very sort of thing to which Rotten, at least, thought they were supposed to be diametrically opposed. More than the rest of the band, he seems to have despised what the Sex Pistols had become.

McLaren cynically and foolishly takes the remnants of the band—not a band at all, with Rotten gone and Sid, barely conscious, also in absentia—to Rio to record a few last, garishly bad tracks and finish the awful *The Great Rock 'n' Roll Swindle*, McLaren's stunningly ugly ode to himself. Quite possibly the very, very worst rock 'n' roll movie ever made, it will luckily be tied up in litigation for many years and seen only in rare glimpses. Astonishingly, McLaren's claims that he created the Sex Pistols, punk rock, and punk culture in general will go largely unchallenged by a generation of pop culture "scholars." (Julien Temple, the director, would return to his subject twenty years later to make *The Filth and The Fury*, the Sex Pistols documentary he should have made in the first place.)

Sid Vicious dies of an OD one year later. For many fans and critics, February 1979 marks the very death of punk rock itself. Punk Rock, RIP, 1977–1979.

John Lydon (McLaren had gotten a court order preventing the singer from using the name Johnny Rotten, which McLaren claimed to own, and it took years of wrangling to get it back) soldiered on with Public Image Ltd and made a couple of pretty decent records, very different from what he had done with the Pistols, showing more influence of the jazz and even jazz-rock bands he had always listened to. The first couple of PiL albums were still "important" to those who were listening—diehard punk rock fans despised them as sellouts, but more progressive listeners liked the trance-dub drone of tracks such as "Swan Lake." At any rate, the rest of the world wasn't listening at all: It was remarkable how quickly and completely Johnny Rotten was ignored and forgotten by the mass media he had so scandalized just a year or two earlier.

As the years passed and he aged, he became, increasingly, the old punk rocker with the funny hair, growing increasingly portly and comfortable-looking in Los Angeles, getting by on his past glory and the occasional Mountain Dew promotion.

It was terrible that Sid died so young and wastefully. For all his fucked-upness he was the other genuinely charismatic member of the band, a gawky, drugged-out Keith Richards to Rotten's Jagger. Had he shaken off the heroin and the guilt over Nancy's death, gotten past his own bad-boy Sex Pistol punk-rock image, maybe he could have gone on to . . . well, who knows what? A film career, perhaps.

Or maybe it had to end there. Maybe Johnny only sang about there being "No Future," and Sid truly lived it. The sense that that's true has always fueled Sid's cult image as the one true and ultimate punk rocker. The classic and only watchable moment in *Swindle* is the grand finale, Sid's big production number, his punk rock "My Way." It's a great bit, a timeless fuck-off to everyone and everything—to the world itself. Probably it's just hindsight, but you really get the feeling watching it that it's Sid's fuck-off farewell to the world. He said to an interviewer around this time that he would be dead in two years. In actuality, he cut that time in half.

Comparing young, skinny, pimply dead Sid to the middle-aged, excruciatingly self-aware Lydon making soft drink commercials twenty years later, you have to wonder which one of them did the right thing.

Then again, Johnny Rotten *did* die. McLaren and Lydon killed him. He was a stage character anyway, an act that Lydon was reluctant to take on and deeply ambivalent about the whole time he was doing it. His short and stormy career with the Sex Pistols began with a tortured "audition" in front of a jukebox, lip-synching Alice Cooper's "Eighteen," and was marked throughout by his disgusted tantrums. He stormed off stage midway into more sets than the band ever successfully completed—pissed at himself, at his band, at the crowd, at the whole charade. His two most memorable lines as Johnny Rotten were "God, this is awful" and the final send-off, delivered at the butt end of the band's last concert, in San Francisco's Winterland: "Ha ha! Ever get the feeling you've been cheated?" An American audience that had come to see what was being touted as the most important new rock band in the world literally watched that band disintegrate before their eyes, in a single song—the Pistols' cover of Iggy's "No Fun." (Not that it stopped the promoters from picking the bones. The Pistols played to 5000 people, grossing something like $21,000; by the time promoter Bill Graham and the Winterland et al. were done taking their huge cut, the band netted a princely $66.)

That iconic "Ever get the . . ." line is often cited as the ultimate punk rock Sex Pistols Johnny Rotten kiss-off to the world. What a perfect line to end a band's career with. If you had scripted the movie you couldn't have written a better ending. In fact, it was Roger Ebert who wrote the movie. Rotten adapted his kiss-off from the last line in the screenplay for the aborted Sex Pistols film *Who Killed Bambi?*, written by Ebert, the roly-poly B-movie screenwriter and movie critic from Chicago. The project had been cooked up by McLaren and Ebert's B-movie mentor Russ Meyer, for whom Ebert had scripted *Beyond the Valley of the Dolls*. Trace elements of the abandoned *Who Killed Bambi?* can be glimpsed in *The Great Rock 'n' Roll Swindle*. In the final line of Ebert's script, Rotten was to turn to the camera and address the audience: "Ever have the feeling yer bein' watched?"

Lydon did a lot of talking in his 1995 memoir about never repeating yourself, never looking back—don't rehash the past. Then, just one year later, in 1996, the Sex Pistols announced they would reunite for a twentieth anniversary tour. Shouts of horror around the world were ignored. How funny is that (I mean sad)—the specter of the Johnny Rotten of the Future bellowing "No future" at an audience of potbellied accountants nostalgic for their punk-rock 1970s?

To his credit, Lydon was candid about at least one motivation for the tour. The long years of legal battles with the intractable McLaren had finally ended in the band's favor. The Pistols could be the Pistols again, earn money from their songs. They called it The Filthy Lucre Tour—both an admission that, as the Mothers of Invention had joked many years before, they were "only in it for the money" and a wry nod to a *Daily Express* headline of 1977 (after EMI sacked the band but let them—i.e., McLaren—keep the money already paid to them) that screamed "PUNK? CALL IT FILTHY LUCRE." Still, by 1996 this kind of punk irony was old hat and embarrassingly tame—and an act of self-hagiography ostensibly at odds with the punk aesthetic. No one in their right mind really wanted to see the middle-aged Sex Pistols get back together and perform middle-aged-men's versions of "God Save the Queen" and "Anarchy in the U.K." No one.

It was the original lineup that reformed, with Glen Matlock back on bass. The tour began at a Finnish outdoor rock-and-drinking festival, after which it was scheduled to straggle through Europe to the U.K. and various dates in the United States.

Of course it was a disaster. How could it not have been a disaster? Smarter fans stayed away in droves. Stupid ones went and tried to relive the past. American punk-rock music writer Gina Arnold attended the Finnish concert and seemed surprised by what a fiasco it was. The Finnish kids, very drunk, many of whom had not yet been born when the Sex Pistols had originally performed, were unaware of the momentous historical occasion they were privileged to be witnessing and bored by the old farts acting like punk rockers on stage. Rotten, hilariously, was outraged when the kids started pelting him with debris and complained, "I am not your target. There are worse things than me in this world. . . . You should be fucking grateful I'm here." The kids, bless them, chucked more junk at him. The band stormed off. When they returned, the only song in the set the kids responded to was the encore, "Anarchy in the U.K.," which they all sang along with, in English.

An anthem is an anthem.

Arnold attended one more show of the tour, an outdoor concert in a park in London, that sounds even more ghastly and unsettling: droves of grizzled old punks nodding over their bangers and mash and tea as their old idols rip through "Pretty Vacant."

In the United States, the Pistols sold out a few of their smaller venues in New York City and L.A.—music industry strongholds where critics and comped label reps most likely made up significant portions of the audience. Elsewhere they played to half-empty arenas and halls papered with still more give-away-ticket-holders. They got some press, of course, but it was mostly in the form of a bemused shrug. They drew the same type of audience virtually all reunion-touring middle-aged rock bands do—middle-aged boomers reliving their "wild" youth. It was clear that although the tour proceeded more smoothly than the 1978 one had, the band was just as miserable as they had been their first time in America. The new live record documenting the tour came out and flopped dismally, as it should have, and was instantly forgotten, being a flabby, mortifying travesty that made anyone with a sense of decency cringe and feel very, very sad.

(My pal Gilbert completely disagrees with everything I've just written, by the way. He saw the show in New York and says it rocked. He bought the CD and thought it rocked. Everybody's got their rock 'n' roll heroes, even a cynical East Village surfer punk.)

At the time of this writing, Lydon's been riding the punk-revival wave back into the limelight yet again. A new Sex Pistols film documentary, *The Filth and the Fury*, was released in 2000. That year, the forty-four-year-old Lydon also started hosting a show on VH1, the elephants' graveyard of boomer rock, called *Rotten TV*, an adaptation of his program for the BBC, and attended the Republican and Democratic national conventions that year, video crew in tow, to play a rather tame provocateur, a kind of middle-aged brat, more annoying than anarchic. Alan Cabal ran into him in the crowd that had gathered outside the Democratic National Convention in Los Angeles to hear a free concert, with the usual full complement of proselytizing, by Rage Against the Machine. Cabal asked the portly, orange-haired Lydon what he thought of the band. Lydon shrugged: "This year's amateurs." (Rage's music incited a scuffle between the audience and the surrounding police that night. Stones and bottles were thrown, rubber bullets fired, and some thirty-eight young people were arrested. Score half a point for Rage, zero for the Stones on the Street Fighting Man riotometer. Then again, rock concerts had been inciting riots for nearly fifty years by then. Hiphop was good at whipping the kids into a frenzy as well. It says nothing for Rage's aspirations as agents of social change. Lots of loud, fast bands without a political thought in their doped-up heads could get the kids to smash things up.)

In 2000, Lydon himself was espousing a mild type of Rock the Vote participatory democracy, renouncing anarchy and the aimless young protesters who gathered to heckle both conventions. "You will only change things by involvement," he told a *New York Times* interviewer. Anarchy, he declared, was "mind games for the middle class. . . . I'm not sure who gains from chaos, but I know it's not the poor folks in the council flats." No "Anarchy in the TV" from the middle-aged Hollywood demistar. Watching this spectacle, Doughty recalled a line from a Foo Fighters song: "There goes my hero/Watch him as he goes!"

○

Punk did not die at the end of the 1970s, just because the boomers were getting too old to play it or pay it any mind. Instead, it just went "underground" in the 1980s, becoming a fringe preoccupation out of the media spotlight. Left to its own in the relative gloom, it metastasized into the various subgenres of hard core, straight edge, hate edge, street punk, skinhead, Oi!, emo, etc. In some of these various iterations it flourished through the 1980s in places like Los Angeles and Washington, D.C., and Manchester in the U.K. In due course, the mainstream was ready for punk rock to make a "comeback," which it did in the late 1990s, both in a pop-oriented, mass-marketed form of new punk (e.g., Green Day) and in a new wave of nostalgia for the '70s brand. In terms of both sheer numbers of fans and having the full weight of media support behind it, punk rock enjoyed arguably more American interest in 1997 than it ever had in 1977.

In the 1980s and '90s, as the original punk-rock generation aged, the audience for punk remained teens and adolescents. My friend George Tabb, of the punk band Furious George, told me that the older he got, the younger and younger his audiences became. At thirty-six (too old, I agree), he found himself playing for fourteen-year-olds. By 1999, Furious George's bass player was a kid young enough to be Tabb's son who had grown up being a Furious George fan and styled his looks so closely on Tabb's that Tabb dubbed him Mini-Me. And Tabb's look was already a studied emulation of the Ramones'.

One afternoon in the fall of 1999, George came by the *New York Press* office all worked up because somebody had just tried to auction off what was reputedly Sid Vicious's bass on eBay. The bidding closed without a sale, because the top bid of $99,100 was less than the seller demanded for it.

Here's the seller's description:

1975 Fender P-Bass That Sid Vicious had used during the time he had played with the Sex Pistols. The Bass is white and has stickers that Sid had put on just before his passing. The bass was acquired from Anne Beverly, (Sid's mum) The Bass Comes with the original strap that says "SID". The bass is as Sid left it, it still has some blood on the bass (His I presume). The bass comes with a notarized letter of authenticity and documentation. This bass is well documented and was Sid's no. 1 Bass (He had 2 including this one). . . .

George couldn't get over it. Imagine, $99,000-plus for a bass Sid never learned to play. Meanwhile, all those punk kids today are out there learning how not to play on $30 pieces of junk. A sacred Sid relic, complete with his holy blood.

George suggested eBay might be a handy way to assess how people value the whole range of rock artists. Name a band or star and chances are good somebody was selling something related to it on eBay. How much people were willing to pay for memorabilia might be a crude register of how "important" a given star or band was. For instance, we found people bidding up to around $2,500 for a plastic toy Beatles guitar. Not bad, but it's no $99,100. There was a Marky Ramone drum kit that fetched $3,000. Elvis items always did okay, naturally, as did Stones items.

Black Oak Arkansas memorabilia, on the other hand, mostly went for a buck or two.

What this says for Jim Dandy's legacy is obvious. It's a bit less clear why we couldn't find anybody outperforming Sid's bass. To George, this was irrefutable proof that punk rock *rules*. But it might just have been an indication that the late-boomer punk generation, whose members were by then in their mid-thirties and up, had the excess shopping power to overbid on lost-youth nostalgia items, just like their '60s-boomer older siblings trawling for Elvis and Beatles trinkets.

That same punk-rock nostalgia was expressed in other media as well. While Tabb kept punk-rocking into his thirties, some of his age peers left the rock halls for the halls of academe and became what sounds like an oxymoron: punk-rock scholars. If it's axiomatic that very little rock writing has ever really rocked, it's even more true that very little punk-rock scholarship was ever very punk rock. Much of it has attempted to force punk rock into a Marxist-Situationist-subversive mold long rejected by most of the actual practitioners of the music. British writing on the topic tended to come from academic Marxists who even invented a whole new branch of study, Cultural Studies, as a venue for overthinking and overwriting about punk rock as a subversive movement.

If you were a late-boomer British academic, naturally you defined punk rock as subversive, because that was how you wanted to remember it. It was the punk rock of your youth, and it ended, just happenstantially, when your youth did. It's the classic fallacy of rock histories. Beatles boomers, such as James

Miller in his *Flowers in the Dustbin*, remember that their rock died the day punk rock was born. For the 1950s rock 'n' roll fans who came before them, real rock was dead by the time Elvis went into the army. The foundations of an historical literature on the Day the Rave Died were laid in the 1990s. And so on. People miss their youth.

Even granting that punk was more of an identifiable social movement in the U.K., where *everything* is a more definable social movement than in the U.S. (it's a small place, crowded with people who take their group identity very seriously), the impulse to cast U.K. punk as an authentic revolutionary movement is romantic and naive. One of the more reflective punk-rock scholars of the late 1990s questioned his fellow academics' need to identify an "authentic" ur-punk that was pure and revolutionary, and later sold-out and commodified. As though there had been an elite originating core of pure punk idealists, Situationists and revolutionaries all, led by that genius master-strategist Malcolm McLaren. Then all those other trendy kids and record-label managers piled on and ruined it, man. This is the elitist, trickle-down, Great Man theory of punk—an art-school version of punk. It started with McLaren himself, who always appropriated for himself a far more important role in the creation of punk than he deserved, and whose need to overlay punk rock with much unformed political theory was rather shockingly taken up with no questions asked by the punk-rock academics. "All the talk about the French Situationists being associated with punk is bollocks," Lydon wrote in *Rotten*. "We didn't sit around and wax Situationist philosophy. Never. I understood who the Situationists were . . . I always thought it was foolishness—art students just being art students. . . . Plus they were French, so fuck them." Or as Steve Jones says, "Everyone in the planet knows Malcolm's full of shit."

Danny Fields, the former co-manager of the Ramones, said to me that McLaren's slapdash attempts to put a very '60s, hippie-revolutionary spin on the punks' working-class nihilism created a tension that in fact helped pull the Pistols apart. After all, the ridiculous and punishing itinerary for the fiasco of a U.S. tour was his idea of a political statement: the band would get away from the big city sophisticates on the East Coast and would go meet the real working people of America in the South and West. As it turned out, the real working people of America, when they weren't busy providing Sid with drugs, either despised the Sex Pistols or laughed at them, but were hardly moved to anarchist revolt by them. In America, punk rock was never a working class art form. The American working-class rock fan liked hard rock, arena rock, and heavy metal. In America, punk rock was for disaffected middle-class kids and art students.

By 1971, even John Sinclair—writing from jail—had reached the conclusion that rock was an imperfect tool of revolution. He wouldn't have used a term like commodified—revolutionaries in his day read Marx and Mao, not Adorno and Habermas—but his short-form explanation of how the music was sold out was similar:

> [T]hey saw that our music was the lifeblood of the alternative culture, the thing that held us together and showed us how to live with each other outside the system, so they moved in and took it over by buying off the musicians and turning the music into a simple Amerikan commodity which could be bought and sold like anything else. They cut the bands off from their roots in the rainbow community and made them into big P\*O\*P\*S\*T\*A\*R\*S who could be manipulated any way the owners wanted to use them. . . .

The academic Marxist version of punk-rock history is no more sophisticated and no less romantic. *The Great Rock 'n' Roll Swindle* is just The Man Stole Our Music with a mohawk. Punk's negativity only made it *seem* more worldly. The party line on punk, especially in the U.K., expresses a sense of youthful idealism betrayed—and has there ever been a generation which, as its members reached the end of their youth, *didn't* feel betrayed? British journalist Suzanne Moore questioned the need for a bunch of aging, academic former hipsters to authenticate their youth by turning it into history. "If punk is the ultimate fuck-off then what kind of truth are we trying to tell these days?" she asked. "That I truly understand the meaning of fuck off? That I fucked off first? That once upon a time a 'fuck-off' meant something that it just doesn't mean these days?"

As late as 1999, punk academics in the U.K. were still writing as though numerous versions of punk rock had not continued to exist after 1979, representing some vital pockets of youth subculture activity into the twenty-first century. No doubt the messy fact that some of the best punk rock being played at the turn of the century had skinhead-fascist, or at least patriotic, blue-collar and conservative associations, made it very difficult for leftist scholars to treat it as punk rock at all. But the swastikas, Dago jokes, and flirtations with the National Front were part of the London punk scene from the earliest days, and they resist left-apologists' attempts to shrug them off as simple fuck-off fashion gestures. The fuck-all nihilism, despair, and anger of the British kids who made and embraced punk rock could be driven either left or right by any adult—McLaren, the National Front—who cared to try to use the kids' anti-establishment rage for political purposes. Remember the Dead Kennedys' song "Anarchy for Sale."

Tracking punk's politics through the 1980s and '90s, one might see how punk's fascination with extremism, with the marginal and the outcast, made the form attractive to both the ultra-left dogmatism of D.C. hardcore and the ultra-right rhetoric of the neo-Nazi skinheads. For every lefty band like Fugazi and lefty punk movement like Positive Force, there has been a racist punk band like Skrewdriver (distributed in America by the white-power label Resistance Records) and a neo-Nazi organization like the National Alliance. Bands on both sides "refused to sell out to the corporate interests" who ran the major labels and big tour-promotion companies (admittedly, in the case of a racist skinhead band this was clearly a default position). Both sides tried to use punk music very much in a John Sinclair mode, as a motivating wing of a broader attempt at cultural revolution that included grassroots organizing, commu-nity action, and "consciousness-raising" publications (even though the levels of bumper-sticker sloganeering, kneejerk cant, and preaching to the converted on both sides were so high as to prohibit much resembling political discourse). And generally, despite some small achievements on both sides, one has to con-clude that punk rock has performed dismally as a political organizing tool for both the Left and the Right. On both sides, despite the Fugazi fans' claims of great social significance for that long-suffering and well-intentioned band, or the paranoid media fretting about a global Nazi conspiracy marching to the beat of racist skinhead rock, the hard truth is that punk's total political impact over the years has been even more nearly nil than that of the '60s political rock-ers. The great mass of punk-rock players and fans have demonstrated little political awareness, from the Ramones (the twilight-years single "Bonzo Goes to Bitburg" does not a socially aware band make) to the time of this writing.

○

In 2000, George Tabb was being sued for naming his band Furious George. Houghton Mifflin, publishers of the popular Curious George series of children's books, felt that he was infringing on their trademark and sullying the good name of their product. They felt that consumers might be confused by the resemblance between a punk rock CD and a children's book.

Who knows? Maybe they were right. In one surreal moment during pretrial depositions, a Houghton Mifflin representative disputed with Tabb's lawyer whether or not a punk rocker such as Tabb could legitimately claim that he was "furious" (rather than simply hijacking a handy pun from the Curious George books).

"Punk-rock musicians—it's your opinion that punk-rock musicians are not angry?" Tabb's lawyer demanded.

"They're playing at being angry is my position," the publisher's representative replied, "and that's part of the schtick, is what my take on it would be."

In 2000, Malcolm McLaren made a "spectacle" of himself again, running for mayor of London. After garnering a fair amount of press and uttering a number of his patented outrageous statements, he packed it in. Again.

## Post-Rock

### Why Doughty Doesn't Think Any of This Is Important

IN THE APRIL 2000 *Esquire,* former Bill Clinton adviser Paul Begala wrote of how he hated to be mistaken for a baby boomer: then in his mid-thirties, he only just qualified as a leading-edge Gen-Xer. Calling boomers "The Worst Generation," he carped: "At the risk of feeding their narcissism, I believe it's time someone stated the simple truth: The Baby Boomers are the most self-centered, self-seeking, self-interested, self-absorbed, self-indulgent, self-aggrandizing generation in American history. I hate the Boomers."

That was odd, considering that his boss was the boomers' boomer, but I quote him as a good example of the frustration and anger younger people (especially just slightly younger people) feel toward the omnipresent boomer generation. And that's only if they take it seriously at all. Whereas '60s and '70s types like to think that punk rock ended in 1979, for example, twenty-first-century punks have to be reminded that it even existed that far back. A very good historical Website called World Wide Punk listed the Slits, the 101ers, Malcolm McLaren, and their contemporaries—everything I just wrote about in the previous chapter—under the rubric "Ancient Punk Rock History."

Obviously, most of what I've been describing in this book happened before "Gen Y" was born, and before Gen X could be cognizant of it. Members of those generations never saw hippiedom firsthand, for instance, or experienced the era when certain hippie ideals impinged on the music industry. Their only personal contact with something resembling hippie idealism interacting with the marketplace has been the hip capitalism of Jann Wenner, Virgin's Richard Branson, the ice-cream moguls Ben and Jerry, or The Body Shop's Anita Roddick. This might seriously warp their impression of '60s ideals toward the sarcastic and the skeptical, might it not?

Take Richard Branson. Born in 1950, he became an exemplar of the Boomer Billionaire. From a middle-class, English public-school background, Branson showed his entrepreneurial leanings while still a student. In the late '60s he would grow his hair long and join all the other young people (and Mick Jagger) in marching against the war in Vietnam; in the '70s he would place himself at the center of British rock culture. But he was always a businessman at heart, not a hippie nor a rocker (and certainly not a punk rocker). He started his first enterprise, a youth magazine called *Student*, when he was seventeen, and he was soon landing interviews with stars such as Jagger himself. Virgin Mail Order Records, begun in 1970 with start-up capital from his wealthy father, was the seed that grew into the global empire that included Virgin Music (sold off in the early '90s), Virgin Atlantic Airlines, Virgin Cola, and interests in everything from blue jeans to hotels, cosmetics, financial services, and Necker, Branson's private Caribbean island, rented out to celebrities and millionaires.

Virgin Music was always Branson's main claim to hipster status. In its early years it was mostly a home for prog-rockers such as Mike Oldfield and the Giorgio Gomelsky–managed Gong. Branson's decision to pick up the Sex Pistols in the mid-'70s had less to do with his "getting" punk rock than his simply seizing the opportunity to ride with the hottest media commodity then in Britain. It also allowed Virgin to re-brand itself from the flagging prog-rock sound to the newest, hippest scene. Under Branson's ownership, Virgin's aesthetics were largely commercial: Phil Collins, Boy George, Janet Jackson, grandpa-era Stones.

In a figure such as Branson, the boomer generation presented the world with a new genre of businessman, the long-haired, ever-youthful, fun-loving "adventure capitalist" known for his association with rockers and celebrities, his daredevil antics in balloons and speedboats, his piratical brazenness in pitting little Virgin Atlantic against the giant British Airways, his casual and highly personal management style. There was something in him of those rich rock stars Ellen Willis spoke of in Chapter 3, rebelliously luxuriating in their ill-gotten gains. And indeed, he looked and acted more like a guy who would be playing keyboards for Rod Stewart than a traditional businessman. It all lent him a veneer of the anti-establishment, anticorporate "renegade" spirit so crucial to the hip boomer's sense of self-worth.

Ben & Jerry's and The Body Shop, meanwhile, represent a different and, I think, even more significant brand of hipster capitalism and boomer entrepreneurship. These two firms took the celebrity charity ball and benefit concert off the stage and right into the market and mall. Separately but simultaneously, they invented the most literally bourgeois manifestations of hipster capitalism ever, in which what once might have been considered frivolous indulgences and possible signs of the consumer's affluent decadence—beauty products, "super-premium" ice cream—were transformed into good works for the third world, endangered species, the very planet. Eating that pint of super-premium Cherry Garcia ice cream was not an indication that you were a self-indulgent yuppie, but rather the opposite—that you were a sensitive, caring, and progressive citizen of the world.

Ben & Jerry's was founded in 1978 in a converted Vermont gas station by a pair of hippie entrepreneurs, both boomers, Ben Cohen and Jerry Greenfield. By the mid-1980s they had gone public and franchises were popping up like magic toadstools throughout the United States, making the hippie founders wealthy men. As it grew into one of the dominant presences in the super-premium ice cream market, Ben & Jerry's also became a leading representative of the new generation of "socially responsible" businesses, making sure that all of its good deeds, charitable contributions, and ecologically friendly practices were integral, nay, central to its promotions and marketing. For all its New Age inventiveness, Ben & Jerry's clearly understood the wisdom of the old-fashioned salesman's line, "Sell the sizzle, not the steak." More ingeniously still, the company's marketing transferred the halo for these good deeds to the consumer, making the buying and enjoying of super-premium ice cream a charitable act in itself.

Inevitably, Ben & Jerry's encountered the conflicts inherent in this business model. In the early 1990s, the company donated many gallons of diluted ice-cream waste to local Vermont pig farmers, whose swine lapped it up. The story made happy international news as yet another demonstration of the company's innovative largesse and commitment to "linked prosperity" with its local community. So when the pigs starting dying young of arteriosclerosis induced by that fatty ice-cream diet, threatening the livelihoods of the farmers, "[i]t was a minor catastrophe," Jon Entine, a leading analyst and critic of socially responsible capitalism, wrote. Ben & Jerry's then compounded its error by trying to cover up the disaster. A black eye for the company's carefully groomed good-guy image.

While this was an embarrassment for the quixotic ice-cream purveyors, it was nothing compared to the havoc their do-gooding capitalism wreaked in Brazil. To provide the Brazil nuts for Ben & Jerry's "Rainforest Crunch," the company got the well-intentioned idea of hiring indigenous rainforest-dwellers as harvesters. The idea was to show the locals and the world a commercially viable and small-is-good alternative to the clear-cut forestry and strip-mining that were devastating the rainforest. (The Body Shop's Anita Roddick was another big save-the-rainforest booster, as were Sting and many celebrities in Hollywood and the music industry. It was a completely non-controversial charity to back.) Ben & Jerry's received tremendous international press for this effort—and sold millions of dollars' worth of Rainforest Crunch. Only later did the bad news emerge. The indigenous peoples of the rainforest, knowing they could never make as much money harvesting the nuts as they could from selling off their land to miners and foresters, were accordingly never too keen on the project (the harvesting was, in fact, done mostly by workers brought in from outside). And because of Rainforest Crunch's wild popularity, Ben & Jerry's demand for Brazil nuts soon greatly outstripped the rainforest project's capacity. Indeed, the company was soon buying 95 percent of its Brazil nuts from huge South American agribusinesses notorious for their sleazy practices. As the final irony, these giant corporations proceeded to buy up the land that belonged to the indigenous groups the project was conceived to support.

As the 1990s wore on, Ben & Jerry's image slipped further. Reports of widespread employee dissatisfaction emerged. Sales slid as more and more aging boomers forswore high-calorie treats such as ice cream for more spartan, health-conscious fare. The stock price sagged and stockholders complained. Finally, in spring of 2000, they forced the founders to sell out to the corporate giant Unilever—much to the horror of diehard Birkenstock-wearing fans of Wavy Gravy.

To Entine, Ben & Jerry's gaffes were classic examples of the "reckless idealism" of hipster do-good capitalism, and of the pitfalls that await when smart marketers play off the guilt of "[a]ffluent baby boomers [who] no longer try to change the world so much as 'shop for a better world.'"

Even more than Ben & Jerry's, Anita Roddick made herself an icon of this hippie-dippy "capitalism with a conscience." Born in 1942, she is a few years too old to be officially counted as a boomer, but she certainly represented a '60s entrepreneurship boomers easily identified with. Starting with one simple store in Brighton in the late 1970s, she created an international empire of mostly franchised Body Shop locations, making herself great wealth. Like Ben & Jerry's, The Body Shop convinced boomers that they could pamper themselves without guilt, that rainforest soaps could wash away any feelings of decadence, that every tube of shampoo helped to save the whales. Roddick clearly enjoyed creating and maintaining her image as a kind of Mother Teresa of shopkeepers, the most progressive, caring, and enlightened self-made multimillionaire in history. As with Ben & Jerry's, cracks in the facade eventually appeared. It was revealed that even by corporate giving standards, The Body Shop (unlike Ben & Jerry's) had a lousy record of charity contributions. There were accusations that its high-priced, high-minded products were also high in petrochemicals. British animal-rights activists sued, claiming that the company, despite its public stance against testing cosmetics on animals, in fact used animal-tested ingredients in its products. Roddick stepped down as CEO in 1998, and by 2000 she was claiming to have forsaken the business world altogether to devote herself solely to social activism.

In social and political terms, the feel-good mojo these companies were selling their customers engendered something more like magical thinking than critical analysis. A host of imitators such as Putumayo, Starbuck's, and countless fern-bar-decorated, indigenous-peoples-invoking retail establishments sprung up in the '80s and '90s. Socially responsible credit cards and mutual funds took this process a step futher, toward something more like a pure form of consciousness-capitalism dubbed "armchair activism"—a kind of *unconscious* conscious-capitalism. (Ironically, global oil conglomerates and giant mining firms proved quite adept in the 1990s at borrowing this hippie "sizzle" and selling themselves to the public as eco-conscious, even Green corporate citizens.)

These companies achieved something closer to Situationism than anything Malcolm McLaren ever managed to pull off with the Sex Pistols: a *detournement* of symbols of luxury and decadence into those of charity and conscience. Here was Debord's "commodity as spectacle" made manifest, wherein the act of using your credit card was, in and of itself, a good thing. Here also was Debord's "surplus of collaboration from the worker," whereby the consumer is portrayed back to herself not as a mere purchaser of soap, but as a heroic purchaser-of-soap-who-is-saving-the-rainforest. "This worker," as Debord wrote, "suddenly redeemed from the total contempt which is clearly shown him [in the workplace], finds himself . . . in the guise of a consumer, seemingly treated as an adult, with zealous politeness."

Here was consumer democratization allowing millions to participate in effortless philanthropy, once vouchsafed only to the enormously wealthy. As an example of a new genre of hedonist philanthropy, it was even more striking than the self-congratulatory ritual of attending a celebrity charity concert where you got to see your favorite rock artist *and* free Mumia.

The casual billionaire, the caring capitalist, the armchair activist—leave it to the boomers and former hippies to have dreamed all this up. It is one of our signal gifts to the world. I think it would be very difficult for an intelligent young person in the 1990s *not* to have become skeptical.

○

Younger musicians and music fans could be forgiven for considering boomer opinions of youth music—youth culture generally—to be utterly clueless. One way I differ from some of my boomer peers—especially boomer rock critics—is that I don't consider my liking or not liking new rock music relevant to its value in any way. A man approaching fifty is so far out of the context in which new music is made and received as to make any aesthetic opinion he may have of it totally irrelevant. As I write this, the major journalism venues are lousy with first-generation boomer rock critics still churning out reviews of records, bands, and concerts they have no business discussing in a public forum, especially in influential media centers such as the *New York Times* or *Rolling Stone*, where their reviews, however daffy, might seriously impinge on the careers of young musicians.

In 2000, Robert Christgau, the self-proclaimed "dean" of rock criticism and inventor of a quasi-academic A-through-F grading system for record reviews, was approaching sixty and still writing about new bands and acts for the *Village Voice*. He had first written about music in *Esquire* in 1967. The *New York Times'* chief rock critic, Jon Pareles, was in his mid-forties. The *Los Angeles Times'* Robert Hilburn turned sixty in 2000. Greil Marcus was in his mid-fifties. Numerous less-well-known writers at numerous other newspapers, magazines, and electronic venues were also still writing about rock despite having passed into middle age or beyond.

These old men of rock criticism were the precise equivalent of Mick, Pete, and the other old men of rock. They were simply too old to be making credible rock criticism. Why don't these older writers move on to write about mature people's music—the opera, jazz, the blues, even geezer rock? Believe me, I understand: they're boomers, constitutionally unable to stop liking and caring and writing about rock. But there is something inherently wrong with their passing aesthetic judgments on music made by young musicians for an audience of even younger people.

"Bands like Rage Against the Machine are not meant for people in their 40s," Robert B. Ray of the Vulgar Boatmen told the *American Journalism Review* in 2000. He identified two problems. On the one hand, there was "critical senility": the simple, inescapable inability for a rock critic approaching sixty to really get with a new band—or even worse, a whole new genre of music. What, for instance, could a white man of sixty, who was raised and had his critical faculties honed on folk and rock and soul musics, possibly have to say about hiphop or electronica or rave culture? At how many raves of the 1990s did Robert Christgau dance the night away on E? How could he possibly expect to understand that culture well enough to hand out grades to its musical products? In the same *AJR* article, "Dean" Christgau made the astounding claim that he "got" hiphop, whereas some other old, white rock critics might not, because he listened over and over to Parliament-Funkadelic in the 1970s until he got *that*, and this self-education in P-Funk back then somehow prepared him for hiphop and rap later. Dusty Springfield would call that wishin' and hopin'. That he had to listen to P-Funk over and over before he got it in the first place suggests a serious funk deficiency that could only *dis*qualify him from passing judgment on hiphop twenty years later. And it seems a terrible "White Negro" condescension to assume that getting George Clinton in the '70s automatically grants one access to the music of, say, RZA twenty years later. By 2000, an entire generation of young listeners had grown up listening almost exclusively to hiphop and rap-based popular musics. How could their grandparents possibly hope to understand that world as it was lived by the young—or explain it back to them in a way that was relevant to their experience of it? Ray also spoke of "overcomprehension," a term he borrowed from film studies; it means a tendency for older critics to overhype new acts even if they don't understand them, for fear that they'll miss the boat on the next Elvis or Sex Pistols. When I heard an old boomer rock critic claiming to be down with the Wu-Tang, I smelled overcomprehension.

Defenders of older critics argue that they bring a "wealth of experience" and "wisdom" and a "depth of knowledge" to new music that enriches the understanding of it. I would argue the opposite: if you've been reviewing rock records for thirty years, all you can bring to a new one is a lot of baggage and fossilized preconceptions. Youth music needs to be heard with fresh ears, the way it's played, with a sense of discovery and possibility and forward momentum.

And, of course, older rock critics tend to overhype older rockers as well. Enshrining Lou Reed, Clapton, Patti Smith in a pantheon of rock gods, older critics hear the music these people make exactly the way older fans do: with nostalgia and lots of denial.

It's no wonder a younger person would think that any boomer writing about rock had to be full of it. One young music writer I know told me about seeing one of these famous middle-aged rock critics at a Ricky Martin concert at Madison Square Garden in 1999. In the midst of a mass of screaming, swaying teenage girls, there was the old scribe hunkered down in his seat "with his frowny face, his earplugs, and notebook," the younger critic laughed. "I was feeling like a dork until I saw him."

Mark Gauvreau Judge is a Gen-X—and conservative—pop-culture critic who sometimes wrote for *New York Press*. In the *Wall Street Journal* of July 21, 2000, he delivered a stinging rebuke of boomer rock critics and their adolescent obsessions. Titled "Bohemians Like Them," it was subtitled, "Aging critics pine for rock as revolution. How embarrassing."

"Greil Marcus needs to grow up," the piece began. Marcus had written in the *New York Times* that the female band Sleater-Kinney signaled that "rock can be born again." "Maybe rock can be born again," Judge sniped, "but rock critics never are. Like the culture that supports him, Mr. Marcus—together with many of his colleagues in the press—is apparently trapped in the mind of a 16-year-old. A 16-year-old, that is, in 1968 with a subscription to *Ramparts* magazine.... [T]he mandarins of the rock establishment cling to the old hope that Life Will Change once the forces of authentic music-protest are unleashed on the world. They're Castros in a world gone cheery and capitalist.

". . . Sadly, Mr. Marcus is not alone in advancing the rock-as-social-revolution paradigm, although it has been generally discredited by America's intractable bourgeois ethos and capitalist economy, which quickly absorbs rock rebellion by converting the street-fighting tunes of yesteryear into commercials for Nissan."

Judge cited *Washington Post* and *Washington City Paper* critic Mark Jenkins, still writing about rock in his forties. "To him . . . music 'is about social change.' Mr. Jenkins is perhaps best known as the world's biggest Fugazi disciple.... Mr. Jenkins recently called Fugazi 'one of the most influential and popular underground rock bands in the world.' . . . [T]his is akin to being the world's best maker of typewriter ribbons."

He also lambasted Ann Powers, the *New York Times* rock critic (and former protege of Christgau) who had authored a book on bourgeois bohemianism called *Weird Like Us*. There, Powers wrote about a thirty-year-old rock critic named Barry Walters, whose apartment was filled with Barbie dolls and other toys. Powers praised Walters' ability to transform adolescent fixations into a career. Judge retorted that Walters was "a perfect symbol for the 'respectable' rock critics who never moved beyond adolescence and its juvenile politics."

Was he being too harsh? I don't think so. Time and again, boomers proved themselves in the dark regarding youth culture. In the spring of 1999, to cite one glaring example, two deranged boys strolled into Columbine High School in Littleton, Colorado, and proceeded to blow away fellow students. It presented an opportunity for adults to display their utter ignorance of and lack of empathy for young people and "youth culture." For two weeks, media pundits of all types engaged in the age-old pursuit of trying to figure out how to blame it all on rock 'n' roll. The struggle united liberals and conservatives, political analysts and "opinion" columnists.

For the first week of coverage they were having trouble nailing which genre of rock 'n roll the Littleton killers were supposedly into. Some pop-music-challenged journalist saw the boys' black trench coats and misidentified the killers as "Goth" kids, and for the rest of that week the entire media industry was getting it wrong, conflating kids who wear eye shadow and dig the Cure with Nazis, satanists, skinheads, Oi!, death metal, and *Doom*. The Milwaukee *Journal Sentinel* referred several times to the killers as "Gothic outcasts" and confused Goth kids with neo-Nazis. In Tacoma, Washington, the local *News Tribune* noted at the end of that week: "Someone labeled the killers as Goths—incorrectly, real Goths say—and since then, Puget Sound–area students who favor Goth garb have been called Nazis or murderers. People have threatened to beat them up and, in some cases, have done it."

By the second week, they believed they had gotten it straight: The problem wasn't Goth music, it was very definitely black metal music. Suddenly we had grampuses like Joe Conason in *Salon* pretending to know black metal music from Black Flag roach spray. "The killers' fascination with Hitler and their targeting of Christians and blacks," Conason wrote, "combined with their apparent preoccupation with 'industrial' music, together suggest the possible influence of a fascistic youth subculture that has inspired horrific violence else-where." Pretty soon we are descending "into the dank milieu where screeching, atonal bands with names like Mayhem, Morbid Angel, Deicide and Darkthrone exploit satanic, pagan and Nazi imagery to create an atmosphere of shock.

"Both the sound and the fascist fetishism date back to the early days of punk rock, when Malcolm McLaren marketed swastika accessories in his trendy London boutique, Sex." Another culprit, "the early post-punk group Throbbing Gristle, which glamorized the Nazi SS and Goebbels' Ministry of Propaganda, [was] the precursor of certain ugly elements in today's 'industrial' scene. A more current example is the suddenly famous Marilyn Manson, whose stage name refers not only to the murders inspired . . ." etc., etc. Before it was over, he had thrown his net wider to haul in John Waters and *South Park*, Howard Stern and Damien Hirst: all virtual co-conspirators in the Columbine murders.

I thought leftists were supposed to *resist* this kind of stop-the-music *entarte kunst* ranting. Conason's "liberal" take was little different from that of ultra-conservative R. Emmett Tyrrell, posted on the online version of the journal *American Spectator.*

> The origins of the Colorado high school massacre go back many decades. They go back to the 1960's when youth culture emerged as distinct from American culture, which is to say a culture shared by all age groups. They go back even further to the 1920's and 1930's when loony theorists—usually from continental Europe—theorized about zoo sex, violent individuality, psychic flumdiddle, all the nonsense that found its way into Nazi thought, left-wing thought, and other aberrant notions. The origins of Columbine high school's unspeakable massacre go back to the nihilism and evil of earlier centuries. Yet it is in the Twentieth Century that nihilism and evil found their proper marketers.

Meanwhile, in the *Village Voice*, columnist James Ridgeway, who sees a neo-Nazi in every woodpile, threw in his two cents' worth, trundling out dire warnings of a fascist youth culture in underground revolt. Ridgeway's piece carried the subhead "Lords of Chaos," echoing a Feral House book about black-metal bands in Europe, *Lords of Chaos: The Bloody Rise of the Satanic Metal Underground,* by Michael Moynihan (himself often accused of neo-Nazi sympathies, an accusation he always denied) and Didrik Søderlind. Ridgeway wrote:

> The Nazi symbolism flaunted by the teens accused in the mass murder last week at Columbine High School in Littleton, Colorado, has renewed speculation about neo-Nazi influences in the counterculture, specifically in certain areas of Black/Death Metal or "extreme" music. Also within the last week, the British racist group Combat 18, which is intricately involved in the White Power music scene, claimed responsibility for two bombings in minority neighborhoods in London. Although only a few people involved in Black Metal music have neo-Nazi leanings, squirreled away amid the goths, Satanists, and Odinists are some Hitler lovers. Racist right political leaders are always on the lookout for ways to recruit malleable foot soldiers, and in recent years the fringes of the music world have proved a rich resource.

This is classic yellow journalism. Notice the instant segue from the real world—two kids who went nuts in Colorado—into the realm of fantasy and circumstantial paranoia, with a racist right mind-control conspiracy stretching its inky tentacles around the globe to transform innocent youth into brainwashed storm trooperettes. By this point, Ridgeway had been writing about the rise of this global neo-Nazi cabal for so many years he seemed incapable of wondering anymore why such a vast and disturbing movement would need a couple of severely depressed high school kids in the middle of Nowhere, Colorado, to do its dirty work.

It was all moot anyway. Months later, it was revealed that the two boys belonged to no group or cult (neither satanist nor Goth nor neo-Nazi), were not abnormally fond of rock music, and hated everybody and everything equally. They were loners, complete outsiders at school and in the world. Their shooting spree was, at bottom, a suicide pact; they just figured they would take a few of their despised classmates with them when they went. The frenzy of ignorant psychobabble in the (boomer-dominated) media suggested less a society fearful *for* its youth than a society fearful *of* them. Smart young people exploit this frightened fascination: gangsta rap, for example, milked it for many millions of dollars' revenue.

A horror of youth violence also warped the media reaction to the "riots" that ended Woodstock '99, forever besmirching what had been perhaps the boomers' most cherished locus of hippie-rock nostalgia. Woodstock '99 was another example of hip capitalism foisting itself on its children. Young writers (such as nineteen-year-old Philip Guichard in *New York Press* and Gen-Xer David Samuels in *Harper's*) described a temporary, walled-in concentration camp created by predatory boomer entrepreneurs. Where those of us who were drawn to Woodstock in 1969 felt we were all part of a coherent "freek nation," a separate tribe as it were, the kids who came to Woodstock '99 came only to see the big-name acts and bared tits. Samuels spoke to a middle-aged assistant to the organizers, a veteran of the original Woodstock, about the differences:

> "We wanted to get out of Brooklyn," she says, when I ask her about the dreams of her youth. "We all did. We wanted to get out of the Catskills. To create our own world. It was going to be fun and funny. We would do away with racism, with classism, with all the gossipy, parental stuff that people thought was love. Everything was focused on expansion, even the drugs. It all had something to do with improvement, with improving yourself, improving the world." She leans back in her chair and sighs an imperious-old-Jewish-lady sigh. "Then somehow we gave birth to that," she says, gesturing out the window toward the trash-strewn campgrounds and the noise of the bands and the kids on the runway still beating on the trash cans. "And the thing that puzzles me is—how?"

I thought the young people were right to "riot." High-energy youth music had been inciting youths to riot for half a century. For a couple years in a row, the hiphop magazine *The Source* couldn't hold its annual gala awards ceremony without it degenerating into bloody melees of East Coast/West Coast, Crips/Bloods, winners/losers factions. People have actually died in the crush of crowds at Who and Pearl Jam concerts. And what was Altamont if not a rock concert riot in slow motion? The young people packed into Woodstock '99, burned by the sun, barraged by the music, and ripped off by rapacious vendors of $4 bottles of water, spent the weekend stoned, drunk, bored, and sullen, yet they waited until the very end, after the very last band had played, before indulging in their short fit of vandalism. The organizers and promoters had been robbing and mistreating them for three days and nights, and they struck back, inflicting financial damage on their tormentors. It was like a big stadium event, only worse—set on an airbase like a giant skillet—and it provoked a soccer-hooligan response. The nostalgic peace-and-love veneer was as thin and transparent as Body Shop soap scum.

Writing in *New York Press*, Gen-Xer Adam Heimlich took special umbrage at the notion, expressed by more than one smug boomer media pundit, that the difference between the two Woodstocks proved that the 1969 generation was inherently superior to the 1999 one. "Korn, Limp Bizkit *and* the Chili Peppers, but no cops inside?" he wrote. "What the hell did they expect? That the name of the festival guaranteed peace, maaan? Because a name is all Woodstock '99 and Woodstock had in common, long before the bonfires. . . . Why no reporter could recognize the resemblance Woodstock '99 bore to the end of rush week at State U. is beyond [me]. To claim what happened demonstrates how rock has changed, or how Xers are different from Boomers, is to insult the intelligence of anyone who understands white American youth." The first Woodstock, he pointed out, had gathered hippies and freeks; the second one, fratboys and meatheads. It wasn't as if fratboys and meatheads didn't exist in 1969; they just didn't go to Woodstock. (They were more likely to go to Vietnam.) Woodstock '99, however, was precisely the Fratboy Woodstock.

". . . If it was teen rebellion, it wouldn't wear a baseball cap and chant, 'Show! Your! Tits!'—that's mainstream U.S.A.," Heimlich argued. "Woodstock '99 could have featured actual, establishment-challenging rap and metal acts, but the promoters didn't want a fringe party (less money in that, as it requires good security—black kids and working-class whiteboys mustn't ever be allowed to get too rowdy). They wanted a jarhead party. They got one."

And let's remember that the peace-and-love generation was not above its own acts of vandalism from time to time. Shortly after I got home from Woodstock, I went to a nighttime "rock festival" staged at a racetrack in Bowie, Maryland, a semirural area midway between Baltimore and Washington, D.C. It was not a part of the world particularly conducive to a hippie rock love-fest; it was redneck, working-class, farmboy territory. The night I went to the festival the weather was blustery and damp. The bands played on a flatbed stage, and the audience sat in wooden folding chairs. As the bands played on and the night grew colder—I think the Mothers of Invention were playing—some longhairs near me, weary of the chill and no doubt fucked up on drugs, made a small pile of their chairs and patiently set them on fire. Other people near them added their own chairs, and pretty soon we had a decent bonfire going and were all warming our hands and watching our breath smoke in the damp air. It was simple, thoughtless vandalism, and I don't know that we would have stopped there if a squad of Maryland State Troopers hadn't suddenly descended, dousing the fire and dispersing us.

Who knows why we didn't revolt at Woodstock? It was chilly and damp there, too. I don't believe it was because we were morally superior to subsequent generations. According to Ellen Willis, one might even find our placid stoicism just a little bit disturbing. Maybe we were just in no condition to rebel. Maybe, as John Sinclair might say, it was the acid.

○

As I was working out some sections of this book in the pages of *New York Press* in 1999 and 2000, naturally we received emails and letters to the editor from readers opining what an idiot I was, how wrong I was about rock. This was not unexpected. Years ago I had learned that, next to a perceived insult to readers' ethnic identity, nothing stirs people up like a perceived insult to their *pop music* identity. I once wrote dismissively of Creedence Clearwater Revival's tub-thumping rhythms and received an ocean of hate mail that didn't recede for weeks; someone even took out a classified ad in the back of the paper to denounce me. Everyone who has written in any way critically about popular music is familiar with this phenomenon.

From the tone and the internal references, it seemed that the mail I received denouncing me for the ideas expressed in this book was mostly from defensive late-boomers, guys who had grown up on and identified with the 1970s rock I find so awful. These were guys who had spent their whole lives feeling under the historical thumb of '60s types like me, and they were sick of it. Who could blame them? If I were a '70s boomer I might well despise '60s boomers myself.

By far, the most thought-provoking responses I received from such '70s types did not exactly come "over the transom": they came from Bill Repsher, who was writing about music occasionally for *New York Press* and more regularly for an online zine called leisuresuit.net. Bill got into the habit of firing off an email response that kicked my butt every time I wrote about rock history, interviewed somebody like John Sinclair, complained about the Rock and Roll Hall of Fame. With his permission, I reproduce a few extracts here, because I find what he had to say challenging—and humorous.

Bill was born at the very tail of the boom, on June 18 (Paul McCartney's birthday, he points out), 1964. Getting into rock as an adolescent in a largely blue-collar eastern Pennsylvania area in the wasteland of the 1970s, he remembers that the first album he ever bought was Elton John's *Goodbye Yellow Brick Road*, "a mammoth two-record set I got at Woolworth's for EE price, $6.99, which was an arm and a leg back then . . . bought it with lawn-mowing and snow-shoveling money." The first single he can remember buying was Gilbert O'Sullivan's "Out of the Question," in the summer of 1974. He was also a fan of Electric Light Orchestra, the Raspberries—a lot of what us '60s guys considered '70s dreck. In their teen years, he and his working-class friends got into heavy metal. Punk rock, he says, completely passed them by. Punk rock was for arty college students, not guys who were going to graduate high school and go get a job at the warehouse or the lumber yard.

"As a 10-year-old, in '74, I was supposed to be out there buying the New York Dolls second album, and what, *Metal Machine Music* by Lou Reed? I was listening to pretty much what a 10-year-old in '74 would listen to," he recalls. "Speaking from a pop music sense, I'd have loved to have been born 10 years earlier and absorbing the Beatles, Stones, Dylan, etc. Shit, even the Monkees! I think the real deal comes into play in your late teens—where you either get with the program and start branching out, or, as with most people I know, you simply stop listening to new music and cling to whatever sounds you associate with your wacky and wild teenage years. I moved past that point when I was about 14—I think buying the *Kinks Kronikles* and that two-album Jimi Hendrix greatest hits set was the onset. And from that point forward, I'm like a feather on the breeze of pop, John.

"I'll tell you, John, one of the boons of the 70s was that people of your age, i.e., cool older siblings as compared to uncool parents, were always telling us how much 'our music' sucked. Sort of broke us in for the future, where it's become a financial and cultural necessity to scoff at everything that came before. When you were raised in the 70s, you were already well equipped with that sense of musical dislocation. People older than you in the 60s may have told you *your* music sucked, John, but chances are you thought they were a bunch of out-of-touch greasers who never got over Elvis. Most kids my age made mopey faces and said, 'Yeah, you're right.'"

For all that, Bill found my '60s rock attitudes very foolish:

"John, every time you write about rock, it's like the proverbial bunch of blind men feeling an elephant. Only you're that one sick fuck among the blind men who's felt elephants before, feels his way around to the elephant's penis, and spends the rest of the time stroking that massive penis, knowing full well what he's doing. While all the other blind men are giving different descriptions, you pick that one perverse part and know exactly what you're feeling....

"[Y]ou're attaching all this sacred bullshit to rock that isn't real— you're coming off like a little boy carrying on about his favorite baseball player, when his favorite baseball player is out getting his dick sucked and speeding on a handful of crank on his night off. I don't go for that 'sacred' vibe—rock music is as mummifiable as anything else wrongly incarcerated in a museum or hall of fame."

He disagreed with me less on the notion that rock is young people's music. In this regard, in fact, he could sound harsher than I have:

"I have a 'should have gone down in a plane crash' theory on many acts," he wrote. "Iggy goes down after *Raw Power*. Brian Wilson goes down after *Pet Sounds*. McCartney goes down after *Band on the Run*, although I won't argue with anyone who says side two of *Abbey Road*. Elvis goes off to the army and gets killed in an on-base accident in Stuttgart. Mark David Chapman hits New York a bit early and gets Lennon during the *Mind Games* sessions, just after he cuts the title track and before he finishes the rest of the album.

"There are damn few incidents where fate does its thing and knocks someone off near to or at the height of his powers. Sam Cooke. Otis Redding. Buddy Holly. And plenty of bands who broke up at the right time. The New York Dolls. The Sex Pistols. The Velvet Underground. The 'unlucky' hordes left behind do what they're conditioned to do: go on making money as performers. And you're right, a whole grisly culture has sprung up around baby boomers trying to deny that they're not cool anymore. I see it all the time with friends my age, too, trying to pretend they like rap, or whatever other load of crap is coming down the pike and being sold to kids who don't know any better, but know their parents don't like it, and that's all that matters. 'Cool' is a product to be sold to kids, and I'd hope most adults could give a shit and simply go on with the rest of their lives. My dad used to laugh at me for making fun of his big band records—he had the right attitude, and I got more than a few big band CDs in my collection."

Nevertheless, I could never get him to buy the second clause of my rock-as-youth-music thesis: that rock was also youth *rebellion* music, and that its co-optation by balding old men—whether onstage, in the audience, in the back office, or in print—was a sad thing.

"My question to you," he responded once, "is what's the ultimate point of teenage rebellion? It seems like a mirage to me, always has. Why? I think the ultimate teenage rebellion would be to kill yourself the night before your 20th birthday, wouldn't it, if the only issue was rejecting the values of adults. Only, kids seem to play at rejecting the values and don't really rebel against anything—all they have are lousy attitudes, which is fine and relatively harmless in the short run. They're not rebelling—they're whining, but often in ways that can be entertaining.

"I think the ultimate problem is boomer hubris—they can't stand the idea that this 'wild' generation, the one that ran around getting stoned and fucking in wheat fields, can't possibly be topped by anything that follows," he continued. "And, unfortunately, the idiots following you are sitting around pretending that everything they liked at the age of 16 is the coolest thing since Brando. It's this sick youth culture we've constructed in post-war America that started out with a bang and has turned into a pure money-making machine, the more slovenly and stupid the better, explaining the preponderance of wiggers ['90s white boys affecting hiphop styles] as the century came to a close. (I can't wait for wiggers to get older—should be interesting.) How do you handle a pop culture that over-emphasizes anything youthful? Ignore it? Pretend that your youthful chapter was the only thing that mattered and cling pathetically to the memory? Pay lip service to it and pretend you like the new stuff?

"Fuck all of the above! One thing I realized when I turned 30 a few years ago that I didn't know before then and wish I had: it's all open field running. Always has been and always will be. If you want to tie yourself down to a generation, be my guest, but you will go down with the ship. . . . You have to become a ghost of pop culture and float over the graveyards and maternity wards of cool. That's the ticket."

And in one of his most devastating and hard to refute critiques, he responded to my baleful ranting about the Rock and Roll Hall of Fame:

"No one asked me my advice on the Hall of Fame, either. I'd make it one room. Have a dummy made up to look like a skinny, acne-scarred kid sitting in a bedroom. There's a window in the bedroom, and it looks out on a street, where five attractive girls, the kind who would never look twice at a loser like that, are practicing cheerleader moves on a summer's afternoon. The only thing of note in the kid's room? An AM radio and a beat-up pawnstore acoustic guitar. That's rock 'n' roll, John, straight down to the heart: loneliness and the search for pussy. Eat my dick, Jann Wenner."

○

Which brings us back to Mike Doughty, with whom I began this book. Six years younger than Bill Repsher, Doughty's rock experiences began in the 1980s. By the turn of the century, Doughty had spent seven years earning a living in the record industry, and he liked to counter my romantic, '60s-guy theories about rock's lost opportunities with his insider's practical, hard-won knowledge of how the industry was actually run in the 1990s. That was the core of our differences: Whereas I thought about rock as culture, in his experience it was all business. He found all distinctions between rock and pop meaningless. He grew up and lived in the context of what John Seabrook has dubbed "Nobrow," the new all-embracing cultural marketplace in which all distinctions between highbrow and lowbrow, between art and commerce, between making art and marketing it, between the cult and the masses have become obsolete. Indeed, in the world of Nobrow, Seabrook argues, the very concept of culture has been degraded into nearly meaningless buzz. A survivor in this world, Doughty thought of me simply as a silly boomer pining for the good ol' hippie days—a charge, of course, I could fight only so far. Like all interested guys of his age cohort, Doughty was a very good rock historian, but that's all rock made before the 1980s was to him: history.

Doughty is an army brat, born in June 1970 in a U.S. Army hospital at Fort Knox. His family followed his father, a military historian, to Germany, Belgium, and, when Doughty was in the sixth grade, finally to West Point, where his father ran the history department. Doughty left home for college when he was sixteen and moved to New York City when he was eighteen. When I met him in 1991 he was twenty-one, studying at the New School and working as a doorman at the Knitting Factory, then next door to *New York Press*. He started writing music criticism for us. A couple of years later, he broke the news that his band, Soul Coughing was up for a major-label contract. We were encouraging but skeptical. Our little pal Doughty a rock star? It seemed unlikely. His music was too arty; he was too much the bespectacled poetry-writing music critic geek. We patted him on the back and told him to go for it, and we promised that when it all fell through he could come back home and be a music critic again.

In the end, both Doughty and the hardnoses at the *Press* turned out to be right. From its beginnings in 1993, Soul Coughing was a bigger success than even Doughty could have expected. Signed to a major label almost as soon as they were formed, they put out their first album, *Ruby Vroom*, in 1994 and instantly earned much critical respect and a devoted cult following. ("Dean" Christgau, Doughty hastens to inform me, wrote some nice things about them.) They toured extensively in the United States and Europe on major bills for much of the rest of the decade. Their second album, *Irresistible Bliss*, came out in 1996. By the end of the '90s, having put out a third LP, *El Oso*, in 1998, including their most obviously hit-potential single, "Circles," they still had that large and devoted cult following—and yet, that was all they had, and it wasn't enough. They had never quite turned the corner to really big hit records, a mass following, riches and fame. WEA, Soul Coughing's label, shipped 400,000 copies of *El Oso* to the stores. That's a lot of records. But it's not a gold record. (An album is certified gold when 650,000 copies are shipped to retail outlets.) And after seven successful years, the band felt, a gold record was not too much to expect. They were frustrated and restless. When they broke up in the spring of 2000, Doughty was back writing for *New York Press* again. The rock star thing hadn't fallen apart as quickly or as completely as we had originally and cruelly predicted—Doughty, now frequently touring as a solo act, was still a big draw, and there was major-label interest in where his career would turn next. When he stood at the mic center stage with the little acoustic guitar he had adopted for solo touring ease, adoring young women still pressed themselves to the lip of the stage and gawked and sighed and bopped their heads, very much the twenty-first-century version of bobby-soxers worshiping at the feet of the young Sinatra.

Only, Doughty in the year 2000 wasn't *quite* so young anymore. He turned thirty that summer, shortly after he and I had the following conversation.

"My first band was in 1983," he tells me. That would have been when he was thirteen. "It was somebody else's idea. Decided I should be the bass player. . . . [It was] a funky Jethro Tull band." Next he joined "a hardcore band called the Jagged Edge." He laughs. "We were not good. We decided we were punk. Oh yeah, we're punk." This was in affluent Putnam County in New York, up the Hudson from Manhattan. "Garrison, New York. A rich kids' town with punk rockers. Also, it was on the side of the river that the train was on, which was not insignificant, because they could get on the train, come down to New York City and go to the [all-ages punk and hardcore] matinees. Me and friends started coming down to the city, pretending that we lived here. 'Do you think people think we really live here? Do we look like real punks?' Later on I found out what 'actual' punks who live in New York do. It wasn't really that different, except that they didn't go to the train station at the end of the evening. And they could buy beer."

His next band was a funk metal band, Dada Dred. "We invented funk metal in a vacuum," he smiles—they were unaware that funk metal was already being played elsewhere. "I remember hearing the Chili Peppers for the first time— 'They took our sound, man!'"

When he moved to Manhattan in '91, "I went folk, because I had no choice. That's the thing about New York City. Where are you gonna get a rehearsal space?" We met around then and he started writing music criticism for *New York Press*. Through his job as a doorman at the Knitting Factory, the avantish jazz and rock club, he had a free place to rehearse and even record. "I just started asking people at random to be in bands with me." One of the results was the band Isosceles, a jam band that could throw as many as twenty people on stage at one time.

Soul Coughing's name came from a poem Doughty had written "about Neil Young throwing up on a bus." At first it was just a name. "What I'd do was, I'd book the gig at the Knitting Factory, then I'd go get the band." The other members of the band were several years older than Doughty. Drummer Yuval Gabay, a Moroccan from Israel, brought in upright bassist Sebastian Steinberg, "who was such a mercenary at the time. As bass players are wont to be, because there are no bass players. They're all guitar players and saxophone players." Keyboardist Mark Degliantoni came to a rehearsal with no keyboards, just a video camera for taping the music. Classically trained, he had never been in a band before. Pretty soon he was laying down richly textured samples over Gabay and Steinberg's churning rhythms.

Whereas many bands struggle for years—or forever—without attracting major-label interest, Soul Coughing was drawing A&R reps to its earliest gigs. "It was completely out of nowhere. We had Imago, Capitol, Atlantic, Columbia. A guy from Blue Note showed up. He actually had a contract, brought it backstage." Why did they all come? "I have no idea," Doughty responds. Then he adds that the early 1990s, the "alternative" years, was "a very weird time" in the music industry. "Nirvana had hit. Everyone was thinking, 'Anything can happen.' It was the first time in fifteen years in the record business when *anything* could get big—you know, when it wasn't just a matter of having a single. All the formats were changing."

Still, Soul Coughing didn't immediately strike one as a sure-fire hit factory. They made cool, brainy, beatnik jazz-funk over which Doughty laconically rapped obscure, druggy lyrics. At its most lively it tended to turn ingeniously syncopated and polyrythmic in ways not always conducive to white-folk dancing. To an out-of-touch fortysomething like me, it was hard to picture this complex sound drawing great flocks of young people.

Doughty is willing to concede that the "white rapper" novelty factor might have helped sell the band to the label representatives. Ever since the Beastie Boys had hit in the mid-'80s, the industry had had a perennial hunger for the next big white rap group or artist. "We were on a bill once with Everlast and

Vanilla Ice," he laughs. "It was so great. I was just like, if in 1991 I'd ever thought, 'Someday Everlast is going to go on before you, and Vanilla Ice is going to go on after you . . .'"

I show my age when I press Doughty to categorize Soul Coughing for me—was it a white hiphop group? Jazz-funk? Alternative rock? Doughty just shrugs. "It's all the same, *papi*," he smiles. "It's all pop music." I, of course, tell him he's wrong, and we proceed to discuss the Carducci principle. When I insist that he choose a genre, he replies, "Then it's rock. It's a live band, and everybody in the band decided to make music based on the rock they were listening to. That makes us a rock band." But he then cites hiphop's heavy influence on his music and tastes. Much of what he liked about hiphop—its willful crossing and mixing of genres, its willingness to borrow or steal from any type of cultural resource whatsoever, its blithe disregard for musical "rules"—showed up, in some form, in Soul Coughing's music, and that of many other white groups in the 1990s.

"We had to make a *business decision* to be a rock band," he explains. What he means is that when Soul Coughing started out in the early 1990s, and indeed into the late-'90s, "there was no touring market for hiphop. Rock promoters wouldn't touch it. If we had come out as a hiphop band, we wouldn't have gotten the bookings." It would make a difference, I ask, simply what kind of music the band *said* it made? "Yes. I don't think at any point we actually sat down and said, 'Okay, we are not a hiphop band.' But we did explicitly say, 'Okay, we are going into the rock world,'" which meant playing in rock clubs, touring with rock bands (everyone from Dave Matthews to Cop Shoot Cop to Sunny Day Real Estate to the Violent Femmes), getting on the bill at the big rock festivals (Lollapalooza, the H.O.R.D.E. tour), and seeking exposure on rock radio.

When asked if rock 'n' roll is dead, Doughty the turn-of-the-century rock star can hardly summon a display of giving a damn. "See, when I hear 'rock 'n' roll,' I think '50s music. Is rock 'n' roll dead? Nah. Because the bulk of musicians who are playing out there in the year 2000 are still rock-identified and started playing rock as kids back when the only people saying rock was dead were the Sex Pistols."

But then what does he think of the James Miller thesis, that by the end of the 1970s rock was a fully formed art, and that kids playing rock at the turn of the century were, in effect, speaking a dead musical language? "Well, I'm not so sure that the majority of rock bands were really stretching the language in 1968 any more than they are today," Doughty says. In fact, he argues, if you take the historical long view, everybody has been playing "the same chords since the field hollers, and the sea shanties, and the Irish jigs. You know, 1-4-5 [the stereotypical blues-rock-pop chord progression] doesn't change."

However, he goes on, there is one sense in which you could say rock is dead, and that is "in the sense that no one *believes* there is rock anymore. In the sense that there was a moment when rock came into existence and was 'a force for social change'"; and that moment—that boomer definition of rock—clearly passed a long time ago. On that, we can agree.

Throughout the late 1990s one heard that rock was over, that electronica and raves and hiphop were "the new rock." If rock didn't die, what happened?

On the one hand, Doughty says, rock didn't die, "It went away. But it only went away in the sense that the media wasn't paying attention to it. And that's totally different from what's selling records and what people are actually listening to." At the turn of the century, rock still had a large and enthusiastic audience. As hard as MTV pushed rap and pop throughout the '90s, the kids calling into the station's request shows were often begging to see the latest videos from hard rock and heavy metal bands. The three youngest people contributing to *New York Press* in the spring of 2000—Philip Guichard, Ned Vizzini, and J. T. "Terminator" LeRoy—were nineteen or twenty, technically on the cusp of Generation X and the millennials. Guichard seemed truly "post-rock" in his musical tastes, totally into rave culture and dance clubs. But Vizzini was playing bass in a Rage-like rap-metal band, and Terminator was totally into hard rock. That's three white males, a tiny sample, but young white males were always rock's core audience. Most of the twentysomethings around the *New York Press* offices were also pretty heavily, and in some cases exclusively, into rock. Twenty-first-century rock bands were in heavy rotation on the office boomboxes. Granted, maybe all rock in the twenty-first century has to wear irony quotes—it's not rock, it's "rock—that is, a conscious recreation." Still, it's what they were listening to and talking about.

On the other hand, Doughty counters, if rock didn't exactly die in the 1990s, it certainly became an endangered species. "When you're talking about rock you're talking about guitar bands as dance bands. You will actually be able to say rock is dead when everyone is going out and listening to DJs playing records or guys playing sequencers, and there's no live music anymore." And the way things were heading at the turn of the century, that day might not be so very far into the future, he predicts. "It's just more efficient. It's cheaper to have a guy with a bunch of records [than an entire band]. It's cheaper to have a guy who just brings a little hard drive to plug in and play a little sequencer. Also, the nature of digital technology is such that you can have at your disposal the whole history of recorded music. It's become more and more feasible for smart folk to listen to the old stuff. . . ."

So live music will become obsolete?

"Yeah, I think so. Gatherings of kids will not become obsolete," but they won't need live musicians to entertain them, he suggests. He tells me of a DJ friend who, when he goes off to a gig, flies there by himself, carrying all his equipment in a case or two; sets up and works the gig; collects his fee; and flies home to a big, beautiful house in L.A. "He probably gets paid less per gig than my band does, but my band puts nine people on the road, plus the cost of the bus and the hotels. Musicians are learning to become DJs, and they're going to earn more money. I personally am doing a folk thing, because I can make more money."

But is a DJ really a substitute for a live band? Isn't the DJ electronica rave culture really a substitute not for rock, but for disco? There's something visceral about being in the same room with a live drummer, seeing live musicians onstage, that is a wholly different experience from the electronic dance club scene. Not more valid, just different. I think that explains why, despite all the predictions of its death, rock seemed to be making yet another comeback at the turn of the century.

I ask Doughty what he, at thirty, thinks of my contention that rock is music best played by young people for young people. For obvious reasons, he doesn't completely agree, though he admits that most rock is certainly aimed at and consumed by people twenty-five and under. By the time you hit twenty-five, he posits, you begin to hunger for something a little different in your musical diet, and rock begins to sound too familiar, limited, and repetitive. You have to abandon rock. "That nobody knows how to reach this listener is so bizarre," he muses. "No one in the record industry knows how to reach the twenty-eight-year-old."

But maybe they shouldn't, I respond. Maybe by the time you're twenty-eight—

"—You don't want to listen to good music?" he cuts me off.

But you can't keep repeating the rush, I insist. You can't keep pretending rock is new and exciting and wonderful into your forties and fifties (unless you're a rock star or critic, and paid for your arrested development).

"But Muddy Waters was making great records in his forties," Doughty argues. "Why is that a whole other case?"

Because maybe rock 'n' roll is music meant to stimulate things you can feel only before the age of twenty-five, whereas Muddy Waters's blues is music for adults, like jazz, like classical. Most musicians lose their energy for rock in their forties, or more likely their thirties, whereas blues guys, up to a point, only get better as they age.

"I can't refute that," Doughty concedes. "However, genre is just what you know. Everybody puts everything they like into the music they make. So the musical language of the guy who's going to be the Muddy Waters of tomorrow is rock."

He remembers seeing the Rolling Stones one time, on the *Steel Wheels* stadium tour in 1990, and watching Jagger race back and forth across the vast stage "for no reason that I could see, other than to say, 'Look at me! I can still run!' And yet he sold out Shea Stadium, what, eight nights in a row? There's *nothing* to tell this guy he should stop. Yours is a quintessentially baby boomer argument: *I don't like this. This displeases me. Take it away. This is no good anymore.*"

But it's patently not any good anymore, I respond. Doesn't he think rock should have some purpose in the world?

"I don't think so. It's entertainment. I'm not romantic about it at all."

It shouldn't serve some larger purpose?

"Fuck no! *No*," he laughs at me.

My generation believed it did.

"Yeah, when you were twenty!" he scoffs, still laughing. "When I was twenty, I also believed that the reason I loved records was that they connected me to a higher purpose, that there was a genuine intellectual purpose to it. And of course, as when you get down to all things academic and intellectual, you find it's basically all bullshit. It's pleasure. It's entertainment."

Then why does he do it?

"It's what I do for a living," he replies. "And there's nothing wrong with that. Because I still like it when I do it. Because I still have something I'm chasing after."

○

It was only later that I decided I heard a contradiction—and maybe a sign of hope—in that last sentence.

I don't know. Who's right? Maybe Bill Repsher and Doughty. Maybe rock is/was just a branch of pop, just entertainment, just a business, and any romantic notions that it might serve some larger purpose were always ridiculous. Certainly we '60s types are to blame for having sustained a world in which the following generations could come by this cynicism so handily. From the moment we took over the media, the music and entertainment industries, the marketing of fashions and ideas, we were selling rebellion and coolness and anti-authoritarian ideals to the mainstream and devaluing them in the eyes of intelligent younger people. We maintained a commercial culture that co-opted anti-establishmentarian ideas so thoroughly that the few apparently sincere, though often insufferably self-righteous, voices of protest—such as Fugazi or Ani Difranco—had to opt entirely out of the system, while those voices of protest who operated within and benefited from the system—Rage Against the Machine, the entire Ice-T generation of rappers—were inevitably compromised. You simply can't accept that Grammy and fight the power at the same time. This is not a new condition of the marketplace—the young Jefferson Airplane helped to sell "hip" jeans to the mainstream. But were we not the generation that was going to change such conditions rather than master the techniques for maintaining them?

Is it silly for a man approaching fifty to be worrying about all this at such a late date? Yes, I suppose it is. It's the boomer in me.

Or maybe Ellen Willis and Tuli Kupferberg are right. Maybe we did make a revolution—just not the one we had talked ourselves into believing we would make. Ours was a cultural revolution—quiet, nonviolent, slow-motion, yielding no abrupt or sweeping changes to the economic or political order, but creating profound adjustments in morals, values, and attitudes. It incorporated the environmental movement, the women's movement, the gay liberation movement, and the sexual revolution, affecting not only attitudes but actual civil rights and personal opportunities.

At the heart of this transformation stood the civil rights movement itself. White people have always taken too much credit for their role in that, as they generally do for any improvement in American race relations. To the extent that race relations have improved, credit for racial tolerance belongs mainly to the consciousness-raising efforts of the original civil rights and Black Power movements, the achievements of courageous, visionary, and occasionally obstreperous black people.

Premiere among the boomers' claims to have caused great political change is that our marching and draft-resisting and protest-singing "ended the war in Vietnam." This is, of course, a gross overstatement. A man named Ho Chi Minh and his army ended the war in Vietnam, by winning it. We did a bit to help by distracting our leaders.

But what lasting effect did this antiwar activism of our youth have on our skepticism toward warmongering in later years? Very little, it seems to me. Americans, boomers included, overwhelmingly supported President Bush's Gulf War; it caused his Gallup approval rating to shoot to a stunning 89 percent. Clinton's approval rating also peaked, at 78 percent, when he made his own airborne, remote-control war on Iraq—although Americans were roughly equally divided on the morally and politically more complex air war in Kosovo. It may be that my generation's youthful resistance to the Vietnam War was a unique "attack of conscience," stemming perhaps, as Danny Fields believes, from selfish motives of self-preservation rather than anything more noble.

It strikes me that many of our "greatest achievements" have been personal and perhaps selfish. Forget the Me Decade—maybe we were the Me Generation. In *our* declaration of independence, the pursuit of happiness has pride of place. If we're women, we can get better and more fulfilling jobs than our mothers ever could, and we can have sex and have abortions. If we're gay, we can be so more openly and freely than any previous generation. We eat better than our parents did, work smarter, live longer. We are healthier and more active, and we have more time and money to spend in the pursuit of fun. We want to keep on rockin'. We made the personal political. We did not invent the computer, but we did invent the personal computer.

We've carried our '60s and '70s notions of personal enrichment and fulfill-ment through our lives. For us, it was never enough just to work, eat, sleep, pro-create, and die. We wanted life to have meaning, however naive that seems to the young people we've helped turn into skeptics. We wanted our lives to have a purpose, and the purpose, once, was to change the world.

That we have not fulfilled the promises we made to ourselves in our youth is obvious, even to be expected. But is what we have accomplished enough? It's certainly not the revolution we started out to make. Remember that cynical Ten Years After lyric? Love to change the world, pal, but I'll leave it up to you. Was that more like us all along?

## Rock in New York

### The Sounds and the Stories

"Rock in New York" was Giorgio Gomelsky's idea. One gloomy, snow-laden late afternoon in February 2000, George Tabb and I were sitting in the small kitchen in Giorgio's third-floor apartment over the Green Door. We were in the midst of the series of interviews that yielded Giorgio's story in Chapter 2 (and much more). A guitarist with a big amp and a lot of sustain was practicing old-fashioned Hendrix-like runs down in the ground-floor hall; the fluid wails and seagull cries rose up through Giorgio's linoleum-covered floor as if he had the very ghost of '60s rock chained up down there. We had brought a bottle of Chianti and Giorgio had made us a delicious Italian-style bean soup. ("You can eat a plate of soup, can't you?" he had called down to us as we trudged up the dark and narrow stairs to his aerie.)

Giorgio was in a mood for hatching schemes. This was not unusual, George later informed me. He had known Giorgio for maybe twenty years by then, and Giorgio apparently always had ideas for projects, some more grand than others. One project Giorgio tried to talk us into that day was to help him organize a larger version of the mass mooning he had been involved in half a century earlier in Zurich. He wanted us to assemble at a secret time and location—preferably fashionable fifth Avenue, in the midst of a busy shopping day—2000 disaffected New Yorkers who, when a prearranged signal was given, would all simultaneously drop their pants and bend over. There would be video documentation, of course. We might call it *2000 Asses in the Air*. The owner of each of those asses would be briefly interviewed on camera, each explaining his or her own motivation.

A great idea, but George and I felt it was a little beyond our time and ability to orchestrate. But, looking back, it couldn't have been more of an organizational nightmare than Giorgio's next scheme, "Rock in New York." He was inspired both by the interviews we had been doing with him and by interviews he himself had been videotaping with various rock figures for public-access cable, with an eye toward eventually putting them online. (He taped a fascinating rant by John Sinclair that inspired me to go to New Orleans and seek him out myself.) Giorgio's idea was a kind of casual symposium to which we would invite a large number of rock figures, specifically from New York, and gather some *Please Kill Me*–style oral history from them—only we would do it live, in front of an audience, as well as videotaping it. Informally, we would simply goad them to tell "war stories" about making rock music in New York City. We would try to steer it away from nostalgia, toward authentic oral history. Giorgio's notion was that there was still plenty of useful material to be mined, not just from the performers, but from the producers, managers, club owners, roadies, and such, who are not often asked for interviews. My contribution was to suggest that instead of interviewing just old-timers, we should aim for a cross-generational spread, including kids just starting to play in the city's rock clubs at that point. George added the idea that there should be music, with a lot of New York bands and musicians playing short sets. Finally, we agreed it should be a benefit for charity. We spent the next three months pulling it together, cajoling New York rock celebrities into participating, juggling their schedules and massaging their egos; collecting background information, photos, and videotape to give the event an authentic and accurate historical context; designing ads and publicity; renting tables and chairs and amplifiers and stage dressing. *New York Press* sponsored it, and Bowery Ballroom, an excellent rock hall, agreed to host it.

The event went off on Sunday, May 7, 2000, pretty much according to plan. There were a few flaring tempers and walk-offs, and one older rock figure with stage jitters who got falling-down drunk before he was due to go on and had to be eased out a back door. MTV's Kurt Loder, who was going to help MC the event, was a late cancellation. Then again, Joey Ramone, who we feared would not show up, came and lurked in the shadows. We started in the middle of the afternoon and ended after midnight with a drunken jam to the tune of "Louie, Louie." Along the way, the event touched on over forty years of rock 'n' roll in New York City, from doo-wop through the Fugs to Blue Öyster Cult, Max's Kansas City, CBGB, the New York Dolls, the Ramones, Sonic Youth, and Soul Coughing to the teenagers Marianne Nowottny and the New Mexikans. Danny

Fields and Jim Fouratt, both long-time New York rock figures, MCed the bulk of the stories session. After the stories, there were performances by Nowottny, the New Mexikans, the Brain Surgeons, the Rattlers, Bebe Buell, Furious George, M. Doughty, Starr, Noel Ford & the Fanatics, and special guest Ronnie Spector, whose six-song set went from the Ronette's "Baby I Love You" to Johnny Thunders' "You Can't Put Your Arms Around a Memory." (A doo-wop quartet and Tuli Kupferberg had incorporated brief performances into the storytelling part of the evening.)

Yes, I did feel that some of these people were too old to be up onstage rocking, but the event being a team effort, I didn't press it. A few who did play, not to be named here, more or less proved my point. But Tuli and Ronnie Spector were great. There are exceptions to every rule.

Here are some brief excerpts from some of the stories that were told that evening. They just skim the surface.

○

**Tuli Kupferberg:** The Fugs "startled" in 1964. I was a poet monkey—I was a poet *manqué,* living on East Tenth Street between B and C. We poets would all read at Le Metro cafe, an early, *cheap* coffeehouse on Second Avenue just north of St. Marks Place. We spelled that Marx. Actually the proprietors made their money as a bookie joint, and all the faux antique chairs and tables were for sale. So this coffeehouse became the place, and any poet of any renown who came to New York would read there . . . Ginsy, Burroughs, Corso, et al.—especially Al—would read there often. Among the lesser luminaries were myself and Ed Sanders. . . .

After reading, we would all retire to a local Polish bar in the cellar of the Dom on St. Marks Place, and the fat-ass poets would drink beer and attempt to dance to the jukebox tunes of the early Beatles and the Rolling Stones. One night Ed Sanders said to me, "We poets can do better than these dimwits. Let's start our own rock and roll band." I loved that idea, and I picked the name Fugs from Norman Mailer's *The Naked and the Dead.* . . .

. . . Our first gig was in Ed Sanders' Peace Eye Bookstore, a former kosher butcher—the kosher sign was still in the window—at 383 East Tenth Street. In the store Ed sold beatnik poet pamphlets and other esoterica, like a set—and this was sorta unique—each in its own glassine envelope, of pubic hairs of the poets. . . . Our first concert was held in the store in 1964. . . . We next played a few gigs in Diane DiPrima's repertory theater in the Ukrainian Communist meeting hall—you remember that hall? remember Ukrainian Communists?—on East Seventh Street. . . .

[W]e played Izzy Young's Folklore Center on Sixth Avenue near Bleecker. Izzy loved to boast that he hosted Bobby Dylan's first New York concert. We then moved into weekends at Jonas Mekas' Cinematheque at St. Marks near Third Avenue. We were an instant hit there. The whole East Side hippie community attended. They came up alongside the stage to sing along, to laugh, to scream, to break furniture, and they even helped to write some of our early songs.

And the rest is a mystery—no, a history. And the rest is a mysterical history . . . a hysterical mystery.

Now I'd like to sing a song from that period. . . .

[He sang "Doin' All Right," to raucous cheers.]

○

**David Johansen:** . . . I went straight from being a really terrible student in high school to being in the New York Dolls. We had a great time. It's not that much different than what people do in a frat house. Except in drag. . . .

[The Dolls] had kind of like—this sounds really sick—we had kind of a blessed existence. We kinda got together and rehearsed for a couple of days. We were the biggest thing in town two days later. After that whole thing transpired, *that's* when I started paying my dues. What I would do is get in a van with about six guys and travel back and forth across the country, opening for heavy-metal acts in hockey rinks . . . kind of like officiating at Hitler Youth rallies.

When I was home I used to hang out at Tramps, 'cause I lived around the corner. People would do residencies there. Charles Brown would play for a month, Big Joe Turner would play for a month, Big Maybelle would play for a month. I used to hang out there and read the paper to Big Maybelle and go to the track with Charles Brown. It was great.

[Tramps] was open on Monday, but there was nobody singing on Monday. I thought it would be a good idea to do a show for Mondays, which was the Buster [Poindexter] thing. So we started out with like three guys and it got really hot. I started working there two or three nights a week. I was making as much as I [had been] schlepping, and I was actually able to stay home and get a life—if that's what you call this. . . .

When I was a kid, in the '60s, when I was you know fourteen, fifteen, Bleecker Street and MacDougal Street were really rocking. The Night Owl and the Cafe Au Go Go, you could see really great acts. Like you would see Paul Butterfield *and* Muddy Waters for three dollars. . . . You could see three great acts for three dollars, totally diverse acts, it wasn't so homogenized as it is today. And then when we came around, there was really no place to play. All the places were boarded up. I think there was some situation, the cabaret laws or something, some kind of fascist dictum had come down and a lot of the places had closed.

So we kind of just fell into the Mercer Arts Center. Eric Emerson had a band called the Magic Tramps, and he said to me one day, "You know I'm playing at this place, the Mercer Arts Center. Do you want to open for us?" And, I was like, "Yeah." We would play anywhere, 'cause we didn't have anyplace to go, really. So we went and played for him, and then people liked us a lot. The guy who owned the place, or ran the place, his name was Al Lewis, he was like an old-fashioned showbiz guy with a bowtie and his hair parted in the middle, like an old-fashioned agent kind of a guy. And he was like, "Oh play again, play again," after Eric played. So we played again and then they offered us a night of our own every week in the Oscar Wilde Room. So finally we had a place to vent, which was good, and all these people started coming to the show who had seen each other on St. Marks Place but hadn't really had a situation to get together in. And this kind of brought this whole scene, an instant scene, together. Because so many people were looking for some kind of outlet for their rock 'n' roll ideas, and we were very fortunate to be in the center of that at the time.

○

**Deborah Frost (Brain Surgeons):** I was in this band, Flaming Youth. I had answered an ad in the *Village Voice*, because at that time I had written plays—I was very precocious, I couldn't wait to get out of Westchester. So at sixteen I had written a play for Joseph Papp, who said, "You're the voice of your generation." And I said, "Voice of my generation! What do I do now?" I freaked out and ran out of the Public Theater. It was also because I had to work with grown-ups there and I didn't know how to deal with that. So I did the next best thing. I wanted to be in a band like the Rolling Stones, but I really wanted to do it with girls. . . . Nothing really worked out until I got into this band, Flaming Youth. They took me to this apartment on East Tenth Street. . . . It turns out that this guitar player, Denise Mercedes . . . was involved with Peter Orlovsky, and they said, "Here's your bed," which was usually Allen Ginsberg's bed. . . . He wasn't always there, but they gave me his bed. There was this Buddhist shrine. I said, "Why does this Jewish person have a Buddhist shrine?" I knew I'd come a long way from Scarsdale. . . .

○

**Danny Fields:** [I went to a Beatles convention] a few weeks ago to sell my book on Linda McCartney, and it was 3,000 Beatle fans. The women were okay—they kissed the pictures of Paul McCartney and George, that's okay. But any male who's a Beatles fan—if he's young, it's like arrested development, and if he's old, he's just, by definition, so pathetic that it makes the Star Trek people look like . . . Nirvana. These people were loathsome. They all had bodies by Homer Simpson and hairdos by Meathead. They actually wore Beatles things, Beatles buttons and Beatles beanies. They stood around a lobby singing fucking "Rocky Raccoon" and "Strawberry Fields" all day—songs that sucked when they first came out, and they suck even more now. You know, it's like music for grandparents. And they had these like sixty-year-old losers, with their thirty-five-year-old loser children all dressed up in Beatles, and their little *babies* already—like *hostages* to this lapse in taste. I mean, I liked [the Beatles] when they first came out. They had long hair and I could throw that back at my father and say, "Look, these people are so famous, on the cover of *Life*. They have long hair—how can you yell at me?" *Rubber Soul* was sweet. I liked *Rubber Soul*. But after that—ho hum.

**Jim Fouratt (Hurrah's, Danceteria):** I grew up in Rhode Island, working-class family, precocious, only child, and I used to listen, under my pillow when I was seven years old, to Alan Freed and the Hound Dog. I didn't know at that age who they were, what they were, one guy came from Buffalo, and they were playing what was called rock 'n' roll, which was sort of a mixture of black rhythm-and-blues music and early . . . Bill Haley and the Comets, Bill Doggett, the Del-Vikings, you know, those kind of songs. A little tiny kid, and I'd listen under my pillow when I was supposed to be asleep. Why I did that I don't know. It took me to another world. . . .

[to Danny Fields] Do you remember the Dom?

**DF:** Yeah, I remember the Dom when Andy Warhol moved the Velvet Underground into the Dom, around '66 or '67. It was a show called the Exploding Plastic Inevitable. Don't ask. . . . The Velvet Underground were trying to play their wonderful music on the stage at the Dom and [filmmaker Barbara Ruben] had a wonderful idea to run around with a film projector and cast polka dots on them. . . . It was not a visual aid, it was a visual detriment to their music. I'm sorry if Barbara has a lot of fans here, and we loved her very much . . .

**JF:** Remember the night?

**DF:** What?

**JF:** The night that we all went to see—

**DF:** I don't remember any night in particular.

**JF:** Well let me refresh your memory. We all went down to the Dom one night, and you were with Niko, to see this new young singer. And we all walked down into the downstairs of the Dom—which became the Electric Circus later and was totally destroyed. It was an old Polish or something kind of bar on St. Marks Place. Anyway, the whole Warhol group went down to see this young artist, and Niko said to Danny, "*Look* at him." And it was a young—

**DF:** —Jackson Browne, at the age of sixteen. . . . Jackson and Niko quickly became lovers, and he accompanied her and she sang his song on her first album. He was sixteen. He was the most beautiful little thing. . . .

**JF:** David [Johansen] didn't talk about his job at Max's Kansas City.

**DF:** He was one of the very distinguished busboys there. We called them Phoebes, because *All About Eve* ends with Eve herself—who has usurped a position high in the Broadway theater—being attacked by a younger generation of climber called Phoebe. So we called the bus boys Phoebes. . . . And there were the waitresses, who were very beautiful and leggy, and they wore black and they all married rich people.

**JF:** And there was [owner] Mickey Ruskin, and there was the back room. Why don't you describe what it was like to walk into the back room of the only place in the world that mattered at that time.

**DF:** Well, it was a real restaurant in the front. In the back room, there was no doorkeeper, but there was a distinct vibration of you belong here or you don't. In fact, Patti Smith and Robert Mapplethorpe both told the story of the two of them cowering in the doorway of the back room: "Oh look at all these incredibly trendy people, there's Andy Warhol and Janis Joplin . . ." *We* were saying, 'Who are those adorable people? Is it a boy and a girl? Are they two girls? Are they two boys? What are they? Why don't they come in and sleep with all of us?" So we sat there staring at them, and they stood there trembling about us, and finally I just said, "Sit down." And that was the invention of Robert Mapplethorpe and Patti Smith. . . . And I'm not name dropping, they'll verify this—well, she will. He's not in a position to do very much. . . .

Steak was $2.95. Coffee was free, you could keep taking it yourself. You would run up—Mickey was so wonderful, you would just sign the check "Fatty Arbuckle," "Donald Duck," whatever, it didn't matter. As long as you signed the check, they would take it away. We thought we had big tabs. We had tabs three or four thousand dollars. . . . But the heterosexual abstract-expressionist alcoholic artists at the bar, like Frosty Meyers, had checks of $60,000! For alcohol! In 1968. I mean, how do you *do* this? The drinks were 95 cents! They had 60,000 drinks there! And Mickey would just let it flow. Until he went out of business.

**JF:** Let's talk a little bit about how live music came into Max's Kansas City under Mickey Ruskin.

**DF:** This is not my favorite thing that ever happened there, because it suddenly became not exclusive—because you had the kind of people who want to hear rock 'n' roll, and they were not the kind of people that you wanted to sit with or drink with or . . . sleep with, maybe.

**JF:** They didn't get into the back room, Danny. They went upstairs.

**DF:** I know. . . . It was just dark and it was very wonderful and it was a place to play. Peter Crowley is here, and he booked it, and he was very creative and imaginative, and wonderful people were there. But originally, it was just a discotheque upstairs. There was no live music. Jane County, formerly Wayne County, was the DJ. Every night closed with "Gimme Shelter." That was the last dance. You'd go upstairs and dance, and then you'd go back downstairs and you didn't have to see anybody who'd lined up on the street to hear Bruce Springsteen or something like that—coming to play at Max's Kansas City! It was a revolting turn of events!

**JF:** Young boys from New Jersey—

**DF:** Aerosmith—

**JF:** Well, Steven Tyler fit in the back room. I don't think Bruce ever got down there, did he?

**DF:** Please. What would he do? Who would he talk to? Who would talk to him? No, no . . . He was like the antithesis of everything we were. . . .

**JF:** Do you remember [the club] Salvation?

**DF:** One Sheridan Square.

**JF:** . . . Which later on became where Charles Ludlum did his theater company. . . . They tried to sort of be [Steve Paul's midtown club] The Scene meets Max's in this tiny club. Jimi Hendrix used to hang out there.

**DF:** . . . It was okay. It was not memorable, but I remember that much about it.

**JF:** But the owner that ran that club, Bradley—

**DF:** —Bradley Pierce, who invented Ondine's, which was a club on East Fifty-Ninth Street. His idea was to bring Whiskey-a-Go-Go, Sunset Strip bands to New York. So he brought Buffalo Springfield and the Doors there in '66. That was their New York debut.

**JF:** . . . This is before the Doors were famous. And we all went up to see them, you remember?

**DF:** Yes, because all the girls came running down to Max's screaming that there's a gorgeous lead singer at Ondine's and you have go see him, so we all went up there. . . .

○

**Peter Crowley (Mother's, Max's Kansas City):** The Fast were one of the first bands that came over [from England] and played Mother's, because they owned a PA, and none of the big headliners [here] owned a PA. Television, the Ramones, the Heartbreakers, they didn't own anything. I mean they barely had clothes on their backs. And so the Fast, and I think Neon Leon and a couple of others of those bands, owned PAs, so they got to always be the opening acts.

○

**Hilly Kristal (CBGB):** Actually what had happened, that I recollect, I think I was putting up the sign, the awning or something, and I think Tom [Verlaine] and Richard Hell were walking by—I think I was on a ladder—and they asked what I was doing, and I said I was starting this club and this and that. . . . So I think two, three weeks later, Terry Ork came by . . . and he said, "Well, you're closed Sundays. Can I put in a rock band Sundays?" So that's what started. He managed Television, and he just wanted a place for them to play. . . . Max's wasn't open at that time, that place [the Mercer] literally fell down, there was nothing. I think there was a place in Queens . . . and there was a place on Fourth Street that was a transvestite place that was open a couple of days a week. . . . So I said okay, I'll try it, and they put Television in. I think we charged one dollar. . . . I thought they were horrible. Nobody came. I was used to hearing the best jazz, you know, and at that point they didn't play that well. The sound system—we didn't have the sound system we got a couple years later, so it was not wonderful sound for loud music. For softer music, okay. But . . . at first, they didn't have it together. They were experimenting, they were fooling around. They could only play in their lofts. So I said never again. . . . Because nobody came, hardly anybody, and it was sad.

[Ork] said, "I have this band from Queens and they have a following." So we got the Ramones. So the Ramones and Television played. The Ramones were worse! It was awful, awful! They'd start, they'd stop, they'd start, they'd stop. Their gear broke down, they'd yell at each other. . . . But you know, that was at the beginning. . . . As they went on, they certainly got better and better.

You need a place to play. You can't just practice. You have to play. It was a growing thing. It was playing and playing in front of people. That was very important.

○

**Lee Ranaldo (Sonic Youth):** When I moved to New York, and a lot of other people moved to New York, there were a lot of people moving here as artists of one sort or another, writers, people involved in the theater, painters and musicians. It was a very interesting time, because there was a lot of cross-talk between these people, there was a sense of community, where you weren't an "artist" or a "writer" or a "musician." Everybody was here trying to do creative activities, and there were a lot of people trying different things....

JF: Why had it changed? In the '50s and the early '60s the abstract expressionist movement had been consumers of jazz, and some of them actually made jazz, but there was this popular culture which they didn't participate in, and rock 'n' roll had become a popular culture.

LR: Well, it certainly did, and in the wake of the Beatles and the British Invasion and Dylan—I mean, Dylan, a crucial element of rock music in New York in a certain regard. People just came here. It was a much more freewheeling time, in a sense.... I mean, all of the people involved in the music of that time, the New Wave bands of the late '70s and early '80s—Blondie and Talking Heads, Television, Richard Hell—they all came here to do different things.... Tom Verlaine and Richard Hell came to be writers.... But music had a lot of access, and had a certain sort of fun quotient, that some of these other activities didn't....

When I moved here, and other people that are sort of [Sonic Youth's] peers, people that graduated college in the last half of the '70s or early '80s, the New Wave scene was really big, bands like Television at CBGBs and the Voidoids, and all that stuff was completely incredible. It was taking this music that had gotten overblown and involved with the spectacle of arena rock and bringing it back down to what were the roots of rock 'n' roll.... A lot of people at the end of the '70s were disinterested in that [arena rock] music, because it wasn't really very personalized anymore, it was a very large spectacle thing....

○

**Bebe Buell:** . . . One time my girlfriend Liz Derringer and I were tripping on mescaline that Danny [Fields] gave us. . . . Liz was married to guitar hero Rick Derringer at the time. [Rick and Todd Rundgren, Bebe's boyfriend at the time] went off to the other room, to do whatever geniuses do when they're peaking. So Liz and I went straight into the bathroom to do our little beauty rituals, and we wanted to try this new electric razor that Rick had gotten. It was supposed to be the state of the art, the newest thing, hottest razor on earth, so we wanted to try it. We were gonna get artistic.

**JF:** Where?

**BB:** You know, all over. So Liz wanted to clean the razor. She dumps out the whiskers and they're albino! Johnny Winter had used the razor. We're tripping and we're looking at the whiskers and going, "God, that looks just like cocaine!" So we took it, we wrapped it in tin foil, we went straight down to MacDougal Street and sold them for twenty bucks.

**JF:** One of the things that you just brought up, by mentioning Johnny Winter, is Steve Paul's The Scene.

**DF:** It was a basement on Forty-sixth Street just west of Eighth Avenue—a large, sprawling basement where Steve Paul sat and welcomed the great musicians of the time. Jimi Hendrix played there. Tiny Tim was the house band. Took his ukulele out of a shopping bag and sang between acts, "Tiptoe through the Tulips." It was very great.

**JF:** It was the only place uptown that catered to rock 'n' roll culture and all the Zeppelins and all the big bands that came across the water. . . .

**BB:** How about Iggy Pop upstairs at Max's? . . . That was one of the best shows in rock 'n' roll. I know you [Danny] didn't like music up there, but Iggy was brilliant. That was an incredible night. Everybody was piled in there. I think our booth there was Alice and Todd and me and everybody. . . . That night was exceptional, because you just never knew with Jim [Osterberg, a.k.a. Iggy]. . . . But that particular night, the glass-cutting night, he was extraordinary. I don't think I've ever seen a more incredible rock 'n' roll show. It had everything—danger, art, sex, and the music was phenomenal. This was before

[Mayor Giuliani], my friends, this was when New York City was really wild and fun—

**JF:** Well, it was also before crack and AIDS. . . .

○

**Albert Bouchard (Blue Öyster Cult):** We got together on Long Island and we didn't really play together in the city in the early days. We played at Stony-brook—you know, mixers and stuff like that. Oh, I guess we came into the city a few times. We played at the Third Annual Blues Bag at the Cafe Au Go Go, and that was kinda cool. I got to meet Muddy Waters. You know, I came from upstate New York, it was like a dream come true coming to New York City and seeing all these famous people. Jimi Hendrix, got to meet him. Sly and the Family Stone, Buddy Miles.

Anyway, so we mostly got our act together out on the Island. We came into the city every once in a while and people would say, "Yo, put on some sides, man! Take a break." We weren't appreciated by the sophisticated city audience. And then Steve Paul gave us a break and let us play at his club, The Scene, for a week. We really met a lot of people. We figured out what we had to do to go over. . . .

○

**Mickey Leigh (The Rattlers):** . . . I started playing when I was twelve years old. The first show I did in New York City was at a club called Cafe Bizarre on Third Street. I was twelve years old. We used to come into the city, early '60s, dressed up like Jimi Hendrix, and all the hippies would yell at us to go back to Queens. I was in a band with Johnny Ramone. The first press I got—it was in the *Daily News*—we played a benefit for the men's alimony prison. We did songs like "Communication Breakdown" and "Good Times, Bad Times." Johnny was twenty-one and I was fourteen years old. And then I introduced him to my brother, who was Joey Ramone.

○

**Noel Ford (Continental):** The '90s, they weren't as bad as I know you all think they were. D Generation and Green Door, that pretty much says it all.... They brought fun back into rock 'n' roll in New York.... Rock 'n' roll is not dead, as long as you people want it to stay alive. Gotta come out to the clubs and support the bands.

**M. Doughty:** I just wanna say disco rules and punk rock is for squares! Yeah!

**George Tabb:** If it wasn't for my band Furious George none of you would be here, because we created rock 'n' roll. Thank you and good night.

# BIBLIOGRAPHY

Amende, Coral. *Rock Confidential*. New York: Plume, 2000.

Anson, Robert Sam. *Gone Crazy and Back Again: The Rise and Fall of the Rolling Stone Generation*. New York: Doubleday, 1981.

Arnold, Gina. *Kiss This: Punk in the Present Tense*. New York: St. Martin's Press, 1997.

Bacon, Tony. *London Live*. London: Balafon Books, 1999.

Barger, Sonny. *Hell's Angel: The Life and Times of Sonny Barger and the Hell's Angels Motorcycle Club*. New York: William Morrow, 2000.

Berger, Harris M. *Metal, Rock, and Jazz: Perceptions and the Phenomenology of Musical Experience*. Hanover, N.H.: Wesleyan University Press, 1999.

Booth, Stanley. *The True Adventures of the Rolling Stones*. Chicago: A Capella Books, 2000.

Branson, Richard. *Losing My Virginity*. New York: Random House, 1998.

Carducci, Joe. *Rock and the Pop Narcotic* (revised 2nd edition). Los Angeles: 2.13.61, 1994.

Collier, Peter, and David Horowitz. *Destructive Generation: Second Thoughts About the '60s*. New York: Free Press, 1996.

Davis, Stephen. *Hammer of the Gods*. New York: Boulevard, 1997.

Debord, Guy. *The Society of the Spectacle*. Translated by Donald Nicholson-Smith. New York: Zone Books, 1995.

Draper, Robert. *Rolling Stone Magazine: The Uncensored History*. New York: Doubleday, 1990.

Editors of *Rolling Stone*. *The Rolling Stone Interviews 1967-1980*. New York: St. Martin's Press, 1981.

Fink, Carole, Philipp Gassert, and Detlef Junker, eds. *1968: The World Transformed*. Cambridge, UK: Cambridge University Press, 1998.

Frum, David. *How We Got Here: The 70's*. New York: Basic Books, 2000.

Garofalo, Reebee, ed. *Rockin' the Boat: Mass Music and Mass Movements.* Boston: South End Press, 1992.

Gimarc, George. *Punk Diary: 1970–1979.* New York: St. Martin's Press, 1994.

Goodman, Fred. *The Mansion on the Hill.* New York: Times Books, 1997.

Gray, Michael. *Song and Dance Man.* London: Cassell, 2000.

Gross, Michael. *My Generation.* New York: HarperCollins, 2000.

Hebdige, Dick. *Subculture: The Meaning of Style.* London: Methuen, 1979.

Hoffman, Abbie. *Steal This Book.* New York: Pirate Editions, 1971.

Holland, Jools, and Dora Loewenstein. *The Rolling Stones: A Life on the Road.* New York: Penguin, 1998.

Jeffreys-Jones, Rhodri. *Peace Now!* New Haven, Conn.: Yale University Press, 1999.

Kahn, Ashley, Holly George-Warren, and Shawn Dahl, eds. *Rolling Stone: The 70s.* Boston: Little, Brown & Company, 1998.

Kimball, Roger. *The Long March.* San Francisco: Encounter Books, 2000.

Lydon, John. *Rotten: No Irish, No Blacks, No Dogs.* New York: Picador, 1995.

Marcus, Greil. *Lipstick Traces.* Cambridge, Mass.: Harvard University Press, 1989.

McNeil, Legs, and Gillian McCain. *Please Kill Me: The Uncensored Oral History of Punk.* New York: Grove Press, 1996.

Miller, James. *Flowers in the Dustbin: The Rise of Rock and Roll, 1947–1977.* New York: Simon & Schuster, 1999.

Monk, Noel E., and Jimmy Gutterman. *12 Days on the Road: The Sex Pistols and America.* New York: William Morrow, 1990.

Sabin, Roger, ed. *Punk Rock: So What?* London: Routledge, 1999.

Sanchez, Tony. *Up and Down with the Rolling Stones.* New York: William Morrow, 1979.

Sanders, Edward. *1968: A History in Verse.* Santa Rosa, Cal.: Black Sparrow, 1997.

Savage, Jon. *England's Dreaming.* New York: St. Martin's Press, 1992.

Seabrook, John. *Nobrow.* New York: Alfred A. Knopf, 2000.

Sinclair, John. *Guitar Army: Street Writings/Prison Writings.* New York: Douglas Book Corporation, 1972.

Slick, Grace, with Andrea Cagan. *Somebody To Love?* New York: Warner Books, 1998.

St. Michael, Mick. *Keith Richards: In His Own Words.* London: Omnibus Press, 1994.

Willis, Ellen. *Beginning to See the Light: Sex, Hope, and Rock-and-Roll.* Hanover, N.H.: Wesleyan University Press, 1992.

Wohlin, Anna. *The Murder of Brian Jones.* London: Blake Publishing Ltd., 1999.

Wyman, Bill, with Ray Coleman. *Stone Alone.* London: Ripple Productions, 1990.

# ACKNOWLEDGMENTS

It was Russ Smith, my friend and the editor-in-chief of *New York Press*, who suggested I write a long article responding to the thirtieth birthday of *Rolling Stone*. That article was the basis for Chapter 4 of the present book. Many other sections of the book originally saw print, in one way or another, in *New York Press*. So my thanks to him, and to all my friends and co-workers there.

Colin Robinson, editor at Verso Books, saw that original article about *Rolling Stone* and approached me with the idea of expanding it into a more general book on rock culture. Thank you, Colin, and all the fine folks at Verso. Thanks also to Kate Lovelady for the excellent copyediting.

Thanks to all the interviewees quoted in the body of the book or excerpted in the Appendix: Kurt Andersen, Robert Sam Anson, Sonny Barger, Albert Bouchard, Bebe Buell, John Burks, Peter Crowley, Jim DeRogatis, Mike Doughty, Robert Draper, Danny Fields, Noel Ford, Jim Fouratt, Deborah Frost, Giorgio Gomelsky, Bob Guccione, Jr., Mark Hertsgaard, David Johansen, Howard Kohn, Hilly Kristal, Tuli Kupferberg, Mickey Leigh, Lee Ranaldo, John Sinclair, Peter Swales, George Tabb, Lucian Truscott, and Ellen Willis. Very special thanks to Giorgio Gomelsky, George Tabb, and Don Gilbert, who had as much to do as I did with organizing and conducting several of these interviews.

Thanks to Bill Repsher for kicking my butt every time I write about rock.

This book is dedicated to Diane, who put up with me very nicely while it was being written.